More praise for THE HEREAFTER GANG....

"...*The Hereafter Gang* is almost as hilarious as Larry McMurtry's *Texasville,* and less earthbound; nearly as haunted as Thomas Pynchon's *Vineland,* and less suffocating. Like both those books, it attempts to hold on to America as the century blows us away; like neither of them, it bites the bullet, in language of tensile brilliance....*The Hereafter Gang* is a posthumous fantasy. Like similar work by a wide variety of writers, from Vladimir Nabokov to Flann O'Brien, from John Crowley to Gene Wolfe, it tells of a hero who, after the death of the body, must sift through the materials of the life he has left in order to make sense of his naked soul...It is one of the great American novels."

-THE WASHINGTON POST

"...A remarkable piece of work...that keeps the glamour of the novel screaming ahead at a high quantum level all the way through. *The Hereafter Gang* is the charm of the author's voice. Barrett knows how to write economically and evocatively...His characters are earthy, bawdy, sensual and dimensional. In other words, they live..."

-LOCUS

"...Barrett has an ear for the bedlam din of urban Texas, and a story-telling voice which deposes matters of great subtlety with great shouts, and an exuberance which glows in the dark, and he's hilarious."

-John Clute, *LOOK AT THE EVIDENCE*

THE HEREAFTER GANG

to Mandy- best wishes!

Neal Barrett, Jr.

Dripping Springs, Texas

This is a work of fiction. All the characters, incidents, and dialogue, except for incidental references to public figures, products, or services, are imaginary and are not intended to refer to any living persons or to disparage any company's products or services.

Copyright © 1991 by Neal Barrett, Jr.

All rights reserved. No part of this book may be reproduced or transmitted in any form or by any means, electronic or mechanical, including photocopying, recording, or by any information storage and retrieval system, without permission in writing from the publisher.

Published by Mojo Press,

P.O. Box 1215, Dripping Springs, Texas 78620
www.mojo.com

Book Design by Ben Ostrander

Cover photograph by mojo

Printed in the United States of America

Originally published by
Mark V. Ziesing

ISBN 1-885418-21-3
The Hereafter Gang
Neal Barrett, Jr.

"What we have here is a dedication page," said Doug. "This is what we got to do first."

"What's it for?" said Sue Jean.

"Well, here's where we thank *everybody for everything they did, for getting us where we are."*

"And where you figure that might be?"

"Doesn't matter where, long as we're here."

"We got the whole page?"

"The whole thing," said Doug.

"Shoot, let's do it," said Sue Jean. "Let's fill this sucker up."

First and foremost, this book is for
RUTH,
Who said, "Go ahead and write it, I'll hold down the fort."
She did, and that's why the book is here.
All my love, forever, R.B.

For **JOE** and **LEW**
Who are always beside me when I need them.

For my special band of brothers.
RODGER and **TOM**

For **TOSH,**
Who is holding a table at the Bird,
for his own Hereafter Gang

And for **GENE** and **REFORD**.
Who already know the way.

God bless you all.
N.B.

THE HEREAFTER GANG

I dream a life I've yet to live,
In some far spring or fall.
Pray who is Honda, Cap 'n Crunch,
And what is Underall?

—JOHN KEATS

Next time around, I be something ain't so troublin' as this.

—hooker,
Houston, Texas

THE HEREAFTER GANG

Doug dreams he and Erlene are at the movies. The dream comes early Monday morning after the party Saturday night, and the fucked up Sunday after that. They see *The French Lieutenant's Woman,* which Doug didn't like when he was awake. He thinks Meryl Streep could use a shot of Vitamin B. She has a birdlike pinkness about the eyes. Erlene says Meryl wears silk underwear you have to buy in this one boutique in Paris France. She likes to sit in outdoor cafés between takes. Doug figures none of this is true. He knows where Erlene gets her dope about the stars. Sometime during the movie Erlene takes off her clothes. She's wearing only fishnet hose. Doug has seen these advertised in the backs of magazines. Before you know it, merchant seamen with Slavic features have her upside down in the seat, doing everything Doug likes to do. Erlene doesn't seem to notice. She finishes off a popcorn tub and a Sprite. Meryl Streep gazes longingly out to sea. As soon as the movie's over, Doug sees Erlene is dead. After a moment of regret, he feels as if a weight has been lifted from his shoulders. At the funeral, Sunny D'Angelo slips him a small glass vial. Doug can secretly apply this to his eyes to bring tears.A beautiful girl gazes at him across the grave. Her eyes are gray and knowing. A silent understanding passes between them. They will meet that night at an exclusive hotel. It is late when Doug arrives. The streets are empty, wet with recent rain like a movie about spies. There is no light in the room but he knows the girl is there. He can smell the fragrant oils she's rubbed on her thighs and the tips of her breasts. These oils are hard to get. They can't be sold in this country. He stops beside her bed; she raises a little foot for him to kiss. Her toes taste of cloves and good leather. She motions him to join her. She whispers in his ear and tells him what she wants. She speaks some language he hasn't heard, but Doug knows what she means. Dark things ooze from out of the closet and under the bed. They've been waiting since he was three. They knew he'd forget to leave on the light. They crowd him to the floor and suck his breath. He smells the wet fur of small animals, the same smell the girl has used to lure him to her bed. A commercial starts to happen. A black man bites into a Whopper. Doug feels a terrible loss. He knows what the black man got. "Hey baby, don't look at me," the man tells him, "your old lady the one that done you in…"

THE HEREAFTER GANG

Doug woke from this dream, hung up between dread and anticipation. He seemed detached. The clock beside the bed said 10:35 or something else. He sat and put his feet on the floor. The sun came hot through the window, striping the bed like a bad prison movie. Erlene had the air on full. It was all bills paid, Erlene said, if they didn't use it someone else sure would.

He recalled this was the best day of his life and felt better. He meant to get things done. There wasn't any reason why he couldn't. Fate dealt winning hands all the time. A schoolteacher from Rose Hill North Carolina won eight-thousand bucks on *Wheel of Fortune,* and didn't seem like he could safely open a can. Dumping Erlene and quitting work couldn't be any harder than that.

He stumbled to the shower and let water run in his face. He thought about the dream. Did he really want Erlene to die? He guessed not. That was some kind of symbol. You told yourself stuff in your sleep but you had to figure out what it meant. It didn't always mean what you thought. The water helped him sort through emotions. He'd looked at Erlene at 6:30 the night before and cut her right out of his life. Just like that. They were watching *60 Minutes*. One moment they were still married in spirit and the next, during a Preparation H commercial, he didn't care if she dropped through the floor. The product coming on the screen just then seemed to Doug a kind of omen, that and what happened next. An image of Erlene's mother suddenly appeared, superimposed on the blue and yellow package. It looked like a clever special effect.

This thought triggered another, and he remembered where Erlene had to be. It was the last Monday of the month, the day she drove south out of Houston down 288 to see her mother. Otta Gee Lamprey lived in a trailer north of Clute. The trailer was aluminum, shaped like a giant suppository. Mounted on concrete blocks, it had sat right there since 1958, defying hurricanes and floods and Texas summers. It was set in a cluster of naked pines, trees dying from the kiss of Monsanto and Dow, the hydrocarbon breath of refineries along the Gulf. Erlene told friends Otta Gee was in the antique business, but wouldn't give directions. On Doug's first and last visit to Clute, he learned the antique business was a cardtable set in front of the trailer. On the table were three ashtrays from the Ramada Inn in Freeport, a Houston Oiler giveaway glass, a Dr Pepper bottle stuffed with faded plastic flowers. There was a Donald Duck lamp with the bill chipped off below the eyes. Donald looked surprised.

And that was it, the whole thing. Just this table full of shit people threw out of cars, or dumped at the Shell across the street. Doug wasn't deep into commerce and sales, but he could see the old lady wasn't making any bread out of this. Which meant Erlene slipped her money now and then, and told him it went for something else.

Otta Gee ran the antique shop on weekends whenever it didn't rain. During the week she drank beer and messed around inside the trailer. Erlene wouldn't go inside. She'd sit in a broken lawn chair and talk to Otta Gee, but she wouldn't go in the trailer on a bet. There were close to thirty years worth of Lone Star and chili dog farts locked up in that thing, and Erlene wasn't sure what else. Whom the gods would destroy, they would first drive to Clute, Doug said, which didn't go over with Erlene.

It was a pure marvel to Doug that a long-legged, high-kicking Kilgore Rangerette, a girl with whiskey eyes and a soft and pouty mouth, could spring from the pizza dough loins of Otta Gee. How could a kid slide down that channel of horror and come out cute as a country bug? There was only one answer he could figure, and that was Erlene's father, long gone and never mentioned since. He had to be some South Texas Apollo. Some god-like trucker on a toot. His super-sperm had invaded Otta Gee, scrambled her rotten egg and fashioned Erlene from scratch. Whoever it was had sobered up and gotten out of town fast.

Doug had been married to Erlene four years before he noticed this slim little honey had Otta Gee traits beginning to show. Little things at first. They went to a movie where a psycho in a hockey mask split a lot of teenage heads. Erlene laughed out loud. She laughed until she cried. Doug started looking for other signs. He peeked in her nose and in her ears for any Otta Gee hairs. Nothing. Which didn't prove a thing. A woman who'd fuck a dentist and a shrink wouldn't stop at growing secret tufts of hair.

Doug dried off and wrapped a towel around his waist and brushed his teeth. He decided he didn't look half bad. An ugly Clint Eastwood. Maybe a handsome Charlie Bronson. A full head of hair and no gray. His eyes were dark and the whites were perfectly clear. He felt the lines at the corners of his mouth showed character and judgement. He reached for the razor, set it down and looked at himself again. It struck him so quickly he was amazed. He didn't have to shave. He could do whatever he wanted. Starting right now. He took the razor and the package of blades and the shaving cream and dumped them in the basket by the sink. Damn. Two weeks and he'd be good as Willie Nelson.

Mousebreath padded into the room, curious at the noise. She jumped lightly on top of the toilet. "I'm taking off," Doug told her. "I don't know where but you better come too. Stay here and you'll get your ass gassed." The cat gave him a witless amber stare. Doug saw ancient wisdom and understanding.

He couldn't find clean shorts, and recycled a pair from the bottom of the pile. He felt like a stranger already. The apartment seemed revealed. He felt depressed and unattached. He couldn't imagine he'd ever lived here at all. The walls were painted hospital decorator green. The carpet looked like a badly matted dog. Erlene placed furniture just slightly out of whack for the normal eye, something she'd likely learned from Otta Gee. Sofas and chairs seemed vaguely Target Spanish or maybe not. Plastic flowers sat wherever Erlene could find a spot. The Sunday papers were still scattered about floor. The coffee table held Erlene's book, which was a history of the Kilgore Rangerettes. Beside it were white take-out cartons, cold fries and dried barbecue sauce. Doug figured Robin Leach wasn't dropping by here for a drink.

Erlene had left coffee on the stove. Doug dumped it out and made his own. Even the simplest act of marriage seemed perverse. He tried to imagine the two of them having breakfast. What would he say? What would they talk about? Mousebreath rubbed his leg and he opened *Nine Lives* and dumped it in a dish. She sprang to the counter and nudged his hand aside. Cats don't think about food the same as dogs, Doug thought. Dogs are scared of God and they wolf down everything at once.

The sun was white-hot out the kitchen window. A garbage truck labored up the alley behind the apartment. The small fenced yards below were empty. Rusted K-Mart smokers, houseplants set outside to die. Doug decided this would be a fine night to check the girl in 104. Boy, she was a window peeker's dream, regular as the ten o'clock news. He'd learned her name from the mailbox and arranged to run into her by chance. She cut him down with a look. She didn't want to know him. Yet, Doug knew her as well as her strawberry douche. Window peeking was a habit he'd picked up as youth, and seen no reason to discard. Growing up in Waxahachie, he had a detailed map of every good window in town. Best viewing times, age of peekee, tit rating and personal risk factor. All this noted in Orphan Annie code, and hidden in the closet in a box. He could remember every treasure that was there. A dirty comic book featuring Dagwood, Blondie and Mr. Dithers. A pair of panties stolen from Betty Allwood's clothes line. A picture of Cyd Charise. He left his mark on a hundred clapboard walls and cedar shrubs. The dangers then were dogs, running in packs through the town. Today it was security guards and Levelor blinds.

He felt much better than he'd hoped. Sunday was even worse than Saturday night, Sunday the moment of truth. The garbage they'd dug up Saturday night, after everyone was gone, didn't smell any better in the morning. Saturday was just off-the-cuff sniping. Sunday they were sober, ready for a knockdown HBO title match. Erlene locked herself in the bathroom and bawled. Doug stomped around the apartment. It lasted until late in the afternoon. By then they were limp with verbal wounds, empty of invective. They held each other and cried. It was good they'd gotten it all out in the open. That was the sensible thing to do. Now they could sit down like grownups and work things out.

"We've both been married before," Doug said. "We're not a couple of kids, Erlene. Things happen whether you mean for them to or not."

"Now Doug, not anything happened at all," Erlene said. "Don't you start on that. Pete was just acting up. You know how he is when he drinks."

"I just meant things *could* happen. I mean they might. If they did we'd understand. That things happen."

"Well nothing did."

"Well maybe it didn't."

"Goddamn it, Doug, there isn't a maybe to it." For an instant, her eyes turned Otta Gee mean. "You hear me put a maybe on what I said?"

"Fine. There wasn't any maybes. I'm too old for this shit, Erlene. I don't need some kind of hassle like who's got the tit in the kitchen."

Erlene gave him a sly country grin. "You're not so old. I haven't ever said that."

"I'm thirty-five. That's getting into old."

"Thirty-six."

"I'm closer to thirty-five than thirty-six. That's how you count it, Erlene. What you're closest to."

"You don't act old Doug and that's what counts. You act like a man ten years younger and that's the truth."

"Well I appreciate that. That's a nice thing to say."

"I'm not just saying it. I don't say things I don't mean. You ought to know me better than that. Aren't I right? Isn't that what I always do?"

"I guess you do."

"Don't I always do that?"

"You always do, Erlene."

"Honest to God I wish you'd fuck me now, Doug. You know getting mad makes me horny."

Doug jumped her right there. He knew the other thing Erlene did when she got mad was change her mind. And even if he was already thinking this was surely the end of the line, he wanted her real bad. He didn't like her head but her body hadn't ever done him wrong.

He guided her through fantasies they'd collected in coastal motels with sandy floors. For once Erlene seemed willing to do anything he liked. He shifted from tamer stuff into the Mexican Bandit and Girl Tourist. Erlene stayed in character, bawling with conviction she was an airline stew on vacation and a virgin besides. Doug draped her over the sofa and tied her hands with a kitchen towel. The sight of that magnificent bottom upended brought tears to his eyes. How was he going to give up that? He gazed at her overturned orchid kissed with dew. Thirty-two years old, and still tight as a new gym sock. He hurried down the hall, found his sombrero in the closet. He pretended to rifle her purse.

"Have you ever been fock by real *Mexicano, señorita?*" he wanted to know. "You are een for *muy bueno* treat."

"Ay, steek eet in me," cried Erlene, "steek eet in me now!"

"You don't do the accent, Erlene."

"What?"

"You don't do the accent. I'm the Mexican and you're the tourist. You got the accent too it doesn't make any sense."

"For Christ's sake, Doug, just do it," Erlene said, "you got me hangin' on the edge!"

After that he did Blind Girl and the Biker. The Sunday papers were scattered over the floor. Mousebreath joined in the fun, hurtling through debris like a demon. Doug made Erlene go to the mirror and read WANTED: CONSTRUCTION WORKERS on her ass. He got them both beers and sat on the john while she soaked in the tub.

"That stuff last night," Erlene said, "wasn't any of it worth a hill of beans. What I want to do now is just put all that behind us, hon. I'm sorry for what I said and I hope you are too."

"Let's not even talk about it," Doug said. He was totally fucked out and a little sad, because he didn't care if they worked it out or not.

"Now Doug, I think we *need* to talk about it," Erlene said. "We got the yellin' and the making up done. I think we ought to get to the talking part too." Erlene sat up in the tub. Bubbles broke on her skin like Rice Krispies in a bowl. "You listen to what I'm saying, Douglas Hoover, all right? I love you, hon, and I don't care a thing 'bout anyone else. Pete got the feelies and that wasn't anything at all."

"What about Ham?"

"All right I gave Ham a peck on the cheek. And I mean not on the mouth itself and that's not even kissing. Christ sakes, him and Aimilee've been friends of ours for years. It isn't like you haven't kissed her a hundred times don't say you haven't. And by the way I did *not* poke my tongue clear down his throat."

"Did I say you did?"

"Just about half the night is all."

"Okay."

"Okay what?"

"Okay maybe I did."

"Isn't any maybe to it.If you didn't I shouldn't have said it. We said a bunch of stuff."

Erlene sipped her beer. Doug looked at the tips of her perky tits above the water.

"That isn't all you said. You said stuff that hurt me real bad. You did, Doug."

"I said I'm sorry."

"Look at me? Will you look at me please?" She took his hand in hers. "Just look right at me honey andd tell me. You think I'm fucking someone, Doug? Ham or Stew or someone else? You do I want to know right now. I want you to come right out and say it."

"No, I don't think you're fucking anyone," Doug lied.

"Honest?"

"Honest."

"And how 'bout you?" Her sly grin took him by surprise. "You haven't ever put the old footlong to Shirley or Janet I don't guess. Lord God Aimilee'd give her right foot to get you in the sack I know that."

Doug looked guilty, though Erlene was only partially right. He'd tried to screw Shirley, but so had everyone else. Shirley was a dead ringer for Goldie Hawn. Aimilee was tall and dark, a lazy looking woman with glazed ceramic eyes. Erlene was right about her. She'd go down on him at high noon in the shopping center if he gave her half a chance, right in front of God and Safeway shoppers. Only that wouldn't happen, because Doug was scared to get near her. He knew that come-on smile hid a crazy. The invitation in her eyes was pharmaceutical at best. Her husband was a shrink, and Aimilee ate his pills like jelly beans.

"No I haven't been to bed with Aimilee or Shirley either," Doug said, leaving Janet out. "Jesus, if I had they'd of told you before I got out the door."

"Would you like to? You'd kinda like to I bet."

"Yes," he said at once, knowing this was the right answer. "If I was going to do something like that Erlene which I'm not. They're good-looking women I'll say that."

"Now see? I don't blame you for that, Doug. That's a real natural thing. Lord, I get turned on now and then. I am not goin' to lie. I guess I'm entitled to a tingle once in a while. Isn't a thing wrong with that."

"Who?" Doug wanted to know where this was going.

"What do you mean who?"

"Which one would you get a tingle from? I mean if you did."

Erlene looked irritated. "I didn't *say* I'd get a tingle now, Doug. Did I say that? That isn't what I said you don't listen. I said I was entitled to a tingle is what I said. I said there was some men we know might turn me on if I was so inclined in that direction."

"We're just talking," Doug said. "Like you said. If you were going to who?"

"Oh I don't know." A little Otta Gee smile. "I just never thought about it, hon."

"Well who if you did?"

"Stew, maybe."

"Not Ham?"

"My Lord, no." Erlene made a face, showing how distasteful she considered the idea.

"Has Stew ever tried anything?"

"Stew Geeter? Are you kidding? Why Shirley'd cut off his balls."

"Then who else?" Doug persisted.

"No one else," Erlene said crossly. "Let's not get off of you now, Doug. Don't tell me you go off to Dallas or somewhere one of those little twitchy-ass secretaries doesn't get the hots."

"Secretaries don't get to take trips."

"Uh-huh. Well how 'bout the ones already there?"

"I stick it to every one gets in range," Doug said honestly.

Erlene laughed. "Just get on out of here, you old bastard. Run out and get us something to eat, okay? I don't feel like messing around in the kitchen."

He left her soaking in the tub, grateful this was over. He took the Toyota because the air wasn't working in the Camaro. It was nearly September, but Texas isn't close to Vermont, and Houston doesn't bother with the fall. Concrete pies bake in the mega-city oven from May to October. Doug didn't care. He'd lived in year-round summer all his life and liked the heat. It felt good coming out of cold air and getting the sweats. Putting on his shades against the glare, he drove out of the lot and onto the street, past half a dozen new apartment complexes. It was hard getting home if you were drunk. They all looked just alike and had names like Navajo Cliffs and Hopi Buttes and Zuni Mesa. Some developer had been to Santa Fe or seen a picture, and there were poles sticking out of brown stucco and dead yucca plants along the drive. If you didn't like Indians, you could go a few blocks and be a Viking or a pirate.

THE HEREAFTER GANG

Doug thought the Hanging Judge Barbecue #7 was the best place to eat in the world. There were plenty of things to do. It wasn't like some place where you ate and didn't have anything to look at but ferns. He liked the plastic rope circling neon signs for Lone Star and Pearl beer. There were things to see on the rough cedar walls. Branding irons and horseshoes and early farming implements all faded into rust. A fly-specked frame of old arrowheads, another of Western badges. One wall had signs from Wells Fargo and Adams Express. Another was filled with rusty relics, old guns that had lain out in the dirt a hundred years. A Colt single action had all six chambers still loaded with petrified shells. What happened, Doug wondered? Was the owner too slow, did he fail to get off a shot? When you ate at the Hanging Judge, you could think about things like that.

The floor was brown linoleum, the pattern worn clean where people had walked, cracked the way mud dries in a river. The kitchen behind the counter had a big metal hood, a fan in the window, blades coated with grease, the essence of every herd John Wayne had ever driven up to Dodge. Over the serving counter were sepia-tone photographs of famous outlaws and lawmen. John Wesley Hardin, Bat Masterson, Sam Bass and Jesse and Frank. Doug didn't care for the lawmen, but he knew the personal histories of every outlaw on the wall. He had books about them at home.

He usually got the Bob Dalton Ribs 'n' Fries and the Clay Allison Kid's Plate for Erlene. Fighting with Erlene had made him hungry and he ordered the Cole Younger Ham 'n' Beef Combo for Erlene, and the Charlie Pierce and Bitter Creek Newcomb House Special for himself. Charlie Pierce and Newcomb were pictured on slanted boards bare to the waist in a funeral parlor in Guthrie, Oklahoma. Pierce was riddled with bullets in the left side of his chest. The holes looked strangely like sores or the bites of dogs. Newcomb appeared untouched, except for a hole in the arm, but this was misleading. As the Guthrie *Daily Leader* noted in the legend down below, Newcomb "was transformed into a lead mine," with bullets in his arms, legs and even the soles of his feet. These two were members of the Doolin gang, and victims of late nineteenth century progress. The telegraph alerted Deputy U.S. Marshals to their presence in the area, and Newcomb and Pierce were soon on display. Even in death, Doug thought, both of these outlaws seemed more attractive and even-featured than Otta Gee.

The boy behind the counter was new. Doug had never seen him before, yet he seemed vaguely familiar. He was young, barely twenty if that, a boy with a mop of unruly hair. His face wasn't handsome or ugly, but somewhere in between. Doug was struck by the lopsided mouth that gave him a devil-may-care look. He liked the boy at once. He made quick decisions about people and stuck to that. The boy seemed poor and maybe lacking social grace. He thought such people were better off and had an easier row to hoe. His mother said the poor had a simple kind of wisdom, pleasures they shared with their own. They would pass a small clapboard shack in the dead of night on a lonely Texas road, and she would point to the square of yellow light and say, "Douglas, just look at that light, how warm and friendly it is. Those folks in there are happy. They are content with what God gave them, and we should be grateful we have so much more." His mother was dead ten years now. She lived to be seventy-two, and left Doug a forty-year stack of *Reader's Digest*. When his father heard she'd died, he jerked off successfully in front of a nurse named Felicia at the Autumn Leaves Home.

The boy told Doug he was just filling in, working at the Judge until he could get something more to his liking. The barbecue business wasn't what he wanted to do. Doug watched him work. For part-time help he carved the beef with real flair. He gave Doug the end pieces where the meat was feathered up and crinkly with fat.

"You enjoy now, hear?" he told Doug, and handed him the big brown sacks ready to go. The paper was already translucent with grease, like the windows in the shacks of contented poor.

It was enough food for six. The boy smiled in admiration. "I don't get to fix a lot of them specials"

"I thought maybe I'd do something different."

"Listen, sometimes that's what you got to do."

"I guess you know what happened to Charlie Pierce and ol' Newcomb."

"Those fellas were a caution."

Doug picked up his change and left the boy a nice tip. He looked at Custer's Last Stand and the poker-playing dogs. Those dogs were hard to get and you couldn't buy a Custer at any price. It seemed real funny one foot hitting the floor on target, the other running wildly off the track. Someone hit him in the chest with a major league bat. "Sweet Jesus!" Doug yelled. The pain knocked the breath out of his lungs. He sat down hard on the floor. The poker dogs pulsed in bright colors. He just sat there getting scared. Then the boy was there squatting on his heels looking concerned.

"Mister you all right?"

"I guess. God that sure hurt bad."

"You sit still I'll get the EMS on the phone. Those boys are real fast."

"No," Doug said, "I'm okay. Don't call anyone at all." The boy left and brought back a glass of water. Doug saw his boots were worn at the heels. He helped Doug to a bench. Doug was shaky but felt better. He drank the water then wet a paper napkin and washed his face.

"You got a bad ticker you ought to do somethin' about it," the boy said.

Doug's heart gave a start. He didn't like talk about organs. "I'm all right," he said. "I got some of those Tums in the car."

"Just buyin' this shit won't do it," the boy grinned. "You got to eat it first." He started gathering up sacks; Doug had tossed food all over when he fell. A few fries had come loose but otherwise everything seemed intact.

Doug figured he'd be just fine. For a minute there he sure felt bad but it was gone. Something real serious wouldn't go away quick he knew that. Which left out the heart or some major malfunction of the brain. That kind of thing could happen. On PBS they said little electric sparks made you think. Your wiring could go bad, just like it did in a house. He didn't care for the idea of losing his wits. Uncle Walt Curie on his mother's side of the fence had gotten oldtimer's disease and regularly pissed on rabbits. He got the map in his head crossed up and thought the hutch out back was the bathroom next to his room. Those rabbits which were all purebred got to where they'd climb the back of the cage when Uncle Walt got anywhere close.

Doug glanced up and saw the boy brushing dirt off his sacks. He didn't feel real hungry but maybe he would. Someone coughed and he turned over his shoulder a little surprised. He didn't think anyone else was there. Doc Holliday sat back in the corner pouring salt in a Shiner beer. He wore an ankle-length duster and smoked a pencil-thin cigar. He coughed again and he was gone.

Doug's heart started pounding and wouldn't stop. Oh shit, he thought, my wiring's gone bad. There's an Uncle Walt gene in there and whatever knocked me down shook it loose! Still, he was strangely calm. His heart began to beat at a normal pace. Once Doc Holliday was gone he felt none the worse for wear.

He remembered Doc's hat had a Montana peak. You could check that out easily enough.

"I'm all right," he said aloud, "I'm just fine."

"Good," said the boy. He handed Doug his sacks. "You take care of yourself now."

Doug said he would. The boy offered to go along to the car, and Doug said he could make it by himself. Outside the heat wilted him at once. He turned on the air full blast and started to cry. The tears just started and wouldn't stop.

"Sweet Jesus, I don't want to go crazy or die either," he said, sounding like something was in his throat. "I can't fuck or anything if I'm dead. I sure don't want to piss on any rabbits."

He took a couple of breaths and settled down. The barbecue smell filled the car and he ate half of Erlene's sandwich. The letters on the sacks were shaped like little brown logs. One side of the sack read "Hanging Judge Barbecue #7." The other said, "Food This Good Ought Be Outlawed, Pardner." Doug started crying again. "What the hell am I thinking?" he said aloud."What difference does it make if I leave her or not? Who's going to be any better?" He'd couldn't stand watching her grow into Otta Gee, but what kind of reason was that? You're talking here world-class pussy tangled up in the Sunday morning paper. Sweet and surly Erlene, still small town Saturday night bitch-kitty cute, the taste of you and fountain Coke between her legs. You could always do different, but maybe you couldn't do any better. And every woman alive's got a mean-eyed mama somewhere.

He cried all the way back to the apartment, and knew he couldn't go in like that. So he drove real slow over speed bumps and circled through the complex watching girls walking to the pool. A colty little girl of fourteen had forgotten to bring her shoes. She tippy-toed quick over the asphalt drive hopping like bird on the beach. Doug longed to take her toes in his mouth and cool them off. You could make a mint of money on little girl toes. Wrap 'em up in foil like Hershey's Kisses.

Telling Erlene he meant to leave was something he didn't want to think about at all. Long distance seemed a good idea. He could go and just not say a thing. Erlene wasn't dumb. Two or three weeks and she'd get the picture clear. He tock a couple of breaths and felt his chest. It felt just fine. He wasn't going to die and he silently thanked Jesus for fixing that. Doc Holliday wasn't sitting on the hood and he thanked Him for that, too. It wouldn't be bad having visions if you could do it without a three-base hit.

Erlene was still in the tub, so he waited a minute and knocked on the door. "Hey, you all right in there?" he said.

"Doug?"

"Well who do you think, Erlene? I got your stuff, you want me to put it on a plate?"

"I don't want anything, Doug." A little catch in her voice, and he knew that she'd been crying, too.

"You okay, baby?"

"Just go away, Doug. All right? I don't want to talk to you now."

"Why not?"

"I just don't."

"You think you're going to eat your fries?"

"Douglas Hoover, you can fuck your sombrero for all I care," she said. "Just leave me alone!"

Now what brought on all that?

NEAL BARRETT, JR.

I can't remember wanting to be anything at all, Doug thought. He'd tried to do it right but it never seemed to work. The way other people spent their lives didn't make a lick of sense. When he was little, his father took him to the office and gave him a yellow legal pad. He could sharpen as many number two pencils as he liked. One corner of his father's big glasstop desk was reserved for him. The desk and the chairs were yellow oak. A black Emerson fan droned away in the corner, stirring the hot afternoon air. He'd stand on his father's chair and lean his elbows on the desk and draw pictures half the day. Comic books full of heroes and caped avengers that shot down the Japs. Japs were easier to draw than Germans. Just two slants for eyes and buckteeth. Germans had monocles and scars. He wanted to draw tits on girls but was afraid someone would see. His father and his uncles ran a real estate office and lumberyard in Waxahachie, Texas. This was before the family moved to Oklahoma. The move seemed to do his father in. He tried all kinds of different work, then finally just folded up and decided he couldn't remember who he was. Waxahachie though was fine. Men came into the office to talk business and make deals. They said Doug was a fine little man and gave him Dentyne and Black Jack gum. Uncle George had a nameplate made for the corner of the desk. Doug was proud of that. He loved the smell of business. The mimeograph fluid and cigar smoke and freshly-sharpened pencils. He wanted to make a deal.

School didn't interest him at all. Whatever they threw at him he made Cs. Being left-handed didn't help. At the time, children who wrote upside down were considered handicapped. One August afternoon Cindy Nance showed him the two great secrets of life. She was fourteen and he was eleven. They stole a couple of Baby Ruths from Kresses and ate them in her room. Cindy said if he'd go naked she would too. This scared the shit out of Doug. He agreed almost at once. He knew all the rumors about girls, but nothing had prepared him for the real thing. She slipped the blue dress over her head, catching yellow curls in the collar. Doug couldn't breathe. He learned girls crossed their arms when they took off their clothes, and wondered what would happen next. Cindy moved back in shadow and peeled her underwear down to her ankles and stepped free, leaving two little circles like knots of rope on the hardwood floor.

"Now you, Dougie," she said, "what you waitin' for?"

Doug was waiting for Jesus to *flat* kill him, but he couldn't tell her that. He didn't want to die. He wanted to stand there forever just looking at Cindy Nance. There was too much to see, he couldn't take her all in. If he stood there all his life he couldn't do it. Since he wouldn't do anything at all, Cindy Nance did it for him. She took off his shirt and went to her knees and worked his buckle, and yanked off his trousers and his shorts in a single jerk.

"Oh my goodness!" she said, giving him a silly little grin, a sly look Doug would see in a woman's eyes the rest of his life. His stiff little tool stood straight up and poked him in the belly. Doug noticed girls' tummys were kind of swollen. Not *fat,* just round in a different way. A girl finger touched him for the very first time and he shot all over her apple breasts.

"Well Jesus Christ, Dougie!" She jumped back startled, but he could tell she was pleased with her work.

"I'm sorry." It was all he could think of to say. His face was hot with shame.

"It's okay," Cindy said, "you're supposed to do that, you're just not supposed to do it real fast." She stood and walked to her dresser and got him a Kleenex and came back.

"Haven't you ever done it before?" " she wanted to know.

"Sure. Once or twice," Doug said. Once or twice a night was closer to the truth.

Her feral eyes saw right through him. "You play with it, don't you. I bet you do it all the time don't tell me you don't."

Doug's face grew hot again. She knew everything. There was no use trying to lie.

Cindy took his hand and led him to the bed. "Do it for me again and I might let you do somethin' to me.

"What?" Doug said.

"You'll see. Something fun."

"Huh-unh. You tell me first."

She sat up on her knees and took his hand, guiding one finger between her legs.

"Oh, Lord!" Doug was paralyzed.

Cindy giggled. "See? I told you it was fun."

He wanted to keep his hand there forever. Cindy had other plans. A guided tour with stops at points of interest, her hand telling him exactly what to do. He did whatever she asked, jerking off for her pleasure and his own. Cindy was ready with the Kleenex, an ever-helpful attendant. She told him everything he ever needed to know in a single afternoon. He could put his thing in hers. He could, if she would let him, which she wouldn't. He'd suspected some of this watching dogs. Now the connection was clear.

"Can you do it all the time?" he wanted to know.

"Any time you want. Dougie, everyone does it. Grownups do it every night and can't anybody stop 'em."

Another shock, total disbelief. Not *his* folks. They wouldn't!

He learned French kissing. Touched the tips of her breasts and even kissed them once. Instinct drew his mouth between her legs. He'd never heard of such a thing but reptile memories led him on. Genetic codes dialed a number he already knew. Yet, when he slithered down slyly past her tummy in that direction, Cindy Nance hit him soundly in the head.

"What is it," Doug said, "what'd I do?"

"You're a dirty little pervert, that's what!" she said.

"What's a pervert?"

"A boy who does that."

"Why?"

"It just is, Dougie Hoover, that's why. You try and do that again I'll clobber you good."

Doug wasn't convinced. He knew what he'd discovered. Cindy Nance knew everything, but she didn't know that.

Now Doug knew what he wanted to be. The future was perfectly clear. It was a magical afternoon, hours unreal and only imagined. Cindy's small room filled with the things girls collected. The patchwork quilt and the sun-faded wallpaper a grandmother bride had picked new. Orange paper shades drawn tight against the locust-hot sun. Here he learned the exquisite indentations of the female form. Kissed a girl's skin for the first time in dusty light. Jon Carter, and Thuvia Maid of Mars.

Some time between learning to stick his tongue down Cindy's throat, and his close call with perversion, Doug was told the second great secret of life. It happened by chance and shaped him as surely as secret number one. Cindy asked him what he wanted to be when he grew up. He said a businessman, like his father and his uncles.

"I'm going to make deals," he said. "I'll sell nigger shacks in town to dumb farmers who've lost their land." He had heard Uncle Bert say this a number of times.

Cindy gave him a curious look. "You want to stay in this town the rest of your life? That's what you want to do?"

"What's wrong with that?"

"It's dumb is what it is," Cindy said.

Doug was taken aback. He switched to the attack. "Oh yeah then what are you going to do, smarty?"

"Well," Cindy said, stretching so her tummy went flat, pointing a little toe in the air, "I expect I'll go out to Hollywood and be in the movies a good while. Then I'll marry a rich and handsome man looks kind of like Tyrone Power and he'll buy me stuff like a house in Fort Worth."

Doug began to backtrack in the face of such breathtaking plans. Real estate and lumber no longer seemed enough. "Maybe I'll do something like that too," he said. "Not a dumb movie star but something else. I might go some place and have an adventure."

Scathing laughter from Cindy. She rolled around on the bed. "Like fudge you will," she said. "You can't do that, dummy."

"Why not?"

She sat and crossed her legs, stuffed a rag doll in the spot where Doug wanted to be. "'Cause boys got to go get jobs that's why. You don't have to do it here you don't want but you got to do it somewhere. You got to work and make money so your wife and your children can have the things you didn't have."

Doug felt the cold hand of fate. This last line sounded familiar. It had the awful ring of truth. Still, at this moment, other needs were stronger. The future was a hundred years away, and Cindy Nance was not.

He didn't forget what Cindy said. He put it aside and let it simmer. It was nearly a year later when it bobbed to the surface again. One Wednesday afternoon it occurred to him playing office wasn't the same as doing it every day of your life. He figured maybe he was slow like Uncle Walt. It was there, he just hadn't put it all together. He'd never really thought that his father and his uncles *had* to make deals and sell lumber. That if they didn't, their asses would be out in the street. He kept his eyes open. He saw that this was true. Cindy Nance was dead right. Everyone had jobs and went to work whether they wanted to or not. The truth of this shook him like nothing had before. It wasn't a choice it was a rule! His whole life was planned, laid out right down to the end. Empty years lay ahead. He would buy and sell nigger shacks and lumber for awhile and then he'd die.

Doug had several bad days. Then panic gave way to calm appraisal. The system was faulty, but there might be reason behind it. He had planned to grow up and make deals at Hoover Bros. Real Estate & Lumber. Now, he wanted nothing to do with that at all. Not if you *had* to do it. That took all the fun out of making deals. He thought about the things he really liked to do, and how he might work these into his future. What he liked to do best was walk around and think and fish. Wander along the cottonwood banks of muddy rivers and plunk at turtles with his father's .22. He liked to take peanut butter and pimiento sandwiches and *G-8 Battle Aces* and *Startling Stories* and climb up a pecan and spend the day. He liked to watch squirrels and listen to crows. And now, to that, he could add sticking his thing into girls, and maybe someday getting his tongue in there too.

He liked to do something else. Something he'd never told Cindy Nance or even Joey Grier his best friend. Sometimes he would hike through wooded hills and find the edge of a farmer's field. When he was sure no one was around, he would take off his clothes and bury himself in the cool black North Texas loam, with only his nose above the ground. Soon the hot sun would warm the soil and heat his skin. He could feel green shoots nudge his back, wondering what sort of thing he might be. A rock? An animal they didn't know? Ants established trade routes overhead. Moles worked their subways around him, poking him with pink-finger noses. He could hear things talking in the earth. There was no need to leave. He had everything he wanted right there. Rain would fall in his mouth and his body would draw nutrients from the soil. In the fall, frost would form on the earth. Crows and squirrels would bring him blackberries and pecans as special treats. He would sleep through the winter cold and wake in the spring. Seeds would burst around him. They would sound like grease in a skillet. New corn would slide by and tickle his ribs. With the first fresh rain he would burst free again, stretch and sit up and go home. Everyone would wonder where he'd been.

It was a daring thing to do, even for a short afternoon. If his father had caught him naked in a field he would have shipped Doug to the funny farm at once, where many years later he'd find himself.

Three days before Doug's twelfth birthday, all the pieces came together. Two factors seemed to explain the work ethic. Since their very first all-out naked get-together, he'd been going at Cindy Nance like a rabbit, finally even persuading her to let him get inside. After that there was no turning back. He burned with a fever; he couldn't eat or sleep or sit still. This was it, he knew, the driving force that would shape his life. He knew what he wanted to do. He'd been watching grown men, and learned they were obsessed with this as well. They didn't just do it at home. They did it everywhere. In cars, offices, motel rooms—anywhere they could. They didn't tell their wives but it was clear that some of them knew. Some, even, were getting things stuck in them by husbands of other wives.

There it was, then, as simple as that. A man's purpose in life was to stick his thing in secretaries, and waitresses at the Wagon Spoke Inn. You couldn't do that at home. So you had to have a job. Some place to go during the day. At last commerce and industry made sense. There were compromises to make. Doug figured he could live with that. The prize was worth the price.

Or so he thought. Three days before getting to be twelve. As it turned out he was wrong, and this mistake brought him right up to the now-point of his life with little to show for the effort. The first secret he learned that lemony afternoon continued to drive him, to joy and to despair. The second great truth never took hold at all. He'd had more careers than he could count. Each, to Doug, more pointless than the last. Nothing even came close to walking the banks of a chocolate-brown river, wondering what bass were dreaming about. He kept himself sane through adulterous afternoons, through packs of lanky girls with gray eyes. This, and the promise of the next sweetie to come, kept him alive.

Still, when the do-nothing job of the moment started stringing out his nerves like wires, when the threat of promotion or some new responsibility loomed close, even pouty country girls and commode-hugging throw-up whiskey nights weren't enough. He knew it was time to drive far out of town and bury himself neck-deep in the soil. By now he knew every square inch of good farmland within a hundred miles of Houston, every broken fence and trail through the woods. This was Doug's only real secret, and one he intended to keep. First, because there is little good pussy in your average state mental institution. And more important even than that, he'd come to know, over the years, something too awesome, too wonderful to share. He knew what soil immersion was for. He knew why God had shown him this practice when he was young. The truth was he wasn't thirty-six but fifty-seven. He guessed what was happening by the time he reached forty and still looked nineteen. He managed to make shady contacts and buy a new birth certificate and other vital records. He figured he might die. Someday. If a truck happened to hit him or some pretty thing's husband walked in. If that didn't happen, he'd live to be a hundred and six. As long as the earth renewed his body, leaching out dysfunctions and sending vital rays loosed by the continental drift through his cells, he'd be fine.

He didn't doubt the truth of this for a minute. That business at the Hanging Judge Barbecue #7 had flat scared him out of his wits, run reason out of his head. He'd forgotten what he was. That he didn't have colds or heart attacks. Every vital organ was tended by nature's physician, the good sweet soil of the farmer's field. He'd be sticking his thing in girls for maybe forty more years.

And sitting on the sofa watching Mousebreath eat a plastic yellow rose, listening to Erlene bawl in the tub, he wondered why it had taken him so long to get smart. Why he'd ever thought about hanging around forever with Erlene. He could see himself now, farting around changing jobs about two hundred times, Erlene looking more like Otta Gee every year. By God he wouldn't. He'd spend his nights on the first great secret he ever learned, and he wouldn't waste his days on the second. He wondered if Cindy Nance had gone to Hollywood or stayed in Waxahachie. That was something he'd like to know.

THE HEREAFTER GANG

Another bad thing about jobs is the way they cut into the morning, thinks Doug, giving Monday a mixed review. Morning is a very special time. Doug likes to sit and think. His easy chair has been covered and recovered a dozen times, riding along with him through the different lives he has lived. The upholstery on the arms is worn through and he can see the wooden frame and the tarnished heads of tacks. Sometimes he studies the layers of fabric bared like geologic eras, reminding him of the past. He knows where he was and what he was doing when each of these layers was new.

At Lincoln Elementary he went to the little one room store across the street to buy candy. This was on one side of the school, Mr. Wetzel's model airplane shop on the other. Every kind of candy you could want was on display. Walnettos and Milk Duds and Necco Wafers. Jujubes and Forever Yours and Milky Ways. Kids today don't know what they're missing. The candy of that time was not the same as it is now. There were cardboard tubes of mints, picturing soldiers in the uniforms of all nations. After you eat the candy you can save and collect the tubes and line them up in armies. There are flat packs of bubble gum with pictures of baseball players and fighter planes and bombers. Doug's favorites are the Japanese atrocity cards, picturing the rape of Shanghai and the fall of Nanking. The theme here is Chinese babies skewed on Jap bayonets. Bombs fall out of the sky. The cards are two-color, red and yellow. Yellow for Oriental skin, red for exploding bombs and bloody stumps, the hated flag of the rising sun. Doug yearns for a complete collection. On the top of the glass counter are jars of orange slices, lemon drops, gum drops, jelly beans and marshmallow candy in the shape of peanuts. A penny's worth of candy fills a small white sack. Doug's favorite is cinnamon squares the size of sugar cubes. First there is the sandpapery coating, pleasantly rough to the tongue. Under this the slickness, the warning of hot to come when the fiery molecules of cinnamon are released. His cinnamon square period coincides with the mysteries of Sunday school and the reading adventures of Dick, Jane and Spot. Words that sound the same have similar meanings. Sin and cinnamon. He feels these are strangely linked. He learns this isn't so, but these are formative years. For the rest of his life, sin leaves a good taste in his mouth.

He has other word problems linked with religion. He wonders about the Nazarene church. It seems unlikely they are connected in any way to the Nazis. Still, these are the only two words he knows that begin with these letters.

So this is the way he thinks about the morning. It is a cinnamon square to be held in the mouth and savored, rolled about and tasted as each new layer reveals some pleasant thought, some moment from the past. Doug thinks only of the past. There is nothing he cares to remember in the present, which begins at age eighteen when he leaves Oklahoma City for a seemingly endless series of futile marriages and meaningless jobs. The really good things he remembers are crowded into the years before that.

People tell Doug there are wonderful things to do in the present. Erlene tells him this all the time. The only good thing he can see about the present is that it will shortly become the past.

Doug has a picture on his wall. It is a green and yellow Siemens-Schuchert D III, a bullet-shaped fighter plane designed by Harald Wullf in 1917. His bookcase runs to histories of early Roman Britain, minor English poets, World War I air war stories, and Western outlaw lore. Instead of reading widely, he tries to learn all he can about the narrow range of subjects he likes the best. In a matter of moments he can put his hands on a description of Caesar's clash with the Cassivellaunus. Cockeyed Frank Loving killed Levi Richardson in the Long Branch Saloon. The past is chock-full of such events. Very little of interest is happening now.

By noon Doug is part of the freeway traffic and on the way to work. Houston began as Allen's Landing. The Allen brothers built a wharf and started a store on the edge of a swamp in 1826. Houston is an accident, like Dallas. Many cities in the West were settled in this manner. Ma got sick and grew tired of watching the ass-end of an ox. So they stopped and did a city. The promising town in Texas was neither Dallas nor Houston, but Jefferson. Steamboats came up the Mississippi and the Red River, through Big Cypress Bayou to Caddo Lake and Jefferson. In Jefferson's heyday, there were fifteen boats at a time tied up to the docks. Everyone had a big white house. Jay Gould came to town in 1872 and said he wanted to run the Texas & Pacific through Jefferson. The men who lived in the big white houses said, "Fuck off, Gould.

We're into steamboats here." Gould said grass would grow in the streets and bats would roost in the churches. And they did.

Houston has several downtowns. The real downtown sent concrete rootlings thrusting blindly through the earth. Many took hold and grew. The downtowns all look alike. Buildings no longer wear clothes. There is no place for pigeons to sit. These dominoes of glass are set in tightly-packed rows. Men in white trucks bring toy trees and set them about the buildings in pots. Someday this will piss God off and he will flick the dominoes over with his finger.

Doug sees a pretty girl in a Trans-Am. On the radio, Pastor Jack speaks from the top of Angel Tower in Alvin, Texas. He tells Doug he will boil in his own juices. Houston will be consumed on April seventh of next year. Send a love offering for an illustrated booklet of this event.

Doug had worked for Clinton-Fevre three years, his second longest time at one job. Early in his working career, he discovered the art of getting paid for doing nothing. He learned to seek out positions in the non-functioning departments of large organizations. Rising young executives shunned these dead-end jobs like the plague. Doug avidly sought them out. He found the public relations department of a big ad agency was the perfect place to hide. There was almost nothing to do. Able assistants handled press releases and other puff pieces for favored clients. Doug tried to stay out of the way. His boss felt he was doing a fine job, and often recalled his name.

At work there were two call-slips on his desk. One was from Sunny D'Angelo. He wadded it up and threw it away. The other was from A.V. Annie Tonklin who said she had to see him quick. Sarah Dee came in and sat down. She lit a ciggie and gave Doug a cool appraisal.

"You look like shit, Hoover," she said. "You're hitting the bottle some."

"That's close," Doug said. "Everything all right down here?"

"Don't be ridiculous. Hoover I got to talk to you." She stood and closed his door. She was a tall angular woman with fine bones and a full head of chestnut hair. A whiz at her job, which essentially was Doug's.

"When you going to quit," she said, "and do I get the job when you do."

This took Doug by surprise. "Who said I was going to quit?"

"Lord, Hoover, you're wearing quit like a bad suit. You shucking Erlene too?"

"I guess I am."

"You sure are a mess. Listen, you know Jane Glynis down in media? Works for Tod Griever?"

"The blonde with big tits and bad legs."

"Hush, Hoover. That is my true love you're talkin' about. We're tying the knot next week and I want you to come."

"Jesus Christ."

Sarah Dee looked hurt. "Well I sure thought better of you. I figured you'd understand."

"Sure I understand."

"Don't think I didn't see that look."

"Sarah Dee, I been chasing women a lot longer'n you. It isn't that at all. For a smart lady you sure got a bad case of the dumbs. Amos Fevre isn't about to hire a female person to run this circus. If he did she'd be ugly as a hog. And he isn't going to buy this wedding bell stuff I'll tell you that. Amos is sixty-eight and he isn't into your alternate styles of life. You'll be out on your ass and the lovely bride will be supporting you on secretarial bucks. You're good at what you do, Sarah Dee, and that isn't my job description or even close. You'd fuck up the works in a week."

"It's not fair, goddamn it," said Sarah Dee, raising her chin in defiance. "Why I can do your job in my sleep."

"That's why you're here," Doug said. "Listen don't you think I'd get it for you if I could? You want to let this alone, that's my advice. I put you in for promotion you'll likely lose the job you got. With or without the lovely bride."

"You stop saying that, Hoover."

"All right I will."

"Fuck men. Fuck everyone oh Jesus I'm going to cry. I just about never do that. Pass me a Kleenex, Hoover. It's in your second drawer behind the booze."

Doug gave her the box. She ripped off tissues and fled the room. Doug puttered around a few minutes, glancing at memos passed along the chain of command. Many were from people he didn't know. He felt real bad about Sarah Dee. Her sociocultural needs were like his own. They'd both fucked up the American Dream. The *Wheel of Fortune* wouldn't touch them on a bet. He'd get her a little money before he left. But she'd never leave it at that. Sarah Dee was good-looking, upwardly mobile and mad enough to spit nails. She'd attack with righteous fury, self-destruct with a flair. Maybe march right into Amos Fevre's inner sanctum and pee on the rug. Draped in Sapphic robes and whacked out on tequila. The business world is deadly, thought Doug. How do people live with the pressure?

Doug discovered Annie Beth Tonklin on a stool in a shitkicker bar. Primal urges told him this was a girl who'd fill needs he hadn't even thought about. He was taken at once by the leopard stretch pants tucked neatly into half-Wellington boots, the truckstop beehive hair, the T-shirt with two armadillos flicking happily across the front. A mean-mouthed, long-legged girl with a pack of Salems and change. A girl who knew the Greyhound schedule by heart. She looked up and saw him coming, led him with her smooth-bore eyes.

"You're about the prettiest lady I ever saw," Doug said. "My guess is you're a flight attendant for TWA. I'd say you've been overseas a lot. You model part time and I've seen you on a prime time show."

"Let's get this straight right off," she said at once. "You're nice enough looking and you can stay. Just don't play around with my head. I been mind-fucked by every sort there is, from rock stars to oilmen and back, and a cowboy's the only honest man I ever met. I'm 'bout what you imagine and nowhere as dumb as you hope. I got native wit and cunning that won't quit. A shop teacher in Greenville South Carolina knocked me up when I was twelve. Left me after a month in this crackerbox house with eight dollars and a Graceland pillow. The whole place was full of stuff he'd made. Put a jigsaw in that sucker's hand and he'd go from now till Christmas. Wasn't a straight line in the house. I couldn't stand to drink in there, made me sick as a dog."

"I see," Doug said.

"No you don't. Where'd you get that fucking hat?"

Doug hadn't been aware of the hat. He took it off and saw it was a new black Stetson with a Gene Autry peak and a rattlesnake band. A blurred memory surfaced. Flowered shirts and Tony Lama lizard boots. He was certain the back seat of the Toyota was full of merchandise with pictures of horses on the sacks.

"It's a seven-year cycle," he told the girl. "Drink whiskey and drive fast, buy lots of cowboy clothes."

"And pick up country girls."

"If I get real lucky."

"Maybe you will."

"In here you think?"

"Mister, I can see those wheels turning 'round. I'm putting me a story and a half on this girl, and one of those ol' boys back there is going to walk up and eat off my ear."

"That did cross my mind," Doug said. "There isn't a man here hasn't pissed with Merle Haggard."

"You'll be all right," she told him. "Long as you don't do something stupid."

There was a plastic bass above the bar. A sign about credit and a Remington Arms poster of a grizzly looking mean.

"You're not so out of place as you might think," the girl said, tapping a

Salem down. "There's still country in you. You've gone and let it fallow but it's there. You've let your crops go is what you've done. Billy, I'd like another brandy and Dr Pepper you got the time."

"I'll have the same," Doug said.

"You don't want to do that," said Billy out of the dark. "Matter of fact I won't fix it. Her but not you."

"Fine," Doug said, feeling whiskey bold, "I'll have me a Lamborghini and Seven Up."

Billy looked at him straight on. "A Lamborghini's a eye-talian car. We're not a bunch of Plymouth Rock roosters in here. You might want to think on that."

"He'll have a Black Daniels straight up," the girl said. "Leave him alone, Billy, he's all right. Kinda insecure in his environment is all he is."

"I'm not certain I can hold another drink," Doug said. "I been at it two days or maybe three."

"That's sure some revelation to me, having seen you stumble in here on your own. Your wife don't understand you or so you think. I'll bet my ass she does."

Doug didn't have to answer. Billy came back with their drinks.

"There's a fellow back there in the booth," Billy said. "Bet his friend he can shit in your new hat and fill it up. His friend's got fifty says he can't."

"This fella a Indian you think?"

Billy looked confused. "Now what's that got to do with the price of feed?"

"I saw a Cherokee Indian do it in Anadarko, Oklahoma," Doug said. "He filled two hats bigger'n mine. This was after a four-day domestic buffalo fest in which the Five Civilized Tribes reverted to ancient ways and did a great deal of dancing and throwing up."

"That ol' boy might be a quarter Comanche now I think it," Billy said. "I can go and ask."

"I don't know about Comanches," Doug said. "Except telling one he's civilized offends him."

"You two don't mind," the girl said. "I'm not up to any major sportin' event just now. You coming or not? I think you just got lucky."

Doug followed her outside and drove in fairly erratic style to the Cedar Grove Motel Inn where the girl did something to her hair while he threw up in the toilet.

"My God, you could of done that in the car," the girl said crossly.

"I got expensive cowboy gear in there."

"You goin' to be all right?"

"I will when I get me a drink."

"I guess I heard that a couple of times."

When he got his drink fixed she was sitting on the bed shedding clothes, peeling out of the stretch pants and T-shirt and kicking it all aside. He looked at her hillbilly legs and thought, I bet this girl can sure run. He offered her a drink and she said no.

"I was going with this guy for a while said he had a Ford truck dealership in Dallas. I caught him one day coming out of where he works which is a Nazi bookstore. That told me why he didn't have a good white shirt to his name. So what is it you do? I mean when you aren't Tom Mix."

Doug told her. She said it sure beat the shit out of McDonald's.

"I been there two and a half weeks. I can't look at a burger and fries. I'm on straight peanut butter and canned pears."

"You got tits like a two-dollar snowcone," Doug told her.

"My mother used to work in a Dairy Queen," she said, and settled into his lap. "I usually just go down on a guy till I get to know him better. I'm making an exception with you. Take that as a compliment if you like."

"I think that's what I'll do."

"You are in for chills and spills, I'll tell you that. I holler, groan and see visions and I'm triple-jointed where it counts."

"You're a sweet little honey," Doug said.

"I expect you'll find I am."

In the morning Doug asked her where they were, which turned out to be Pasadena, Texas, the ass-end of Houston. That accounted for the cowboy clothes, and the endless string of shitkicker bars. Going out for breakfast he saw a couple in a new Chevy pickup with oversized tires. Mother, nursing baby and dad all in camou fatigues. Dad went in the store for a six-pack and Doritos. There was a thirty-ought six in the gunrack, with a scope sight suitable for sniping at Voyager II. Bumper stickers on the back:

WHEN PASTOR JACK TALKS, JESUS LISTENS
HONK IF YOU LOVE TEXAS PUSSY

"John Travolta met Debra Winger right over there at Gilley's," the girl pointed out. "You goin' to do what you said last night, or was that just whiskey and lust?"

"I said I'm going to do it then I'll do it," Doug said. "I'm not a man lets booze do his talking. What exactly did I say?"

"Shit." She was irritated at this. "Is your name really Doug or something else? I'm Annie Beth Tonklin and I don't guess you remember that either."

"Sure I do." Doug didn't. "And I intend to keep my promise, Annie Beth."

"Good." She leaned over and gave him a sister kiss. "I don't know a damn thing about that job but I can learn. Honest to God, Doug, I'll flat out puke I ever see another quarter-pounder."

Which is the long way of telling how Annie Beth Tonklin got to be A.V. Annie overnight, Director of Audio Visual Productions, a bogus department of the non-functioning Public Relations Division of Clinton-Fevre Advertising, Inc., an agency with the second largest billing in the Southwest. Doug spent the weekend at the Cedar Grove Motel Inn, writing up the proposal, with Sarah Dee's help. Sarah flirted openly with Annie, and thought the whole idea first rate. The audio-visual part had come to Doug in a flash, bouncing Annie on the bed like an IHOP pancake. Sometime Saturday afternoon, he went out for Dr Pepper and brandy and chili dogs, and a bottle of tequila for Sarah Dee. He had no idea what happened while he was gone and didn't ask.

The concept of giving Clinton-Fevre "complete state of the art audio-visual potential" was Sarah Dee's. The key there was "potential." It meant they could blow maybe four-hundred grand for first-rate AV shit, and not really have to use it. The agency execs could take clients in for a quick look-see after lunch, and lead them away bedazzled. The thing about AV equipment is it shines up good and looks like it ought to do everything but fly. Clinton-Fevre could put the new department in their slick brochure, talk about "total agency service," and continue to send work out to a good reliable shop.

Clinton-Fevre bought the proposal in a minute. Doug was lauded for timely, creative management thinking. Annie Beth's resume said she was formerly head of a large audio-visual house in LA. Everyone was happy for the moment. Except Annie Beth.

The call she'd left on his desk didn't surprise Doug at all, but he didn't have to like it. Trouble was piling up a lot faster than he could handle. It was mid-afternoon and he hadn't quit yet. He still had to face Erlene. She'd be in a badass mood after a day with Otta Gee. He knew what Annie wanted, she wanted to quit. Doug knew he'd made a mistake and Annie Beth knew it too. It was just a matter of time.

He took the elevator down one floor. Annie Beth ran into his arms, cute as a bug in a purple jump suit and spike heels, tears running down her cheeks.

"Doug, honey," she bawled, "good living drives me crazy. I got clothes I don't have anywhere to wear. Some of those outfits I don't even know which end goes on the top. I got more money than I can spend, and I sit here the whole fuckin' day reading paperback books. This Lady Melanie Jane she's panting every time this dude looks down her bodice. What's a bodice, Doug? It's gotta be dirty or he wouldn't be lookin' at it strong. You see what I'm saying? I been here two years, honey. I miss the sound of trucks. Sittin' at a pissant bar with a suitcase and a ticket."

Doug held her in his arms. "Annie Beth, what do you want me to do?"

"Shoot, I don't know. Something." She sniffed on his shoulder. "You quit honey, I sure don't intend to stick around."

"Don't I have any secrets around here?"

"Not from folks who love you, Doug, you sure don't." She kissed him on the mouth. Fritos and Dr Pepper. "I don't belong here, hon, and I knew right off you didn't either. I'd ask you to trail along with me on the road, but neither of us could stand the aggravation."

"Well we've had us some good times," Doug said.

"Lord if we haven't. Doug you've been a pisser and I won't forget you soon." She snuggled in close and made noises in his ear. "You cuttin' out on Erlene?"

"I guess so.

"Boy that's a big surprise."

"I guess not."

"You got someplace you have to go? That Lady Melanie stuff's got me hot and bothered, Doug, and we ought to say our goodbyes proper."

"You want to lock that door, why I'll see if you taste like Fritos on both ends."

"God A'Mighty, Doug Hoover," Annie said, "you've got a cowboy soul, I'll hand you that."

THE HEREAFTER GANG

Doug learned early seeing's not the same as doing. Every kid at school was taken in by slick-haired Asians smooth as glass. Watch the Filipino master. His black agate eyes never blink as he slips the Duncan yo-yo from his pocket and walks the dog. This and other miracles you can do this too, kid, it's easy. Hand over your quarter and in one swift motion he carves a palm tree and a ship under sail. A silver blade with a handle of mother of pearl, fingers stained with Lucky Strikes. You can buy extra strings if you want. Once the yo-yo's in your hands it turns to stone. It wobbles and spins and goes flat. Too late, the slant-eyed man is gone and you'll have to make do with what you have. Don't buy anything from a country that grows rice. Your allowance isn't due for a whole week. Self-abuse is fun, but it won't buy a new *Captain Marvel.* You don't have to spend money on a dentist. To fill cavities at home, chew up a couple of peanuts once or twice. Press selected pieces into hole with tip of tongue. Replace as needed. Save more money by avoiding expensive foods. Gingersnaps are your best nutrition buy.

Incompatibility is the all-time top 40 reason for splitting up. It doesn't say anything bad about you or her either. The judge stamps your paper and that's that. He doesn't ask why, and that's the reason people like it. Incompatibility wouldn't be near as popular as it is if you had to stand up and say, "Lou Ellen found out I was fucking that checkout girl at K-Mart, your honor. We got incompatible after that."

The straight truth is, leaving home doesn't have much to do with money or fighting or even screwing around a lot. Change is your culprit. You get up one morning and say Christ, I can't stand her anymore. I'm going out and get a new cutie at the store. This is really why Doug is leaving home. He tells himself Erlene is starting to look like Otta Gee, getting the whock-eye and that sound in her voice like broken glass. Or that she's fucking people he knows, and maybe some he doesn't. Which he's doing too but that's different. The truth is, he wants what everyone wants. Change rules the world. Sixty-year old men want to be twenty-five. Bankers want to be forest rangers. Cowboys, mystics, and truckstop waitresses know change is just an illusion. They know standing still is the best way to get from where you are to over there. That you ought to find a good beer you like and a favorite song and stick with that. Temptation will do you in. That sly devil change wears many faces. Still here's Doug leaving yet another wife and another job. Change is the nation's number one killer. Like Annie Beth says, you were a cowboy once, but you don't remember when.

THE HEREAFTER GANG

It was late when he left Annie Beth. Their goodbye fuck was full of joy and remorse. They sated themselves with pleasure, parabolic curves of desperation crossing each other where the sum of two needs equaled excess. They washed down the sweet taste of love with Jim Beam and some red and white pills from Annie's purse. Annie couldn't remember what they were, but they might be good for summer colds. Annie did the Waylon Jennings TV Christmas album by heart. Doug threw up on slides depicting metropolitan growth. The world seemed slow as waffle syrup, pleasantly out of synch.

Waiting for the elevator door, Doug had a moment of total recall, coupled with the inability to remember anything at all. He had no idea who he was. Drugs and dangerous audio visual rays had wiped his memory tapes clean. Two men in the elevator studied him from a distance. They talked about a mixed media blitz. They thought Doug looked familiar.

Doug wasn't sure where he wanted to go. Not home, he knew that. He was in no condition to explain his new lifestyle to Erlene. She'd sniff out Annie Beth in a minute. You can't talk sense to a woman you got another on your breath. They won't sit still for it. Which meant he needed a place to sober up and take a shower. He couldn't think just where. He noticed he couldn't see, not anything at all. He might be snowblind in the mountains. Peeking through his hands he found the street, asphalt between his knees. Bits of pill hung from a string out of the corner of his mouth. He was cold and then hot.

"You all right, fella?" A man tried to help.

"I can't walk," Doug said. "I got Donald Duck feet."

"Fuckin' junkie." The man walked off.

He found his car before arrest, before the duck legs melted down to stubs. Well he sure wouldn't do that again. Booze was all right, he could handle that fine. Drugs belonged to another generation. Houston heat had broiled a lizard on his hood, sizzling all the juices and leaving a perfect fossil behind. Doug touched it with his finger. He started to cry. He loved that lizard a lot. The poor little sucker's tiny ribs and crystal eyes were no deeper than a racing stripe. He didn't know if it was real.

He realized driving wouldn't work. He was raving over ducks. He was certain there was *pâté* on the dash. He couldn't get the key in the hole. Yet, he was clearly somewhere else. He couldn't remember getting there at all. Stumbling out of the car he found a street with live oaks. Ahead was a neighborhood bar done in Elizabethan style, phony stucco and slats. It was dark inside. When his eyes began to work, he found himself surrounded by clubby academics. Grad students with beards drank wine and smoked pipes. The air was thick with tobacco ice cream. There seemed to be a lot of skinny girls with thick glasses and no tits, fat boys with tits and no glasses. Clearly not a shitkicker bar.

A cold beer settled him down. Doug's plan was simple. Sip until the sun went down and move out in easy stages. The night would cover faulty driving. One more drunk wouldn't matter. Everything started coming up. He made it to the john and tossed a river of Jim Beam, a logjam of red and white pills. Jesus, what had he done? Could Annie be alive? Resting on the cement floor he read graffiti:

AIR CONTAINS ALL THE NECESSARY NUTRIENTS
FOR A HEALTHY BODY
JANE AUSTEN EATS COCK
BLACK HOLES SUCK
I'LL NEVER GIT A FUCKENG DAGRIE
JO ANNE PEELZER GIVES GOOD ZEN

Doug was surprised to learn educated persons were no funnier than anyone else. He felt deprived. Back in the bar, a student with failing hair sang songs in Old Norse. Doug joined in. No one seemed to notice he didn't belong. He began to make friends and decided he might enjoy taking a course. Everyone got in a Buick and went to somebody's two-story house. There was Bach on the stereo and Japanese beer in the fridge. He learned they were into the social consciousness of John Milton. Doug felt he was making a contribution. A man with a pipe nodded him on. The man giving the party had just learned he wouldn't get tenure. He taught something at Rice, and the cocksucker head of the department was out to get him. Doug knew the man wanted them to leave, so he could fuck a very tall and shadowy student with long hair. The girl was on an academic run and wasn't about to give her body to a loser.

The girl approached Doug. "I've seen you somewhere," she said. "You're anthropology, right?"

"You bet," Doug said.

"You know Howley Duke?"

"Oh sure."

"I had him for this elective. I mean, you've *got* to get out of Lit once in awhile, you know? We had this perfectly gross run-in about Leaky. I mean you've got this jaw thing and a perfectly *obvious* gap of my God a zillion years and that fucker hasn't covered *all* of Kenya who does he think he is?"

"John Fisher was a dead shot either left-handed or right," Doug said, "it didn't matter any to him." Lord, this girl had skin like divinity fudge. "He held Dimmit County in sway. The Rangers couldn't touch him."

"What?" the girl said. "Oh, right. I mean look, you've got tool manipulation just forever before *Homo Erectus,* for Christ's sake. I mean *who* are we kidding here?"

"I sure would like to lick your nose," Doug said.

"I don't think you should. Ricky's on kind of a tear."

"We won't say anything to Ricky."

"I guess you're kind of cute."

"That's a start."

"I'm thinking Drama next semester. I mean Lit's dead on its feet, don't you think?

Doug threw up in her lap. He thought he could explain what had happened. This girl was a sweetie, and he felt they'd gotten off on the wrong foot. Someone put him in a cab. He lay on the seat and watched the lights, trying hard not to get sick. If he did he knew the driver would dump him quick in a high-crime ethnic neighborhood.

Doug woke from a duck dream. It seemed to be eleven in the morning, maybe twenty-four hours since he'd left the apartment for the office. It was clear he wasn't getting on with his life. Soaking in the tub he decided it was vital to avoid doing yesterday again. That meant no more booze, or at least only recreational drinking. His father used to say it was all right to drink if you liked the taste. He said a man who drank whiskey and made a face was a man you couldn't trust. You'd learn soon enough he was a liar and a cheat. A man who cried when he drank was a weakling and a fag. This wisdom, Doug recalled, from the man who said it was lucky to find a penny with the date of your birth, unlucky to find one with the date of your death. Doug was frightened of pennies until he was thirty, and made sure there were none in his pockets.

The first thing to do was tell Erlene. Then drop by the office and quit. And then what? That was the good part. He wasn't going to make any plans. Just go. Throw away about everything he owned. Save two pair of jeans and two shirts, some worn Hush Puppies and some down and out boots. Maybe five good books. He felt the past was his destination. He would drive due north and never even look back. Waxahachie first, and just walk around town and see where everything was. Go by his old house, and the houses of all his friends. The shrub-covered windows of girls who'd shed their clothes in lemon light. The drugstore with the white-tiled floor and the marble counter and wire chairs. The floor would be damp from mopping and smell like sour ice cream. For old times sake, he would steal something from TG&Y.

Everything wouldn't be the same. He wasn't goofy enough to think that. But there'd be enough to suit him. Small towns leave pockets of the past. Whatever was missing, he'd fill in the blanks.

First off he'd find a good place to lie, spend a few hot days in healing soil. Red dirt and sandy loam had kept him going, but there was nothing like the power of native ground, the plowed black furrows where he began. After that, north across the Red River. Oklahoma City and Lincoln Elementary, Wetzel's model airplane shop and the candy store. The old neighborhood, Thirteenth Street and the Ritz Theatre and tree-shaded streets and Veazey's Drugs. Only it wouldn't be there and Doug knew it. He was mooning over cold nostalgia soup. The fat kid who'd bounced his way through junior high was a fat developer now. He'd covered Doug's past with condos and glitz. Doug would have to look but he knew.

And after that? He might be a cowboy then. Or drift up to the high lonesome if he could find it. Get a stake and trap beaver and look out for the Nez Percé and Sioux. He'd make peace with the Comanches, sit by the Snake River and catch trout, drink corn liquor and say the Crow is the white man's dog.

Confronting Erlene was no problem. It put things off, but he was grateful she wasn't there. He'd thrown up on her half of the bed, after his night with the jolly academics. That honey sure had good skin. They might have hit it off.

The idea of food left him cold. He had the weak, not unpleasant feeling that comes with alcoholic cleansing. This time the drugs were in there mixing it up too. Doug could feel the chemical punch. The world seemed slightly out of whack, six or eight inches to the right.

Mousebreath was totally pissed. Doug had introduced a number of bad smells; he was coming and going at odd hours. Doug opened three different flavors of *Nine Lives,* and left them on the counter. "Take your pick," he said, "it's cafeteria day." She gave him a dirty look. That's not the way we do things around here.

Where the hell was Erlene, and when was she coming back? It was irritating to make big decisions and not have anywhere to put them. He walked through the apartment. There was nothing there to tell him where she'd gone. Maybe something had happened to Otta Gee. We did everything we could, Mrs. Hoover. Flatulence is the number one killer in South Texas. Otta Gee buried at a Federal Fart Disposal site in Utah, the trailer towed out into the Gulf. The thing to do was go back downtown and quit work and come back. He dressed in jeans and a blue work shirt and put on a silver buckle and worn boots. A start on the high lonesome. Up the Missouri past Fort Benton; the buffalo shaggy and rust-colored for spring. He opened the fridge for a beer and found the note:

Dearest Doug,

I wish there was some better kind of way to do this but I can't stand waking up face to face and giving you more hurt and me too. We have both been guilty of gross diseat. Don't say you haven't too now honey I know you have. We have meant a whole lot to each other and I am sorry to have to do this I rilly am. Pastor Jack and me have been friends in Christ for some time, and I mean just that, Doug. I know you won't believe there was nothing else but it's true. I am a weak vesil and I guess I would have given up to desire before now except Jack has vowed not to violate my body until I am his legal Christian bride. Marlow Creel is my attorney and he will get in touch with you about the divorce. God it makes me just cry to say that awful word, but the Lord He works in mysterious ways, His wonders to perform. What is happening here is fated and written down in His book. Marlow Creel says half of the checking and savings is legal and right and I think that's fair I hope you do too. He says as a kind of legal precaution only what I ought to do is close up these accounts for now till things get settled more, not that I think any of this kind of thing that might happen with your lesir couples applies to you Doug. I have taken my rings and personal stuff of value over to the place I'm staying. (This is not with Jack now that's not what's happening at all so don't think something dirty.) I will come back later for the rest of my clothes. Please don't try and get in touch with me just yet hon I think that would be too hard on us both. I have taken the TV and the silver grandma Baxter left to me I didn't think you'd mind. I will sure miss you Doug and think of you always with plenty of fondness. I pray you will find the same happiness and peace of mind I have got here with Jack. He is rilly a fine man I know you'd like him. I hope someday you and him can meet under better circomstanses and be friends. Please forgive me for hurting you hon. We each have to find our own road or path in life. I think I ought to keep the Camaro since I'm more used to it than the Toyota if that's all right with you.

Yours in Our Savior,
Erlene Lamprey Hoover

Doug read the note again. His thinking machine was partially unplugged. Pharmaceuticals taped incoming news for broadcast at some later time. When power kicked in he sank down in a breakfast chair. He felt shaken and betrayed. You think you know someone and you don't. This wasn't like Erlene at all, running off with some stranger. Well he knew she was fucking around, but Pastor Jack? Jesus Christ, some asshole TV preacher with that blow-dried hair. Just where did he get off breaking up a person's marriage?

Taking the six-pack with him, he stomped through the apartment. A little two-step shuffle in the hall, to allow for continental drift. The answer to Erlene's betrayal was clear as rain. He bet she'd left clues behind. He meant to follow this down to the roots. Her drawers were sure a mess. Maybe Otta Gee's trailer looked just like this inside. He plowed through panties and bras and hose, jeans and shorts, a jogging suit. Went through quick tossing everything out on the floor. Boy, that jogging suit was a laugh. Erlene's idea of outdoors was a windchime in front of the A/C. The drugs started scatter-bombing again. Boelcke led the *Jagdstaffel* over the French lines. Glass fell out of Doug's eyes. Erlene had a Kilgore Rangerette sweater wrapped up in tissue paper. Doug knew he was getting close. Hijinks start in the backseats of

Pontiacs and Fords. He bet she'd done plenty of that. He found a gold football locket on a chain. Erlene had saved it since highschool, wrapped in a handkerchief with Pluto in the corner. He read the name. Why that team never even made district. Erlene didn't know doodly-shit about sports.

He sat down on the floor. The answer wasn't here. Erlene had covered her tracks. There wasn't a thing to link her to Pastor Jack. He knew what he had to do. Go out to Alvin right now and catch her in that phony Angel Tower. She was staying there and he knew it, rutting around with that preacher in a double-breasted powder-blue suit. He'd knock that sucker's halo clear to Corpus Christi.

It took some effort to find the door. Duck legs failed him on the stairs. The sun stuck needles in his eyes. He'd read your average junkie is sensitive to light. Doug looked around the hot parking lot, not sure what he was trying to find. Maybe a car. Maybe a green Toyota. It wasn't there and he remembered where it was. His legs gave way and he sat down hard on the third degree asphalt drive. Sweat had the smell of dead lizards. The world turned negative 35, the sky black the drive white. The limo turned into the lot. A door whispered open and arms lifted him up and set him gently in the back. Doug hoped this was another hallucination. The arms walked a quarter mile back to the front and got in. The air was cold and smelled of pine, the seats crushed velvet the color of grapes. Sunny D'Angelo sat on the far side of the seat. He made a sound with his nose.

"You smell like pussy and booze," Sunny said. "You don't call people back."

"I'm not up to this," Doug said. "I don't want to ride around."

"You eat anything the last couple of days? Besides you know what."

"I might throw up in here."

"Don't. We'll get some chili. You like ribs? I know this nigger place they got great ribs. Art, drive around and find this jerk something to eat. Chili or get some ribs. No chicken. I don't want any fucking chicken."

Doug leaned back and tried not to think about food. He felt tied together with cheap string. Sunny pressed buttons at his side, a small panel in the door. There were buttons to bring him anything he liked. He reached out and opened the fridge built into the back seat, next to the TV and the three grape phones that kept him in constant touch with crime in several states. There was a bottle of Bollinger in the fridge, Diet Pepsi and Velveeta cheese. Sunny opened a Pearl beer and handed it to Doug. Sunny sat back and looked at nothing, a Buddha in an eight-hundred dollar white suit. A wrestler's body gone to fat, brown Hershey eyes and George Raft hair. Doug wanted out. He was trapped in a grape-fuzz car in a bad gangster film.

"You are an ungrateful little shit," Sunny said. "You won't let anybody help. Everybody needs help what's wrong with that? Sunny D'Angelo needs help sometimes. I need a favor you think I'm too good to ask? I got everything I fucking need I still got to ask a guy a favor. You got nothing you're too good to ask. I find you bawling like a fag out in the sun you don't need any help. What the fuck you doing in the sun?"

"Looking for my car," Doug said.

"So where is it? You don't know, what?"

"In front of some bar. The Reading Room. Something like that."

"Over by the college. I know the guy runs it. Art, call and get someone to pick up the jerk's car. The fucker won't run get him a new one. What do you like, the BMW?"

Color was running down the upholstery like mud. Doug closed his eyes and held on. "Just forget the car," Doug said. "I don't even have the keys."

Sunny thought that was funny. He told Art and Art laughed.

"Your wife left you. I don't fucking blame her."

"How do you know that?"

"I know things, jerk. You don't give a shit what happens to you. I give a shit what happens to you. She move in with some guy? I'll get somebody to talk to him."

"Don't talk to him," Doug said. "Run over him with a truck."

Sunny pulled a little gold pencil out of his coat and licked the tip. "So what's the guy's name."

"Sunny forget about the truck."

"The guy's name."

"Pastor Jack."

"Jesus, kid." Sunny looked wounded. He put the pen away. "I can't do it. He's not my action."

"Pastor Jack's action?"

"Everything's action. You want another beer?"

"I'm getting sick."

"Don't. I been calling you two days you don't answer. You don't have no regard for your friends."

"I'm sorry."

"Fuck you are. You got no consideration. I try to do something for you you don't care. I got this thing going out in the boonies. A little stadium seats maybe nine hundred, a thousand. You got a piece of this, Hoover. From me.

Six points. You got six points from me."

"We talked about this, Sunny." Doug said. "I'm grateful. I can't take it."

"Fuck you can't, you got it. You don't even know what it is, you don't like it."

"It's something like that Girl-of-the-Month Club," Doug said.

"That's franchise now. This is something else. You like football?"

"You're into football?"

Sunny smiled. "No I'm not into football, jerk. Not your ordinary NFL fucking football. This is strictly private. Five grand a ticket, one game only. We get these old guys off the street they got nothing else to do. Bums, winos. They get five hundred bucks. You got to be a octo-whatever to play."

"Eighty."

"Yeah, right."

"Jesus, Sunny."

"Hey." Sunny spread his hands. "The guys get paid."

"They won't last one play."

"This computer guy I got says three, three-point-seven downs. We got plenty of extra players."

"The Ol' Bowl," Doug said, the name coming to him at once.

Sunny's eyes went dark. "Who the fuck you been talking to?"

"Nobody. A good guess."

"Good guesses make me nervous."

"Sunny, I'm in the advertising business."

"Yeah, right. So the name's okay?"

"The name's fine." Doug did a little arithmetic in his head. A thousand seats at five grand which was five million bucks. And he had six points of this sporting event which would wipe out winos in our time. Plus whatever else was in the account Sunny had opened for him in Liechtenstein. Profits from the Girl-of-the-Month Club and the place in Abilene where you could have your way with a badger. He had tried to forget his secret account number. It wouldn't go away. If he had let Sunny's dog become a freeway pancake as God intended this wouldn't have happened. Action is the brother of change, thought Doug, and look where it gets you. All he wanted to do was get out of the car. Max Immelmann was screaming out of the sun, shredding grape upholstery into dust.

"Eat something," Sunny said. "You don't eat you die." He tucked a white napkin under his chin. A little table slid out of the seat. Doug smelled the thick tang of chili in the air. Now when did we stop for that?

"You're on some kind of dope," Sunny announced. "That's a filthy habit.

Whatever you're on kick it."

"I'm throwing up, Sunny."

"Fuck you are," Sunny said, "you got no consideration." He crumbled crackers in his chili. Sausage fingers turned the crackers into powder; chili coated his pinky ring with grease. "You want to take a carton with you? No fucking beans strictly meat. I eat chili with beans I'm farting right into Sunday."

Doug staggered into a sudden wall of heat. He realized the parking lot was his own. The green Toyota was in its spot. He threw up on the curb, aimed for the apartment and missed. The continental drift was getting worse. Great change took place within the earth. Momentum kept him going, arms and legs windmilling, turning him in circles. Goofy learns to skate on the ice. His muffler gets tangled around his face. He slams into a tree and falls flat on his nose. Mickey and Donald laugh. Animated stars circle orbits around his head.

Doug was uncertain of his part in this cartoon. The eternal question of life: Are you outside Goofy looking in, or inside looking out? The pratfall sequence was over. Doug lay flat on his back. The sky exploded and fell like a blimp, tons of canvas made in Essen fell on his chest. Fliers from the aerodrome, returning from a strike on Neuve Chapelle, ran to set him free. Jesus leaned down and looked concerned.

"Are you all right, Doug? You think you can sit up?" Still in flying gear, he tossed his helmet aside. Fine yellow hair flowed free.

"Think I took a Limey bullet in the chest. Are the others okay?"

"Don't worry about that," Jesus said. "Let's get you on your feet."

"I'm okay. Had a couple of bad days, is all."

"I know, Doug." His eyes blue as the sky over St. Mihiel.

"What are you doing here?" asked Doug. "You in the war too?"

"I am about my Father's business, Doug."

"You get a minute, you ought to look into this Pastor Jack. That son of a bitch is going into business for himself."

"I'll do that, Doug."

A red and yellow Fokker howled over the apartment, snarling like a dog. Jesus ran for the cockpit of his battered Albatros. The girl from 104 came over from the pool and looked at Doug. Doug recognized her at once. Seeing her in a swimsuit, secret places now concealed, he felt an odd sense of excitement. She stood well away, as if she had seen this play before, the man lying on the ground pretending to be sick, traces of plastic bile cleverly pasted to his cheek.

"You all right, mister? You okay?"

"I'm fine, and you?" Doug said.

"You don't look too good. I can get the manager if you want."

Doug counted drops of suntan oil in her navel. "If you could give me a hand a minute. Help me get to my apartment."

"No fucking way."

"Thanks. May God be with you."

"Right. Have a nice day." And she was gone.

Another bath, falling asleep in the tub. He seemed to be spending a great deal of time in the water. The vomit-stained sheets had become a permanent odor in the apartment. Mousebreath abandoned the bedroom for good. Doug wadded up the whole mess and tossed it in the closet. Then he looked up the number for Ham Bayliss. The scene outside had scared him enough to overcome his dislike for shrinks, and Ham in particular. His receptionist said he was busy.

"You get him," Doug said. "I got a busload of orphans here and I won't hesitate to make the six o'clock news."

"Will you hold, please?" she said.

Ham came on at once. "Doug, that kind of stuff's not funny. Mental shit isn't any lark."

"I got to see you, Ham."

"How about lunch next Tuesday?"

"I'm talking professional seeing, Ham."

"Well you son of a gun," Ham said. "You sure do sound disturbed. I'm putting Rose back on, pardner. She'll set you up a date."

"I don't want a fucking appointment next March," Doug said. "I'm seeing things, Ham."

A pause on the other end. "What kind of things, Dougie?"

"Jesus Christ."

"What kind of things, Doug?"

"I told you, Ham. Jesus Christ."

"You don't screw around, do you? Anyone else?"

"How many do you need? Max Immelmann. Doc Holliday. Manfred von Richthofen."

"Together, or on separate occasions?"

"Is that important?"

"Dougie," Ham said, "what I'm going to do is work you in here soon as I can. Rose'll put you down on a standby basis."

"I don't want to fly somewhere," Doug shouted into the duckphone, "I want some help. Are you in the help business or not?"

"Give me an hour, ol' buddy."

"Thirty minutes. One second more and I give it to the orphans." He hung up, made a quick inventory of current conditions. His hands were shaking. Residual presence of drugs. That could change any minute. A quick mental picture of the girl in 104. Bound to a barber chair with velvet rope, her more than generous mouth held open by a mail order device. Doug called Annie. It might be helpful to know what he'd done to himself. No answer. A recorded person at Angel Tower said he could leave a message for Pastor Jack. That Doug should remember the Lord Himself would speak to him if only he would listen. "Tell me something I don't know," Doug said.

Traffic had a sobering effect. He felt purged of aberrations. Vision remained normal except for faint peripheral threads. He was as competent as any of these mothers. Chances were good he wasn't the only person on the freeway who gobbled pills and talked to Jesus.

Doug already regretted Ham. Pouring out this shit wouldn't help, and might have the opposite effect. People who knew Ham more than two or three minutes wanted to punch him in the mouth. The longer you knew him the stronger the urge. He made big bucks because his patients grew to hate him even more than they hated themselves.

Coming off 610 he turned onto Westheimer, past the big office tower and hotel complex, the Galleria Mall. Fried glass towers and neo-Mayan heights. Only a week before at one of the posh hotels here he had touched a piece of his past. It had happened as so many things do, the blind hogs of fate sort of bumping each other in the ass and there you are. As he walked out of the lobby into early evening light, an exotic automobile turned into the covered drive. It was a pearl-gray Bentley, elegant polished chrome and tinted glass, thirty years old and still in showroom condition. It whispered to a stop under the blue and white awning. A chauffeur stepped out smartly and opened the back door. The door made the pleasant sound we associate with machines used by the rich. The passenger stayed inside. Doug could see him in bits and pieces, a man lean and well-tailored on oyster-gray upholstery, legs crossed in casual indifference. He wore Italian shoes with tassels. The interior of the car masked the upper half of his face, but Doug caught the bridge of his nose, the clipped military moustache. A Britisher of some means, Doug decided, a man so close to high places, he could call James Bond whenever he liked. A line at the corner of his mouth marked the patience and endurance of a man who carries nothing in his pockets. His eyes were hidden. They would be blue, transparent as Chinese porcelain. Doug would have turned away then, thinking this was all there was to see. But then the passenger moved, brushed his hand quickly over perfectly creased trousers, and Doug was taken back at once to Harding Junior High School in Oklahoma City, nineteen forty something, and Herbert Tarchek, the dumbest kid in the world.

Lightning can strike twice, or even three times as veteran golfers will tell you. Still, Doug was certain even a couple of million volts couldn't change Herb Tarchek into the polished gentleman in the pearl-gray Bentley. Maybe God could do that on a good day, or maybe not.

Doug first remembered Herb in Lincoln Elementary. The kids were a mix of middle class and plain dirt poor. The middle class girls wore patent leather shoes and did their hair like Shirley Temple. They wore long cotton socks, the color of old tobacco. These socks came to their thighs and were held there by lavender rubber garters. If boys had known what to look for at the time, there was plenty more to see. Poor girls wore flour sack dresses and stayed to themselves. They were thin girls with big hollow eyes, frightened as baby rabbits. Boys like Doug who had plenty to eat and had fathers with good jobs wore Ferdinand the Bull shirts and knickers. They carried their lunch in metal lunch boxes or paper sacks, or took two dimes to school knotted in the end of a handkerchief for a hot plate lunch. The poor boys wore patched trousers handed down from their big brothers. They didn't wear shoes or bring their lunch. No lunch and no shoes. That got to Doug. He was a very sensitive kid. He didn't know about the Depression. He knew about dirt-poor coloreds because his father had made a living off the nigger shack business in Waxahachie. He thought being poor was a racial disease. It was scary to move up to Oklahoma and learn white people could catch it too.

Herbert Tarchek didn't have anything going for him at all. He was poor, skinny, slack-jawed and dumb as a post. He never talked to anyone or played with the other kids. Even the other poor boys would have nothing to do with him. Arithmetic and geography were beyond him. Dick and Jane were from Mars. The words beneath the pictures were written in their native tongue. Once near Christmas they gave everyone ice cream. Herb didn't know what it was. He wouldn't eat the cone. Everybody laughed. His nose ran all the time. His tongue was always in motion, like a pink windshield wiper. If it wasn't for snot he would have starved.

THE HEREAFTER GANG

The prettiest and the smartest girl in class was Cully Jean Moon. She belonged to Billy Bass, the smartest and the best-looking boy. Cully Jean was special. She had the magic. Even a fourth grade boy could tell that. Even Herb Tarchek. He followed her around like a dog. Billy Bass bloodied his nose regularly. Herb didn't seem to notice. He kept on following Cully Jean.

By junior high, everyone knew who they were and where they belonged. Herb continued his valuable role as class clown and savior. He gave of himself so that others might not suffer the onset of adolescence. Just as there is one willing girl, one bully, one Brain, one fat kid in every school, there is one Herb Tarchek assigned to each class. These were trying times and Herb was badly needed. Hormonal frenzy was epidemic. Tits were springing up overnight, like curious little buds. Girls began to walk in that mysterious way that girls will, without ever being told by their mothers. Jerkoff fever was rampant throughout the land.

Cully Jean Moon was more beautiful than ever. Tall, lean, and graceful before her time. Dark eyes tilted hauntingly at the corners. During those rare times when she spoke to lesser beings, she tilted her head slightly and focused three inches beyond your head, as if she saw you in a dream. The eyes, and the lazy smile, said, "I already know the answers to your questions."

Billy Bass hung on through the seventh grade. His replacement was Clayton Ricks. Clayton Ricks's father had a Packard dealership and he discovered sunglasses before anyone else. He took over Cully Jean by divine right and introduced her to hand jobs and Lucky Strikes.

Herb continued to follow Cully Jean. While his head lagged behind, his body raced forward without him. In the locker room at gym, boys stared at Herb with grudging envy. At thirteen, he was well on his way to owning a world-class cock. Any boy in school would have willingly traded his keen young mind for the awesome tool Herb was growing. Possession of this tool made his quest for Cully Jean an inspiring sight. He would follow her through the halls, eyes looking nowhere at all, that colossal pole fighting to break free of his pants. It was clear who was calling the shots. The organ, finding no guidance from above, had taken over. It went where it wanted to go and Herb followed.

Clayton Ricks beat Herb to a pulp every time he caught him following Cully Jean, which was three or four times a day. When his fists gave out, he turned the job over to his loyal sidekick, Harley Fish. Fish did whatever Clayton told him to do. He put Herb out of commission. When Herb could walk again, he followed Cully Jean on crutches.

Herb found problems in junior high he hadn't encountered at Lincoln Elementary. There were four social fraternities and sororities in school, and every week there were one or two dances at the Skirvin Hotel or the Black. Kids in one of these elite groups could get a bid to nearly any dance they wanted. Any right-thinking boy went to as many as he could. The stupefying aroma of a hundred gardenia corsages, the strains of *That Old Black Magic* or *String of Pearls,* had a near-magic effect on the female psyche. Girls who wouldn't kiss you goodnight on a picture show date would submit to dry fucking at a dance. It was an opportunity not to be missed.

Herb could follow Cully Jean through the halls, or stare at her house for hours. But he couldn't get into a dance. First you had to be invited. For Herb, this was as likely as a West Texas blizzard in August. Herb approached the problem the same way he approached, and finally conquered, Dick and Jane. He chewed over the problem until he eliminated every possible answer that didn't fit. He'd seen the purple stars on the backs of kids' hands and learned what they meant. There was a man at the door at every dance, usually the gym teacher, Mr. Ficks, or Denton Ames who taught geometry and shop. He had a stamp pad with purple ink, and he'd stamp your hand with a star so you could go in and out whenever you liked. This saved time looking for crashers, tough kids from the other school who wanted to taste the good life.

So Herb had the answer. Or at least he knew where to find it. There was a street behind the Biltmore Hotel called Reno, a street of shabby bars, winos and over-age whores. Half a block from life as Doug knew it, it was as foreign as the streets of Shanghai. There was a Chinese tattoo parlor on Reno, and this is where Herb got his star. It was his ticket to paradise. In his mind, he saw himself walking into the dark and magic room at the Skirvin Tower or the Black Hotel, and dancing the night away with Cully Jean. Maybe not all night. Maybe once. Once would be enough. He would hold Cully Jean and he would touch her and smell her hair and then Clayton Ricks would have Harley Fish kill him. Herb didn't care. It didn't matter.

Why the tattoo instead of simply buying a stamp pad and a star? Because it never occurred to Herb. This wasn't the way the answer appeared in his head. Maybe he didn't know about the stamp. Maybe he thought every kid in school was tattooed. If you were Herb, you went with what you had.

He got the right clothes somehow or close enough, and rode the elevator up to the dance, which was held that night at the Black Hotel. The lights on the dance floor were blue, and Herb could hear Gru Hackley's band and the lilting strains of *Racing with the Moon.* He was close. Almost there. He held up his hand and kept going. The man at the door didn't even look at his hand. He looked at Herb. He was Denton Ames, geometry and shop, and he knew who Herb was. He knew a pig dressed up like the Pope might get an invitation but Herb wouldn't. Mr. Ames knew Herb was slow. Geometry and shop had taught him patience, and he wasn't an unkind man. Herb could drive a nail in wood without risk of crucifixion, which was more than some of the brighter kids could do. He asked Herb nicely to leave. Herb didn't move. He held his star under Mr. Ames's nose and stared into the blue-lit room, into the cavern where music seemed to come out of horns, and not from the radio. The room where he would dance with Cully Jean. Herb knew he was being detained. It was clear that something was wrong.

Mr. Ames asked Herb to leave again, only not so nicely this time. The third time Herb stuck a star up in his face he yelled at Herb and told him to get his ass out and do it quick. Herb was too spellbound to listen. He wondered how they got the lights blue. Maybe they brought the moon inside.

Mr. Ames grabbed the lapels of Herb's coat, which was two sizes too big and had come from a rack in a diner by the Santa Fe tracks. He shouted in Herb's face. Couples began wandering out from the dance. One of the kids ran back and got Harley Fish. Harley's date was Nancy Lash, who was fat and sweated a lot, but would do whatever Fish wanted to get out of the house. Harley walked up to Herb. He spotted the star. He saw what Herb had done. He turned and shouted the words that would make him immortal, part of the Herbert Tarchek lore forever:

"Jesus fucking Christ, the dummy's tattooed a star on his hand!"

The laughter began, swelling until the room could scarcely contain it. Herb turned to watch. He couldn't imagine what was funny. Sometimes people laughed and sometimes they didn't. He was pleased to be a part of whatever it was.

An instant later, he forgot the others were there. His eyes found Cully Jean Moon. He saw her, yet he didn't see her at all. He saw a vision of Cully Jean, an image of all the fragments of wonder he'd created in his head since he'd spotted Cully Jean the first day of kindergarten. Before that day he was next to nothing, a spark barely lit and growing cold. Ghost parents he couldn't comprehend. People who asked questions that hurt his head. Cully Jean had blown his spark into life. He dimly understood that it was her presence that kept him going. And now all the Cully Jean pictures had come together in a picture too hot and too bright. A Cully Jean with shiny sparkle in her hair, a thousand lights dancing in her eyes. He gazed in wonder at parts of Cully Jean he'd only imagined. Bare throat and bare arms and breasts snuggled in pink candy gauze. It was more than Herb could take. Tears blurred the Cully Jean vision. Somehow, at that moment, truth reached the dim recesses of his mind like a new dentist's drill, and he knew this was as far as he could go. That he was standing in the presence of a bright holy light; that he would never dance with Cully Jean Moon, that the Cully Jean fire would burn him if he touched her, burn him black as the toast he always left in the oven and forgot. Out of all the bright confetti that had drifted through his head and just as quickly drifted out, he saw a schoolbook picture in vivid yellows and reds. It was a boy in a funny sheet who tried to fly too close to the sun. It was the first abstract linkage he'd completed since Dick and Jane. It was exciting and scary at once. Neurons that had closed shop and given up took notice. He was that boy in the picture. That was Herb Tarchek himself. *I am the flier, and Cully Jean Moon is the sun!*

Herb began to shake all over. He staggered blindly toward Cully Jean. He knew he couldn't reach her, but he knew he had to try. That was what the picture was all about. The projectionist in his booth began jerking dusty cans off the shelf, running every film he could find at triple speed. Words raced through Herb's head at a dizzy pace:

Throw caution to the winds...

It is required of a man that he should share the passion and action of his times...

Mitt der Dummbeit kaempfen Goetter selbst vergebens...

What this country needs is a good five-cent cigar...

Herb had no idea where these thoughts had come from or what they meant. They burst into flame the instant they appeared. He could feel their heat surging through his veins. He could see the golden image of Cully Jean, coronal fires exploding about her head. Suddenly, the laughter around him died. You could slice the hushed silence with a knife. The crowd stared in wonder. Herb stopped abruptly, not half a yard from his goal, a light-second away from the sun. His tongue hung out of his mouth, his body began to jerk in violent spasms. The couples about him gasped, all eyes riveted to a single, central point on Herb's body. Something enormous there was struggling to break free, to reach Cully Jean, to go where no man had gone before, not even Clayton Ricks. It thrashed wildly about, beat its swollen head, determined to have its way. Herb gave a final, terrible cry. His limbs jerked out of control, and a Gulf oil spill spread over his pants.

No one heard the words Herb uttered, or if they did they didn't remember. But Herb did speak, the words were there, tossed out of that nearly empty hopper in his head, because Herb had to have them, because he couldn't just turn belly up in the water without a sound. *"Death before dishonor!"* Herb cried, then fell in a dead faint at the feet of Cully Jean....

There are more questions than answers to this story. Doug thought about them all in that small part of a moment when the man in the car brushed his hand over the crease of his trousers and he saw the purple star. If this polished and elegant dude was really Herbert Tarchek, how had he gotten from there to here? After the night when his legend was born, no one saw him again. He simply disappeared. Where had he been for more than forty odd years? How did he get to be rich, one of the privileged few? More puzzling than that, how did he get to be smart? Divine intervention, Doug decided. The genius of Swiss doctors. If this was Herb Tarchek, he'd not only learned to come in out of the rain, he'd learned how to do it under the pearl-gray roof of a Bentley.

The only logical answer was this wasn't Herb at all. The man in the car who had 007's home number had a star, but he wasn't Herb Tarchek from Harding Junior High. Maybe the story of this man's star was as interesting as Herb's. If it was, Doug would certainly like to hear it.

At that moment Doug sensed rather than saw the bright flash of color in the corner of his eye. He turned and saw her walking out of the hotel and toward the car. A slim and elegant woman, whiskey-colored hair, cool and distant, her eyes flecked with shavings from some rare and precious stone. A whisper of exotic perfume as she passed. Her eyes met Doug's, and discarded him at once. A nearly invisible wire stretched from the Bentley back to the girl. A tiny German motor made of quartz reeled her gently to the place where she belonged. The turn of a perfect ankle, a peek at a lovely thigh. The chauffeur closed the door, and in an instant the man and the girl were gone.

Doug watched the car disappear in traffic. He knew, now, the man was Herbert Tarchek after all. And the girl was Cully Jean Moon. Not someone who *looked* like Cully Jean, but Cully Jean herself. And that, he knew, couldn't be. They had all grown up together. If he was fifty-seven so was Herb. And so was Cully Jean. She might still be a beauty, but she was not this breathtaking vision barely twenty. And if she wasn't, then who was she? Doug borrowed Herb's labored system of deduction, eliminated every possible answer, and came up with the startling truth. He knew how Herb had gotten smart, how he'd learned to read the Dow Jones instead of Dick and Jane. Cully Jean Moon had fired Herb's ignition the first day of kindergarten. That spark had kept him alive. Instead of frying him to a crisp on the night of the fateful dance, the fire had grown to nuclear proportions. Herb had *willed* himself to make it. Forced himself up through the web of his spidery thoughts. He clutched that holy image to his bosom and made it work. Maybe it took ten years to sweep out the billion gray rooms in his head. Another twenty to figure where the chairs and the lamps ought to go. A frightening task for sure—but what else did he have to do?

Doug decided getting Cully Jean's daughter was maybe the easiest part of all. Like Sunny D'Angelo said, if you had enough money you could get whatever you want—or figure out some way to make it come to you. So someone who knew someone introduced the pretty young girl to the rich older man. Hoodlums steal a baby girl and have her raised by Asian nuns. Whatever. The point is he did it, and Herb was happily rutting with a Xerox copy of his dream. Doug imagined black silk sheets made only in Flemish mills. Imported devices of chrome and leather, hidden in a secret teak cabinet behind the Degas. The girl wears eight-inch heels, a cheerleader sweater that barely covers sweet babychick down. The sweater is white with green letters, and says Harding Junior High.

Doug doesn't know all this. But he knows.

THE HEREAFTER GANG

The Chinese tattoo parlor is gone, and so is Reno Street and the Biltmore Hotel and a lot of other places. Doug has no idea what became of Cully Jean and Clayton Ricks and his faithful sidekick Harley Fish. He can't say if Mr. Ames is still alive and teaching plane geometry and shop, but it seems unlikely that he is. He guesses Nancy Lash is still fat. He doesn't know what happened to these people, but he knows what became of Douglas Hoover. He grew up and did very little at all, which is close to the game plan he had in mind. Only he hoped to have a lot more money to do it with. Now, with Erlene splitting and beating him to the punch and fucking up the bank accounts, he thinks twice about throwing money away on Ham Bayliss. It would be a lot cheaper to buy a good bottle of booze and put up with Jesus and Doc Holliday. They'd both be better company than Ham, or some other good buddy who might or might not have humped the future bride of Pastor Jack. At the moment, life seems undefined. The high lonesome is still far away. Happy trails, Gene, or maybe Roy. Mr. Peanut's in a home for old nuts. Krazy Kat got hit by a Chevy van.

NEAL BARRETT, JR.

Past the tinted glass wall of Ham's office, Doug could see the washed-out crowns of olive-colored trees, the roofs of low-rent houses in a patchwork of concrete and tar stretching south to the ship channel and the chemical haze beyond. Orange steel beams rose out of the flats to herald new office buildings and condos with names like Happy Oaks. The *barrio* would have to move its tacos and red potted plants and make way for a high-rise tomorrow.

"I need someone to talk to," Doug said. "I'm pretty sure it isn't you."

"So why are you fucking up my day?" Ham said. "I don't need any of this."

"Something's wrong with me."

"What do you think it is?"

"I don't know. Real peculiar stuff."

"What kinda stuff?"

"Crazy stuff. I don't feel real crazy but I got all the shit to go with it."

"You better be foaming at the mouth," Ham said. "I don't have to put up with you. I can sure throw you out on your ear. You gave Rose oral abuse."

"I guess I feel better already."

"Don't you play sensitive with me, Dougie boy. I'll take every phony baloney mood you can possibly dream up and toss it right back in your lap. You're not dealing with your newspaper syndicated shrink. You don't like me any, do you?"

"Not any," Doug said.

"All right. I can accept that." Ham brought his fingers together and tapped his nose. The nose helped shape his abrasive manner. It was overly wide and thick, flat on top and ending in a blunt set of nostrils shaped like tiny commas. His cheeks hung in folds beneath sad muddy eyes. There was no chin at all. He looked to Doug like a basset or one of the French breed of spaniels. He watched Doug with these intent but vacant eyes, a look that said he'd like to go out and tree a squirrel. Doug wondered what he was doing in this place, sitting in something that might be a chair, talking to a dog in a tie. The chair was fake yellow suede, hung in a pyramid of chrome. You sat in it like a sling. The chair matched the painting on the wall, a six foot square of acrylic yellow. Ham's desk was a piece of glass with nothing on it. Doug could see his legs and the slight paunch and the bulge of his crotch. He looked quickly away from the crotch. Your head doctor can make a whole case out of a glance. That's the way they do it.

"You don't look comfortable at all," Ham said, watching Doug squirm around. "You want to talk, you get settled down quick."

"I don't like to swing. I got dizzy as a kid."

Ham seemed to take offense. "What that is is your scientifically balanced chair, you stupid shit. Designed by an orthopedic surgeon out of French Lick, Indiana."

"Maybe if I had something broken," Doug said.

"Well that puts the finger on your problem. Goddamn. Just right smack on it. Your all out rejection of the norm, Dougie pal. You got to interface with life."

"I like old furniture you can sink down into a lot."

Ham tapped a finger in irritation. "You forget that chair. We're talking about you. I've known you on a personal and/or social basis, Douglas Hoover. You get smart alecky with me, why I'll put you in your place. Look at you, you haven't even shaved. You're dressed like the nigger cuts my grass. What the fuck, Doug? The child-you is rampant. You don't have a grasp on your goals. You're flat living in the past."

"What's wrong with that?"

"Well shit Dougie boy. It's not real."

"It's real enough to me."

"And what about this talking to Jesus stuff? I guess that's real too."

"I guess not."

"On the phone you said Jesus and who else? Some outlaw or what?"

"Doc Holliday. I only saw him once. At the Hanging Judge Barbecue #7."

"Was he with Jesus then?"

"No. He was just having a beer."

Ham shook his head and made a note with an invisible pen. "All right, who else? Let's get all your spooks out in the open."

"Manfred von Richthofen. Well now I take that back. I can't say if it was him. Might have been his brother Lothar. Manfred flies a solid red Fokker, and Lothar's is yellow and red."

"Christ, Dougie boy, this is heavy shit."

"Just give it to me in layman's terms, Ham."

"Oh well I bet you think this is funny," Ham said. "I'll just bet that's it. You sit there getting snotty about my chair and tell me you and the Red Baron are big buddies. How am I going to help you if you don't even want to get well?" Ham tore off a Kleenex and dabbed his face.

"Take it easy," Doug said.

"Don't tell me to take it easy," Ham said. "I'm the fucking doctor, not you. So how are things at home?"

"Things are just fine."

"In a pig they are. Erlene called Aimilee and Shirley Geeter. That wife of yours has run off with a prime-time TV preacher. Don't tell me everything's just fine. Hoover, these hallucinations of yours aren't the problems they're the symptoms. You got the marital ills and I expect your career's in the toilet. You're on some kind of pills. You hitting the bottle too?"

"No," Doug said.

"No, what? Listen, you talk to Erlene and you work things out."

"I don't want to work things out with Erlene."

"Hey, sure you do. Get your life together. I think Erlene is a great little gal."

"So I noticed," Doug said.

Ham looked hurt. "Now what is that supposed to mean? You want to tell me that? Doug Doug Doug. You see what you're saying, pal? You don't want this woman back. That's one level talking, that's your Doug Hoover number one. This other Doug is flat striking out with this territorial imperative bigger'n shit. This female is *mine* is what this other Hoover's saying. I am pissed at this lady but she is mine. Man, we're getting down to gut feelings right here. Which is the real Dougie, I want to know? What's this boy thinking down where he lives?"

"The real Doug Hoover is the one sitting here listening to this shit," Doug said. "The one that walked in the kitchen to fill up the Doritos and found you poking your tongue down Erlene's throat."

"Oh Jesus. For Christ's sake listen to this." Ham seemed to dry his hands in the air. "Would you just listen to this. Come on now, Dougie, we all get the grabby feelies, including you.

"Have you fucked her?"

"Of course I haven't fucked her."

"You have too. Your eyes moved funny."

"Okay maybe once."

"Nobody fucks anyone just once."

"Hey, you are getting your anger out in the open," Ham said. "That's good.

Go ahead. Shove it off on me. That's what I'm here for. I feel we're edging up on this thing."

"Has Stew fucked her too?"

"Now how would I know?"

"Because you're doctor buddies is why."

"Jesus, Doug." Ham seemed disappointed. "You let this kinda shit get to you, you're going to end up without any friends. You think about it."

Ham rolled back his chair and opened a door in the fake lime credenza. He brought out a bottle of scotch and two paper dentist cups. Doug wondered if he was angry with Ham. He applied self-therapy to the problem. Everyone fucks somebody they're not supposed to fuck. He'd fucked Janet Dauber, the dentist's wife, and the wife of a foot surgeon whose name he couldn't recall. Erlene fucked Stew Geeter the cardiologist and no telling who else, and Fido the psychiatrist who was giving him a drink. What difference did it make? Doug didn't know except it did.

"I hope you aren't going to hold this hanky-panky stuff against me," Ham said. "I don't want that, Dougie boy."

"I hope you don't think I'm going to pay for any of this," Doug said.

"Forget it. Don't think I can handle you, ol' buddy. We're core-group involved. I'll give you the name of a good man."

"I don't need it," Doug said. "I'm getting used to being nuts."

"Don't you get cute. This head shit's not any joke. I'd like you to get yourself a physical while you re at it."

"What for?"

"You don't look good at all. I'd get a hobby if I were you."

"I hate hobbies."

"So do I. Aimilee's into decoupage again. I sure wish she'd quit. We got all the bunnies I can take."

Ham leaned in to freshen their drinks. When he did, Doug noticed a large pistol in the Clint Eastwood calibre attached with spring clips to his chair. It occurred to Doug this was where Ham's eyes had gone when he'd mentioned kitchen frolics with Erlene.

"That's just a precaution," Ham said.

"Against what?"

"Jesus, I deal with highly unstable people in here. Outright loonies if you will."

"That'd stabilize 'em quick."

"What the fuck do you know about it?" Ham said. "I'm out at the AMA range every Sunday morning while you got your head in the funnies. I know my weapon and what it'll do. I wouldn't consider a shot in the kill zone. You mind if we finish this up? I got other Daffy Ducks besides you."

Ham stood quickly and showed Doug another door. It led to a far end of the hall, so no disturbed person would have to encounter any other. Ham gripped Doug's hand. He said everything would be all right.

"You didn't ask me if I'd fucked Aimilee," Doug said.

Ham blinked. "Uh, have you?"

"You mind if I had?"

"Oh I see, I get it. You want to even things up. My misdemeanor cancels yours. That's cute."

"So you wouldn't mind."

"I'd just as soon you didn't. If you are, you better stop. Aimilee's on a pharmaceutical toot, so to speak. That, and a little sexual kink I'd like to get straightened out."

"This is the Safeway kink we're talking about."

"Now I don't appreciate that." Ham looked as if he'd like to scratch a flea. A man who wished his wife would buy a coat and stay out of produce and fruit.

"Dougie, I'm trying to curb this real aggressive feeling toward you," Ham said. "That's not beneficial to you or me either. I'd like you to keep off of Aimilee. That's my professional advice. If you don't, why I'll blow your sorry ass away quick." He glanced at his watch. "I'm sorry, old buddy, I'm running late."

THE HEREAFTER GANG

Doug seems to be running in circles. Trying to wind something up or get started. He doesn't think it ought to take so long to quit work and leave your wife. That's two things to do. Your major executive does six or eight things every day. Erlene hasn't helped, beating him to the punch. He has to admit he brought the rest of it on himself.

There are good and bad points to knowing your own shortcomings, Doug decides. Whatever's wrong with him now will get fixed or maybe not. Knowing what you are is not expecting whole wheat answers from a white bread mind.

Once Doug decided that it wouldn't hurt to look into change. Just get his feet wet and jump out if the water got hot. He bought a self-help book. The author's picture was on the back. A man in his forties with a beard and a sweater from Scottish mills. The man looked pleased with himself. He seemed to offer major solutions. Erlene and her friends were on a self-help kick that year, learning how to reach their inner selves through better bowel movements, and pick up extra bucks in real estate. All this while Doug was meeting Janet at the Ramada on Thursdays, so he heard about BM Therapy and marginal land deals from both Janet and Erlene. Aimilee Bayliss seemed to draw odd conclusions from her class, and ventured into the drug and vegetable scene. So it was a time of learning for all.

Adultery seemed the only adventure left. His friends found pleasure in making deals and buying stock. The joy in this left Doug completely cold. So he kept doing the only thing he liked. Everyone else did it too—but in addition to something else. That seemed to be the rule. It wasn't okay to do one without the other. You had to work and fuck both. Maybe Cindy Nance was right.

One thing he never wanted to be was a doctor. When he and Erlene were first married, they found themselves with friends who were doctors and doctors' wives. The wives seemed to change like chameleons to fit their husbands' special fields. Psychiatrists' wives were mentally on hold. Addicted to the current drug group. They smiled and avoided conversation. Stew Geeter was a cardiologist. Shirley was his second wife. The first was a lean and wiry nurse, equipped with the endurance to put Stew through med school and eat vienna sausage. Doctors choose their second wives from a vast pool of dental hygienists, girls trained for this purpose. Like the doctor's second car, the second wife is picked for speed and racy lines. They are cute as Minnie Mouse and have tits out to here. Few men can stare unscathed at this expanse of young flesh so clinically close to the eye, while the girl on the other end whirs away harmful plaque. Soon the new Shirley is taken down to Cancun where she teaches the doctor things he didn't know about cardiac arrest. His fate is sealed in tequila and Coppertone. Soon after that, there is a new Mrs. Doctor in the group.

Driving away from Ham's, Doug considers Ham's advice about hobbies. He remembers going to college with Howard Plannt, who collected pubic hairs from every woman he'd fucked since junior high. He sorted them as to density and color, and had glassine envelopes neatly labeled "straight," "curly," "wiry," "silky" and the like. Working with a magnifying glass and watchmakers' tools, he fashioned finely crafted miniature portraits of the presidents which he sealed under glass and hung on the walls of his study. He told his wife the hairs came from exotic breeds of cats. He was up to Teddy Roosevelt when his wife learned the truth. Without discussing the matter, she walked out of the house and bought a 12-gauge Remington pump on sale at Sears, and went back and dispatched Howard to other realms. The trial was a sensation in Corsicana, Texas, where this sort of thing doesn't happen every day. The portraits were sold discreetly to a private English collector, and brought a respectable sum. This enabled Howard's widow, acquitted of all charges, to open a nice boutique in Wichita Falls.

Doug's father had a cousin named Billy Dale Hoover, who ran a filling station in White Deer near Amarillo, Texas. He carried part of a German potato grenade in his head from the Argonne, and was pleased with most everything after October of 1918. Billy Dale was obsessed with aviation, though he had never flown himself. He liked to go into Amarillo and watch the planes take off and land. He got the idea that he could raise up hummingbirds from birth, teach them to fly in formation and buzz about in simulated dogfights adapted from actual military records. Half the hummers would be painted with tiny rondels on their sides, and half with the knight's cross. Billy Dale planned to recreate the battlefield of Verdun in plaster of paris, using bits of mirror for water-filled shell holes and cotton for explosions. Toy soldiers and tanks would be to scale. A canvas backdrop would be fashioned to go with the panorama, a genuine oil painting of ominous clouds and darkened sky. All this would be portable and would fit in the pickup truck Billy Dale would take to towns and cities throughout North Texas, and possibly Oklahoma, following the schedule of county fairs. He would charge a modest admission, and felt few could resist such entertainment.

Nothing much came of this notion, hummers having no inclination to be Sopwith Camels or Fokkers. Doug saw part of the panorama when he was a boy and found it quite realistic. Billy Dale Hoover died in 1947 and left the picture of the bullet-nosed Siemens-Schuckert D III to Doug, which he still had on his wall.

At any rate, Howard Plannt and Billy Dale Hoover were two of the reasons Doug avoided hobbies of all sorts, besides window peeking and self-regeneration in the soil, which really didn't fall into the category of hobbies, each having broader parameters than that.

Doug avoided freeways when he could. If other routes added minutes or even hours to the trip, why it was well worth whatever time it took. He held the comfortable thought that in time he'd reach Mary Anne's drive-in by magic or accidental means. The closer he got the better he felt. About the world and about himself. He meant to stay sober. The drugs had run their course except for diehard Kamikaze freaks. It was close to four o'clock on a sizzling hot Houston afternoon and too late to fight traffic and quit work. He could do that in the morning. Pack a few things and put Mousebreath in the car and then off to the high lonesome. He sang a few bars of *On the Road Again.* Considered the merits of the little-known Blackburn Kangaroo bomber. The extended nose gave a wide field of vision. A squadron of Kangaroos was instrumental in dispatching a German sub in the North Sea in August of 1918. Two Rolls Royce Falcon LI cylinder liquid-cooled inline Vs, 255 horsepower each.

The world began to change almost at once. The neighborhood here was past the point of going to seed and well into shabby respectability. People couldn't afford to leave. Doug liked to think they wouldn't if they could. The houses were all clapboard wood or thirties brick and everything cried for a coat of paint. Like people growing old, the houses and the streets relaxed and sighed into final configuration. The trees were past pruning and no one seemed to care. Hackberries and elms formed a tangle of protection. Homeowners prayed for some animated full-color, deep-wood, Walt Disney spell that would keep the city out.

There were secret shady paths and nicely overgrown alleys. Root-buckled sidewalks led to a corner and a small collection of stores. A shoe repair shop showed Catspaw heels in the window, shoe polish dried and cracked in bottles, tins with faded labels. A three-foot replica of a wing-tipped, two-tone, uptown ragtime stepper on display. A walk-in one aisle grocery. The girl on the metal sign had spitcurl hair and a smile. Offscreen surf blew spray across her cheek. She loved the tingly taste of Grapette. A jewelry store with ID bracelets from 1952, and gold heart lockets turning green. A barber shop for old men. Shaved necks and bayrum and *Field & Stream.* On this corner dust was the decorator color, dead geraniums the national flower.

Mary Anne's was on the corner across from the bakery and the used furniture store. The orange and green awning was faded to nearly neutral shades. McDonald's claims umpty-billion sold; Mary Anne's has been flipping greasy buns and brown lettuce since 1936.

Doug cherished this fine familiar ritual, pulling up and rolling down the window and letting in the tinny music. The music, hits of the forties, blared from badly warped speakers mounted directly beneath the awning, each speaker decorated with dirt-dauber nests and sparrow shit. Every note shook the summer homes of spiders. The hot air heavy with the smell of tar and saturated grease, mayonnaise in five-gallon jars that come from the factory slightly bad.

This is me, thought Doug. This is where I belong. This is all the yesterdays bottled up tight and can't anything jerk out the cork. The image overwhelmed him, welling up like an orgasm of the spirit. He was left with syrupy warmth. Ham Bayliss wanted to get this stuff out of his head. Well not on your life, Dirty Harry with a couch. Christ, you had to keep up your guard all the time.

A carhop spotted him and waved. Doug waved back. He watched her prance back to the counter. She giggled with a friend and picked up a tray of malts. He knew these girls by name. He had watched them come and go and he supposed they had written him into legend—or for eight years, at least, the time he'd been in town. They'd passed the word he was okay, a guy who wouldn't yank his dong out every time you brought a burger to the car. So they flirted and popped their gum and promised highschool thrills with their eyes, knowing they wouldn't have to deliver.

Everyone knows what they were doing when something really important happened in their life. You remember where you were when Jack Kennedy got shot. When Tom Landry got fired by the Cowboys. Doug was studying the holes in the green and orange awning, wondering if this very same canvas had weathered fifty hot years of Houston summers. Maybe so, because they made things to last back then. So the girl just appeared out of the blue. He didn't have any warning at all. When she said what'll you have he turned around too quick, like you will when your mind's wandered off.

What did he say? Cheeseburger and root beer? He didn't know. She scribbled something on her pad and stuck a pencil over her ear and she was gone. Doug was stricken with sudden fever. Harold Teen, a little balloon with crazy hearts inside. He'd just seen the girl of his dreams, he knew that. He could say girl of your dreams with a straight face. Doug knew. In one near heart-stopping instant she'd brought the scattered bits and pieces of his fantasies together. She was every girl he'd ever loved. Every girl he'd ever wanted and never had. Every girl he'd followed across the street until she vanished on a bus. Every sun-tanned long-legged pouty-mouthed girl he'd ever seen.

A.V. Annie and Cindy Nance. Erlene the way she'd been when they met. Lord, this was a sweetie and a half! He loved this gum-chewing tight-ass honey, bouncing sassy in a skirt up to here, and those white shiny kicker tassel boots. He'd hungered all his life for this special breed of girls with their disagreeable ways, their nasty hillbilly mouths. These mean-eyed women with their swamp fox jaws and suspicion in their dishwater eyes. Give me a little Bambi-eyed girl, Doug prayed, a girl with apple tits, a lean and lazy girl who can't blink and wet her lips at the same time. A girl who sulks. A bad-eyed girl from East Texas or Alabama or Tennessee who's as jumpy as a cat. I want to count her skinny ribs and watch her toss one hip out of joint. Watch her talk and see the wondrous ways vowels contort her mouth. I want to taste cigarettes and Dr Pepper on her lips. See the awkward whacky bones in her knees. I want to eat breakfast between her legs and suck her toes. I want a girl who doesn't know what I'm talking about at all and doesn't care. A girl who laughs too loud. A girl who barks like a dog when she comes. A girl with cheap whiskey eyes. A girl striped yellow by the motel blinds on a hot Friday afternoon at two. A girl who tastes like otter sweat and stale potato chips. A girl who thinks about herself in bed because selfish is the greatest gift she's got.

Doug remembered them all; in this one instant, they pranced across the screen inside his head. A preview of past attractions, a sweet confusion of aftertastes. The green-eyed girl drinking beer in the morning in a hard-times

Galveston, Texas, bar. They talked a little while, made a joke. She decided without Doug having to ask and led him back to her shabby mobile home. Her husband worked on an oil platform in the Gulf and was gone sometimes for thirty days. He earned good money, more than Doug at that time in some do-nothing mind-fucking job. Where this money the girl got went he couldn't guess. Even if this rawboned sweetie had the will to move mountains, had the drive to move piles of overalls and T-shirts and socks her man left, TV logs and romances and Colonel Sanders bones, there'd be nothing but a dogshit candy wrapper rug there to see. Maybe the girl knew this, too. Maybe Dairy Queen cups and Jurassic onion rings masked a life she didn't care to uncover anymore.

She would lead Doug past this debris and almost shyly turn away, leave him sitting on her unmade bed while she pulled off her Roadrunner shirt and peeled blue jeans down her legs. He loved those long and awkward legs, loved to count the bumps along her spine. Her face and small breasts were alive with copper freckles. She tasted of sweat and salt when he licked the bony hollow of her neck, the fine hair on the backs of her hands. There was barbecue sauce or some other tasty clue to where she'd been. She was awkward when she stood; she walked as if Galveston were as straight up and down as West Virginia. This changed when she came into his arms, drew him to the sheets they'd stained themselves. There was a sweetness in her body, an innocent grace in every limb. In the frenzy of the moment, when the wonder of their coupling overtook her, it was her body that responded. The wide and sullen mouth never changed. Her eyes never lost the sad glaze of desperation. She had resigned herself to looking at a world she couldn't change. Whatever joy she found was filtered through the pleasures of her body. There was surely no resignation there. Doug told her she fucked like a ferret. She didn't know what that was, and wanted to know if it was good. Doug learned nothing at all about her. Her husband got a job onshore; Doug's visits became more hazardous and infrequent. One morning she met him in the bar and said she couldn't see him again, that her husband was getting mean and asking questions. When Doug protested she shook her head. No more sadness in her eyes and no less than he'd seen before. "Honey, you don't want to play redneck roulette with that dude," she said, and Doug decided she was right. He wondered where she'd gotten this line. He'd never seen a trace of humor in her before. Maybe it came from a country song. Or maybe the other way around. Maybe that's where country songs got their start.

Nearly two years later he picked up a girl hitchhiking from Fort Worth to Odessa, certain as he kicked up gravel it was the very same girl. It wasn't. She was a rich man's daughter from Frankfort, Kentucky, fleeing the restraints of affluence, escaping in prefaded designer jeans and calf-length Navajo moccasins imagined in a Lord & Taylor dream. She told Doug money was useless, a karmic drag. The important thing was finding your inner self. And as they whined across Texas at ninety-four miles an hour, she found Doug's basic primal need, pursued it with a fervor equalled only in a Galveston mobile home, Doug staring up at Elvis Presley resurrected, rising out of Graceland in Day-Glo afterlife black velvet splendor on the wall.

It wasn't the same girl but they were sisters under the skin, mean-eyed and lanky and resenting what they were for different reasons which they surely didn't know were the same. Life had fucked them in a way they didn't like and couldn't change. Later, they both had lines in Doug's instant documentary as he waited for the fairest of them all to bring his root beer and burger to the car. Waited for this carhop honey to tell him that the forty years between them didn't matter, that she was dead-on certain no other man could tame her, could release the real woman inside. And then she was right there again, coming at him with a tray under the orange and green awning over the hot melting tar, coming at him with a prancy little walk that would let her hold dimes from her crotch down to her knees.

Doug's throat nearly closed. The magic took him up and held him as she set the tray in place.

"That be all?" she said. "Can I get you somethin' else maybe some fries?"

That voice! Like pulling nails out of a fence. He was right, she was everything he'd dreamed.

Doug couldn't speak. He was drained, wilted from this encounter. The girl gave him a blank-eyed look and danced away. He finished the burger in minutes, the first food he could recall since jumping the reservation and running amok. The root beer vanished. What could he order next? A desperate plan was forming in his head, bursting out like microscopic life on *Nova*. He could order one thing after another and keep her coming. Sleep in the car and be ready next morning. What time did she come on?

He decided he was crazy. Nothing real new about that. Nothing he couldn't handle. No new hallucinations. No Doc Hollidays or saviors on a spree. The carhop queen was real. She wasn't part of that. He still knew real when he saw it.

A horn sounded to his left. Once, like someone had tapped it lightly. Doug turned and saw the boy grinning from a faded blue pickup in the space next to his. The face looked familiar. Then he saw it was the kid from the Hanging Judge Barbecue #7.

"Hey there, how you doing?" the boy said.

"Why I'm fine," Doug said, "real good."

The boy got out and walked around the front of the pickup, leaned on Doug's door and crossed his arms, sungrins closing his eyes.

"I was sure some worried 'bout you. I'm glad to see you sittin' up straight."

"I'm okay. You were real kind to help."

"Nothing a-tall." The boy stuck a cigarette in the corner of his mouth. He wore the same jeans and rough-out boots.

"This your day off or what?" Doug asked.

"Shit. I flat quit that ol' job. Got something better which is no job at all."

"Well I'll say." I like this kid, Doug thought. "I'd guess you're going to drift around some."

"Listen I'm fired up and ready. You won't have to chase me out of town."

They were starting to sound like Glen Ford and Joel McCrea. Doug wanted to tell the boy that he was a drifter too or almost. He tried to get another look at the girl. She was out of sight now or inside.

"Fine looking lady," the boy said, following Doug's eyes. "I'd say that for a fact."

"She sure is pretty."

"She's a gingersnap cookie is what she is."

Doug had a thought. "She's not your girlfriend or anything, is she?"

"Sue Jean? Shoot, that girl'd earn me a free bus ride up to Huntsville Texas. I don't guess I want to go.

Sue Jean. It seemed to fit. "You know if she's got a last name too?"

"Now I did," the boy said. "Why that's right on the tip of my tongue. Shit, don't that beat all. Don't you tell me now. I want to say whipper-snapper. Somethin' similar to that."

Doug laughed. "Whipper-snapper'd fit."

"I'm not much on names."

"I guess I'm not either. Say, I'm Doug Hoover by the way."

"Royce."

"Well okay, Royce." Doug pushed his hand past the tray and found the boy's strong grip. The boy grinned. He had a habit of cocking his head at a five degree angle, shifting his jaw to one side making his face seem slightly unaligned. This was mostly when he listened to Doug talk, like he was maybe on a couple of other channels and didn't want to miss a thing. Doug felt an attack of brotherhood. John Wayne and Montgomery Clift, up in the high lonesome. Why, they could beat the crap out of each other then laugh it all off, embrace in manly fashion and get the cattle up to Dodge.

Royce left the car and walked to the serving counter, coming back with fresh root beers. He set one on Doug's tray, tasted brown foam on his mug and leaned back against the truck.

"Well thanks," Doug said, "that's sure real nice."

"Don't think nothing of it."

"Right here is the best root beer in town," Doug said. "Your bottle root beer's no good. It's different from what you get in a mug. I used to drink it like this when I was a kid. They had these Triple XXX stands up in Oklahoma City. The roof of that place was a great big barrel with real staves down the side. My dad always told me it was full of root beer. I believed him for some time."

"Now that'd be a lot of root beer."

"I wondered what'd happen if it broke. I guess it'd come right up in the cars. You going anywhere special? I mean when you start to drift."

Royce squinted one eye. "See that's what driftin' is. Not knowing where it is you're going. If you know now that's not drifting. That's more like your travelin' or your driving. I don't care a lot for either."

"I got to remember this," Doug said.

"It's not the same as a trip or something else."

"I can see it's not."

Royce looked up like he was following something moving past Doug. Doug followed his eyes and saw a blue-and-white drive by Mary Anne's going slow. "You in some kind of trouble?" he asked Royce. "You can hide at my place if you want. Isn't anyone there but me and the cat."

"Old habits." Royce shook his head. "You take care now, friend."

With that he was gone. He set his mug on Doug's tray and got in the pickup and started up. He tapped the horn again. A fat man came out of the john and blinked at the sun. A fat man with little boy feet. He had a beard cut funny, a black coat big as a tent. The coat seemed covered with flour and soot. He appeared to be confused. His eyes wandered everywhere but straight. He scurried to the truck like a beetle, making waddle-step detours on the way. Royce rolled around to the back and the fat man fumbled with the door and got in. Royce took off down the alley and disappeared.

Now who the hell is that? Doug wondered. Royce hadn't said a thing about him. It might be an old uncle. He didn't look in shape for drifting or much of anything else. Doug honked and a girl came out for the tray. Peggy Ann and not Sue Jean.

"Where's the other girl?" Doug looked disappointed.

"Well I'll say," said Peggy Ann. "Thanks a big bunch. She up and quit is what. Now I got three fuckin' stations instead of two."

"She did what?"

"You want somethin' else?" She blew Doug a bubble.

Doug didn't answer. He left a sizable tip. He suddenly felt lost. The girl was gone and Royce was gone too. He wanted to tell Royce about Liver Eating Johnston and winter trapping on the Snake. No one else had trouble quitting work. Now why was that?

Empty didn't seem the right word for coming home. It was a step past empty, like the furniture and the rugs were all gone, the paint scraped off the walls, planking and wiring exposed. Everything just like he'd left it and nothing still the same. Wadded up sheets in the corner. Books spine up on the couch like birds flying upside down. Everything there, but the residue of life drained away. Bloodless curtains and frying pans. If he stood real quiet he'd see coffee tables and ashtrays and chairs disappear. He didn't intend to hang around for that.

Going from room to room he dragged a cardboard box, tossing in things he wanted to take along. Toothbrush, toothpaste, jeans and boots and socks and underwear. *Life in Pre-Roman Britain, The Battle for Gaul. Great Aircraft of World War I. Famous Badmen of the West. Minor English Poets.* He took the Siemens-Schuckert D III picture off the wall. Grabbed his Mickey Mouse watch. Took a look in Erlene's closet. She hadn't been back. Maybe that fucker was going to clothe her in robes of many colors. He wondered if she'd told him about Otta Gee Lamprey. Now there was a good test of Christian faith. A fleeting image of camping out, buffalo tongue and coffee with Gabby Hayes. He decided against that and left the kitchen alone. A half bottle of Cutty Sark went into the box and Mousebreath's different-colored cans. Mousebreath had stayed out of the way, detached from all this until her food supply became a part of the act. After that she got in the box and stood guard.

One more thing. He went back to his room and pulled *The Search for Alexander* off the shelf. Two twenties guarding the entry to the apadana at Persepolis had been filched. Erlene knew about his stash but hadn't bothered it before. Their relationship was deteriorating fast. In the bathroom, he pulled the toilet paper gizmo off its roller and pulled out the little metal spring. The seven one-hundred-dollar bills were still there. Not much, but better than an apologetic look at the bank.

Mousebreath watched these proceedings, her suspicion of several cat-days confirmed. Order was out of whack. Her person's mate was gone. No big loss there. Her person, normally unsound but entertaining, was more unstrung than ever. The colors in his head spelled trouble. Worse, on the feline scale of bad news, they spelled *change.* Stay close to food. Don't do anything not considered cute. An overnight bag came out of the closet. Mousebreath bit her tongue. She allowed him to pick her up, drop her in and zip it shut. Christ, here we go. He'd better know what the fuck he's doing.

There was nothing in the mailbox but bills. He scratched out his name and wrote: "Sister Erlene, Angel Tower, Alvin, Texas, Go with God." Night closed in, and underwater lights from the pool turned the air a hazy blue. The girl from 104 lay on a plastic lounge chair near the edge. A bald-headed man was in the water. He kept himself afloat by eating the girl's toes. His mouth moved like a typewriter on the blink. Doug understood his need. The girl seemed unconcerned. She waved her drink and Doug waved back.

Doug had always been drawn to the security of motels. When you closed that door and set the heavy brass chain you left your troubles all behind. The room was like a treehouse, a cave on the bank of a creek. No one even knew you were there. You could do whatever you liked. Just anything at all. The church offered sanctuary in medieval times. You could read about that in a book. Now it was Rodeways and Ramadas. They couldn't touch you in there. He liked Ramadas best. The name was done in old-fashioned letters and said *inn.* You might drive up in a coach and get some ale.

Doug let Mousebreath out of the bag. She took one look around the place and retreated to the tub. Doug looked at himself in the mirror bolted permanently over the dresser. He could eat the candy and cookies he'd bought at the 7-Eleven. He could read one of his books. He could watch TV. He had everything he needed. He could call someone and say, "I'm in this motel somewhere but you don't know which one it is."

He ate all his food and watched the news on TV. He never could remember just when he was married to who, but clearly recalled the shows that went along with each bride. Marilyn June from *Perry Como* to *I Love Lucy.* Lindy from *Dinah Shore* to *Gunsmoke.* Erlene from *Dallas* to *L. A. Law.* He wondered where Marilyn June was now. They'd run off from college and gotten married at a wedding factory in Durant, Oklahoma. The idea was to get to fuck legal on Saturday afternoon. Her parents found them out in less than a month. Annulment instead of divorce since they were hardshell Oklahoma

Catholic, a breed apart from any known cult or religion. The month of sin and fun was smoothed over by papal skulduggery, leaving Doug horny and alone. Marilyn June was jerked abruptly offstage, out of his life for good. One agonizing letter finally reached him, smuggled out of a parochial retreat in Allentown, Pennsylvania, a place designed to dry the labial juices aroused by dirty Methodist boys.

After college and ROTC, he married Lindy at Norfolk, Virginia. They settled into a series of dreary army posts. Long-legged, grey-eyed Lindy was a wonder. She fit Doug's standards to a tee, a cross between poor white trash and Scarlet O'Hara, which isn't much different except for luck. She was a dream come true, but Doug wasn't the only one who knew it. Her honey drew flies, and once she got started she slept around as much as Doug. In the end they confessed all their sins and promised to work things out. Which they did for awhile. After the army, Doug found work in Beaumont, Midland and Wichita Falls. They both got tired of pinching pennies, lying about late nights at the office and beauty shop appointments. When Lindy told him she was leaving him for a rich oil and gas operator, he was sad but a little relieved too. He was learning something he'd guessed a long time. That he didn't have the drive to get to the top, or even anywhere near. Work just didn't cut it. It was time he could spend doing a lot of other stuff. He wondered if that was the way he'd been born, or if he'd gotten his fill of business at eleven. Every job he got seemed a lot like selling nigger shacks.

He really loved Lindy, and knew she loved him too. That was the bad part. They had something together real good. She was the only person he'd ever told about the secret healing properties of the earth. Lindy believed him. She'd read a lot of paperback books about Atlantis and the nine-foot giants in Tibet.

He couldn't exactly remember why he'd married Erlene. Except he was going downhill after Lindy, losing jobs on a monthly basis, and carrying the torch for a girl in Fort Worth. Erlene was good in bed but that wasn't much excuse. Lindy had been gone a long time. He was beginning to lose track of job titles. Women's faces were starting to blur. Nothing seemed to work the way it should, so he traded empty nights for some steady fun in bed. And then too late he took a trip down to Clute and saw Otta Gee Lamprey, and a glimpse of the future that gave him the sweats. Nothing was the same after that. Playing Bandit and Tourist with Erlene, in love with her rosy little folds, he'd suddenly imagine Mexican bats flying out of there in droves. It was a picture he couldn't shake.

And then there was the business about kids. He couldn't forgive her that. Half the problems were maybe his but that wasn't. He was sterile as a mule, something he'd discovered years before with Lindy. Lindy wanted children, or thought she did at the time. Doug wanted them too. She loved him a lot and didn't hold this shortcoming against him. Erlene didn't want any at all, and never stopped crowing about awful little rug rats crawling around the house. She was delighted he couldn't puff her like a toad, and told him every time she got the chance. Well goddamn her for that. He didn't have any business raising kids. He couldn't manage to grow up himself. But Erlene didn't have any right to do that. Make fun of kids he didn't need and couldn't get.

Doug's watch said twenty after three. The TV hissed and made gravel. Mousebreath scratched at the door. Doug told her to shit anywhere she liked. He wondered what Sue Jean was doing. He bet she slept in some cute little shortie. Stuffed animals on the dresser, rock stars tacked to the wall. She'd kicked off the covers and that nightgown was creeping up her thighs. My, she looked sweet.

One minute it all seemed fine, lying on the motel bed half asleep. The next something flipped over hard in his stomach and left him scared. What am I doing here? he thought. What the fuck am I going to do next? Seven hundred bucks wouldn't cut it. Three or four weeks tops. Five if he slept in the car and ate a lot of peanut butter. He knew he was handling this the same way he handled most everything else in his life. Which was not doing anything at all. Just letting things happen. He'd registered at the desk as Max Immelmann, occupation: flier. Now wasn't that cute? The motel wasn't a sanctuary at all, it was a trap. The first place followers would look. Why they'd track him down quick. Handwriting experts would see through the ruse in a minute. His prints were all over the room. Mousebreath's shit could be analyzed and traced. The high lonesome was a farce. He was all three Stooges in a cartoon he'd written with his life. Oh Jesus, get me out of this quick.

Filling the tub with water he closed the door and let steam cloud the room. His cock floated uselessly in suds. Therapeutic heat brought an answer he hadn't expected. Just how much money was in that Liechtenstein account? Now that was sure a thought. A hundred thousand? A million? Probably not as much as that. He hadn't saved Sunny's mother from a truck, just his dog. Whatever it was, it was more than seven hundred lousy bucks. The trouble was, that money came straight from one of your major crime enterprise sources. Third graders crowded up by a stinking school toilet shooting crack in tiny arms. They mailed their money right to Doug. It wasn't like that at all, but that was how he saw it in his head. He thought about Europe. There were mountains there and places like the Alps. Which ought to mean hillbilly girls.

They couldn't be that different from the ones we had here. He could learn to speak enough of some language to get by.

This was desperation talking. He wouldn't go near that money and he knew it. He couldn't hardly remember the number anymore. He wondered what Royce was doing now. He yearned to be with him. Windows down on that old blue pickup letting in the good smells of the road. The radio picked up every country station. They had a sack of ribs and a cold sixpack, and they didn't care where they'd be in the morning. Hey now, that was it for sure.

Doug didn't carry trouble from one day into the next. He figured he could pick up something new. A few hours sleep left phantoms lagging behind. Pancakes and sausage finished them off. Seven hundred bucks seemed enough. He wondered why he'd let it get him down. Fear was a virus like the clap and nearly everyone got it now and then. God knows he'd caught a dose more than once. During real bad times, when nothing seemed to go like it should, he'd felt for a minute there were goals he ought to reach, things he ought to do. That poor was a drag and good credit the true answer to life. The light of day and sweet reason nearly always set him straight. He was chock full of reason right now. He wanted to roll down the windows and shout at people in other cars.

The glass slabs of Houston hid behind a wavy veil of heat. Doug didn't mind at all. He forgave the choke of traffic, smiled at the asshole who tried to cut him off. In your big cosmic sense, he and other drivers were threads in the tapestry of life. Life was this pancake sort of folded straight back on itself. Bubbles of batter held it all together, and you and everyone else popped up somewhere now and then. Bubbles that didn't know each other knew you, and you might even know some of them.

The picture in his head got muddy. Batter started sticking to the threads. Which just served to prove Doug's point. The universe has got lots of room for different expressions of itself.

THE HEREAFTER GANG

Sarah Dee sprang up like she'd been poised and waiting for some time. Doug barely beat her to his office, slid into his chair and set the overnight bag on the floor.

"I love that officey look," he told her. "You're sure Joan Crawford on a tear."

Sarah Dee clutched a Styrofoam cup. "You going to play boss long enough for me to talk?"

"I'd say you got something on your mind."

"Real perceptive, Hoover. My lovely bride Jane's got a fool idea she doesn't want to go through with this wedding. It doesn't change things between us. She just doesn't want to come out in the open and get canned."

"That Jane's a solid thinker."

"I don't need this snippy talk from you."

"I don't see a thing snippy about that."

Sarah Dee whipped off purple glasses and drained her paper cup. "Shit, Hoover. Why does everything have to get fucked up?"

"I hope you aren't asking me." He looked at the cup.

"You want some of this or what?"

"I don't know. I might." He studied her a moment, thinking again she was a good-looking woman and he liked her. "This is serious stuff, Sarah Dee. Drinking at work and all. You're earning my respect."

"I haven't even got started. You hang around and watch. It isn't just Jane and you know it. I want your job and can't get it. I flat don't like what you said, Doug Hoover, but I guess I know you're right. They wouldn't put a woman in here if she was Sally Ann Straight. Jesus, what kind of asshole you figure I'll get next? I can't hardly put up with you. I take it you're still going?"

"I came in to quit."

"I think I'll miss you, Hoover." She made a face. "I'd rather throw up sushi than tell you that. I never missed a man in my life."

"I'll miss you too, Sarah Dee."

"My God, this is bad TV." She left and came back with the bottle. It was high price tequila, gold as something you left at the clinic.

"What are you going to tell Fevre?"

"I'm thinking so long or goodbye."

"Well there's something you got to know. I ought to be pissed but I'm not. Doesn't anything surprise me in this circus anymore." She filled Doug's cup. "You got promoted, Hoover."

"Promoted to what?"

"*Senior* director of marketing and public relations. Five more big ones a year.

"These people are unbalanced," Doug said. "I need to get out of here fast."

"Well, you're real good at doing that."

"Don't you blame me for this. I didn't do it."

"Hoover, I don't blame you for anything at all. What I do is resent you getting away with what you do. You don't give a hoot about anything at all. You tell folks I run this place and you think that does me some good. It doesn't do a goddamn thing. Those good ol' boys up there think you're giving the poor dyke a pat on the back. Listen I hate that. I don't even know why I like you except you're honest. I'll give you that."

"Sarah Dee, I do the best I can," Doug said.

"Well that isn't a whole lot."

"I don't guess I'll argue that."

"You just better not. Don't you say a thing. I sure don't want to hear it." Sarah Dee filled her cup, spilling a lot on the desk. Her eyes were starting to wander in new directions. The overnight bag stirred and she jumped half a foot.

"Jesus, what's that?"

"My cat. Didn't want to leave her in the car."

"Well don't take it out. I don't like 'em at all. You know what else? We wouldn't be friends if you could get me in the sack."

"Oh fine, here we go," Doug said.

"Well it's true and you know it. Men don't give a damn about talking to a woman. They want to speak in the other end and that's it."

"I don't want to talk about this."

"Why not? What's so hard about that? If I was upside down you could think of something to say." Sarah Dee poured another drink, tried to focus on Doug and find her mouth.

"Sarah Dee, this has got nothing to do with sex," Doug said. "I don't talk to men either. I can't go two minutes on current events. With a woman there's at least something to do. I can sure do that better'n an hour on the price of power mowers."

"My God." Sarah Dee looked stunned. "You believe that, don't you? They ought to get you off the streets."

"I don't see I'm any threat."

"I *called* you all day and last night. Jane got pissed and walked out. I called you of all people. She won't even talk to me today."

"I wasn't home. I got a room. You and Jane want to work this out, Sarah Dee."

"Oh that's real good. Thanks a heap, Dr. Ruth."

"I'm just trying to help."

"Well don't. I'll flat bean you with this bottle if you try." Sarah Dee sank down and started to slide. "Annie's gone," she said. "Took off looking for a bus. Said you'd already done your goodbyes."

"I guess we did," Doug said. He felt a tug of sadness. Annie was a woman he could talk to. As well as he could do that with anyone at all. He guessed they were a lot alike. They couldn't either one get their lives going straight for half an hour. Helping people out ought to be a major felony offense. He'd fucked Sarah Dee up good. Taken Annie out of a shitkicker bar and gotten her work. Now what if someone had done that to him?

"What if I told Amos Fevre I wanted Jane to take over Annie's spot?" Doug said. "She'd make a lot more and that'd help."

"Wouldn't work," said Sarah Dee.

"Why not?"

"Jane's your basic worker ant. She wouldn't understand the Hoover law of non-achievement. First thing you know she'd try to plug that gear in the wall. Hoover, thanks." Sarah Dee tried to work up her mouth in a smile. Tequila intervened and made her look like Donald Duck. "Your little ol' heart's in the right place. You can't help being what you are."

"Listen, that irritates me," Doug said. "I'll tell you that."

"Well ex-*cuse* me.

"That wasn't real nice."

"Okay, you're a shit. How's that?"

"I thought we kind of liked each other."

"It's a habit, Hoover. I start throwing rocks first just in case."

"Just quit screwing up my goodbye party."

"How's Erlene or should I ask?"

"I'm not filling that woman's Easter basket. We're flat derailed for good." He couldn't remember if he'd mentioned Pastor Jack. Events seemed slightly out of order. "Amos'll be at lunch. You want, I'll take you out to Ernie's."

Sarah Dee laughed and spilled her drink.

"What's funny?"

"Nothing. Except I went out drinking there with Annie. I mean your terminal pollution. We sorta closed the place up crawlin' out." The funny smile seemed fixed. It suddenly occurred to Doug what it meant.

"Sarah Dee, you been playing in my yard. Don't say you haven't."

"Once. Can you believe it? It was Annie seduced *me.* Said she'd never done that girl stuff before. Didn't want me to be embarrassed. I'll say that girl's polite. Lord, there can't be another cunt in the world tastes like Fritos and Dr. Pepper."

Doug laughed and nearly fell out of his chair.

"God," said Sarah Dee, "tell me I didn't say it."

"This sure brings us close together."

"I think I'll throw up and start over. Wish you luck and do me a world-class toot."

"You got a leg on a good one. Wish I could hang around and help." He wanted to say something nice and get it right. "What if I say I like you, Sarah Dee? That okay with you?"

Sarah Dee considered. "As near as I can tell. Just don't push it any."

Doug stood, a little wobbly but all right. "I can still tell Amos about Jane."

Sarah Dee cringed. "Please don't. It's too silly around here already. Just go, Hoover. While you and me are still having fun."

"That's a thought," Doug said. He bent to get Mousebreath's bag. Missed it half a mile. Wondered why his hand couldn't find the right handle. Wondered why his knee hit him squarely in the chin. The floor vanished. He studied fluorescent squares. A Steinway grand fell on his chest. Old-timey jerk-motion black and white film. Hardy tries to haul this sucker up the stairs. Stan fucks it up. The sensation is so complete, so hot and clean and far past anything imagined, it takes him forever to see this is the all-time kung fu Missouri mule kick, the greatest hurt in the world. Grat Dalton fingers *Hoecake Johnny* on the keys. "Hoss, this one's goin' to be right bad," he tells Doug. "Meaner'n a gut-shot grizzly." Doug already knows it. He has all day to watch it coming. When it hits, the second salvo is quick and all consuming and not bad at all. A nuclear whoopee cushion with its own anesthetic. It's there and then it's gone. Sarah Dee wipes his face with a corner of her blouse dipped in tequila. Doug feels strangely detached. Concerned for Sarah's concern. He wants to tell her he's just fine.

"I'm fine. I'm just fine."

"Oh God Jesus. You scared the living shit out of me, Hoover!"

"I couldn't help it," Doug said. "I'm okay. I'm just fine."

"Quit *saying* that. You're *not* okay. Just lie there and relax." She picked up the phone. "I'm getting help. They'll be here before you know it. Just hang in there, honey."

Honey? Doug sat up. "Don't call anyone," he said, "I got some Tums here they'll fix me right up."

Sarah Dee looked dismayed. "Hoover, you had a fucking *heart* attack. Sit!"

"I didn't have any attack."

"Oh well, good. Just what the shit was it?"

"It hurts like hell and it goes away. Now that sure isn't your cardiac stuff I know that."

Sarah Dee burst into tears. "You know what went through my head? I'm going to have to give him that mouth to mouth thing. I thought God if I do that I'll get sick. You made me feel guilty you son of a bitch!"

"I didn't mean to do that."

"You never mean to do anything. It never *occurs* to you what you do might affect some other person. You don't think of anyone but yourself."

"Do you nag Jane like this?"

"You leave Jane out of this. I won't put up with that."

"You're all upset," Doug said. "You're relieved I'm all right. That's your classic stress striking out."

"Oh you think so, do you?"

"I think you're my friend, Sarah Dee. I think we got this bond. I haven't been around here a lot, but I'd like to think we've shared something good, and I'm not talking about Annie at all."

"You're hopeless," said Sarah Dee. "Just get your cat and get the fuck out of here, Hoover. Please. Let me get on with my life such as it is. Oh, you have screwed things up for me. God, what an asshole you are, and you don't even know it."

For some reason, Doug thinks of Jack Bricker. He stops on the way out of town to get a Pepsi and goodies and remembers Jack Bricker likes Butterfingers, too. They discover this mutual interest at the candy machine. Bricker recognizes Doug as a fellow worker, though he can't recall what he does. He draws Doug into conversation before Doug can think of any way to stop him. He asks Doug if the Oilers have a chance. Doug doesn't know what to say. A positive answer seems right. This earns Bricker's scorn. He tells Doug the Oilers are fruits who couldn't goose their way out of the shower. Which is why Doug avoids making friends. This happened the year before but Doug remembers. A lifetime of talking to other people has sharpened his senses. He knows what Bricker wants. He wants Doug to nod his head and agree. Someone talks about drill bits and grubs and you agree. This is what conversation is all about.

Doug can think of one or two people he'd like to talk to again. Royce. He'd like to talk to Royce. Royce wouldn't ask him how the weather was today. He'd look up at a dry afternoon near Amarillo and see clouds like fishbones on a blue china plate and he'd know what the fuck kind of weather. Doug likes to think about this, the two of them together. Royce could tell him things he didn't know, and Doug could think of stories on his own. Now that's talking. Doug decides he'll start thinking of things now. If he ever happens to see Royce again he'll be ready. What a time they'll have. Talking about everything both of them have done. They'll start off with spring and go right through all the seasons every year, remembering something good for every day. That's one of the things about Erlene and most everybody else. What's been they toss out to make room for something shiny and brand new. It scares Doug to think about being like that. Getting up in the morning and having that be all there is. A whole day you don't know. Like jumping out of a plane and hoping you've got a parachute. Sarah Dee is like this. There aren't any yesterdays in her life. Nothing but nows and tomorrows you can't trust. What the hell's wrong with everybody? It gives Doug the shakes. He needs to get on with his life and stop dwelling in the present.

When he walks out of the Safeway with his sack, Doug sees three Mexican girls steal his car. The green Toyota wheels out of the lot and heads south. The girls are dressed in Catholic uniforms. They've left the zipper bag with the cat, and his cardboard box of possessions. Doug feels detached and unconcerned. He's surprised he doesn't worry one minute about the car. He puts it out of his mind, certain nothing can stop him now. A cab takes him out to River Oaks, the haven of Houston's super rich. He gets out a block from where he's going and walks down a well-paved alley. Even the garbage cans are nice. Doug peers through bamboo and sees the palatial home of Parker Symmes the proctologist. He knows Parker Symmes, though he's never fucked his wife. He and Erlene went to a party here once. All the food seemed some kind of organ, and Doug couldn't eat a thing. The lawns are well kept. Three Japanese gardeners are busy with plants around a pool artfully shaped like the small intestine. Doug keeps to the back of the lot under cover of bamboo until he reaches the massive garage. Inside is Parker Symmes's collection of cars that have belonged to Nazi doctors. Doug checks the first one on the end, the Josef Mengele '39 Mercedes. The keys are in the ignition. He places the zipper bag and his box on the seat. The engine makes a nice German sound. Doug waves at the Japanese gardeners. The gardeners wave back. Doug feels good. His setback quota is used up.

Two things occurred to Doug as he drove the Mercedes through the hot afternoon, past Texaco stations and Dairy Queens and uninteresting Texas towns. The first was that he'd taken 290 out of Houston instead of 75. Which meant he was headed for Austin instead of Dallas. He decided it didn't matter. The high lonesome was more of a state of mind than a point on the map. The second was that he'd forgotten to quit work. That didn't matter much either. Clinton-Fevre would notice sooner or later that he was gone. Or maybe not.

For the first time since he'd left Sarah Dee, he let himself look at what had happened. He didn't want to but he did. Never mind it was over, it had scared him out of his socks. He didn't know what it was. All he knew was what it wasn't. He didn't need Stew Geeter to tell him Fokker aces and outlaws didn't go with your cardiac arrest. Jesus, maybe, but not the rest. The proof was he was up and walking around in a minute, not lying in *St. Elsewhere* with Fiscus sticking tubes up his nose. What it was was Annie's red and white pills. Hardy molecular glitches had survived. They were hiding in his system, pharmaceutical terrorists on the run. It was true Doc Holliday had showed up there at the Hanging Judge before his afternoon with Annie. He knew what had knocked him on his ass in there. All that shit with Erlene was enough to jerk anyone out of whack. It might be she was behind the whole thing. *Nova* said there were chemicals in your body just waiting to fuck your head. He sure didn't doubt it. Take away the problem and the shit would go with it. Well, he was doing that now.

Every mile he put behind him seemed to help. The universal wind was blowing true. He could feel it going strong. Communion with the rich and steamy earth had taught him there were signs in nature easy to read as Dick and Jane. He looked for some and found a few at once. In a pasture filled with mesquite and brittle grass, a sorrel stallion humped a mare. A sure sign some belt wouldn't snap in the Nazi car and leave him sitting in the road. A cloud to the north was shaped like a blue-spotted hog. Crows sat on a wire spelling TAB in Morse code. In a moment of clear insight, Doug saw the Toyota's ghost was still with him. It retained traditional properties of the East. His tires were radial prayer wheels, diminishing with each revolution the basic atomic structure of Houston, Texas.

He was content. He didn't need to look for more omens. He turned his attention to finding a place to eat, which wasn't near as easy as teasing secrets out of nature.

Doug's mother used to tell him that the worst part of traveling with a dog was that everyone knew what you were doing when you stopped. She'd make Doug's father do that. The dog would bounce eagerly into the game, gagging on its collar and dragging Doug's dad to an oily patch of Fina station grass. Or better still, a big restaurant window where the folks inside could see clearly what they got with a tuna on rye. The dog's nose would tremble as it learned the names of dogs who'd moved west with pioneers. Doug's father said a dog could do that. He said a dog shits everything it knows, and who's to say how long a memory lasts. The trick was to make sure the dog did its business without watching it occur. Turn away half a second before protrusions appear. Then get the dog in the car and pretend it never happened.

There's no sense bothering with a cat. Doug knew this but did it anyway. He made a leash out of string he found in the trunk, dragged Mousebreath snarling from under the seat where she was tunneling toward a complex German transmission. She hated the car and wherever the hell she was. She had no intention of shitting on a totally foreign planet. Doug pulled her through the grass, a rock on a piece of string, then tossed her back in the car.

The chicken-fried steak was good, thin with a thick brown crust, cream gravy and biscuits, mustard greens and fries on the side. Doug studied the map while he ate. The cafe was off the exit near Hempstead or Brenham. He could stay on 290 into Austin and on north. There was nothing much in Austin he wanted to see. The good times were gone, the Colorado now a lush chemical green, live oaks plowed under by high tech assholes from the east. The only hippie left was stuffed. He stood in the rotunda of the rose-colored capitol, glass eyes accusing, a lid of plastic pot in his jeans. Doug was tempted by the towns on secondary roads. Washington and Millican and North Zulch and Snook. Quarry and Dime Box, and Old Dime Box close to that. And up north of Brenham, Gay Hill, which brought pictures to mind he was sure the solemn founders never intended.

The waitress was fat and tired. She told Doug the cook had done the original oil paintings on the wall. She used to live in Fort Worth. The only other customer sat at the counter. He was old and beat flat, lost in an army overcoat died black. The day outside a hundred and one, but he kept the coat buttoned around his neck. He looked at Doug when he felt Doug was looking at something else. His reaction time maybe half an hour, so it wasn't hard to catch him doing this. Doug liked the cafe. It had slipped unchanged into the present. The menus were mimeographed in light purple ink, as hard to read as third grade handouts when Doug had gone to school. The glass salt and pepper shakers were studded like grenades, the oilcloth cover on the table pictured domestic breeds of rabbits. He gave the place several extra points for the old brass register, scrolled and heavy as stone. The drawer popped open like a good karate chop. A worn glass case displayed unpopular brands of candy, Stone Age Juicyfruit gum.

Doug studied the paintings. One depicted winter ducks in flight. Crazed and wild-eyed mallards with bills like Daffy Duck. They appeared to be on drugs. The other picture showed bright bluebonnets in a field. A lone oak there in the center. A cow or a deer grazed in the distance. When Doug finished his fresh peach pie the old man left his stool and started over to the booth, bringing his coffee with him, sliding in cautious steps as if the floor were slick with ice.

"Now you leave that man alone," the waitress warned from behind the counter. "I won't put up with any bother."

"That's all right," Doug said. It wasn't, and the old man knew it. He was used to reading faces. He knew exactly what they said. He couldn't recall a welcome in recent times.

"I'm not your vagrant or some tramp," he announced at once, easing into the booth. "I'm an educated man fortune chose to kick in the ass. My name's James McArthur Hill Dean and I'm originally from El Paso, Texas. I ran a successful agency for the Prudential Life bunch for forty-one and a half years. I had a wife and a home and two children. One boy and a girl. Their names were Axel and Mary Zane. My wife was the former Mavis Lee Loom of the Corpus Christi Looms, the daughter of Harold G. Loom of whom you've heard."

Doug nodded, though he hadn't. The waitress wandered over and filled their cups, openly disgusted with them both. Doug for putting up with all this, Dean for taking up good universal space. The man was clearly a ruin, his skin unhealthy and transparent. His eyes the color and texture of the fat that doesn't show on chicken in the store.

"I'm eighty-three now," Dean said, "and this is what happened to me. I began my career with the Prudential Life Insurance Company in 1922. On August 12 of 1964, which was two days after I had turned sixty-two, I received a phone call that was to radically change my life. The phone rang at seven in the evening. I can't recall what I was doing at the time. It wasn't something foolish like watching TV or reading a paperback book. I was very likely going over business. It wasn't my custom to get slack. I answered, and without even asking me my name, a man who sounded a lot like Vincent Price said, 'mister, do you believe that life is fair and that we get more or less what we deserve?' Certainly not, I said, who the hell is this? 'The name doesn't matter,' the man said, 'you've answered the question right. I don't know who you are and I don't care. I got your name at random from the book. You might be a saint or a sleeper for the KGB. It doesn't matter any to me. If it's true merit doesn't play a part in daily life, I either will or won't send you a great deal of money in the mail. Depending on the toss of a gold peso I presently hold in my hand. Good night, and thank you for your time.'"

Dean sipped his coffee, holding the cup close to warm his hands. Two brown lines ran down his chin in a course established some time before. "Well, being a career agent for the Prudential Life and of sound body and mind, I took this caller for a loon," Dean said. "He was right, though, and I couldn't fault his logic. There's sure no justice in the world. Any man who says there is is a fool. I was a living example of that premise, a semi-affluent white collar with an average wife and children, a reflection of the actuarial tables of the time. These tables are denied to the public and it's none of your business what they say. I had 'em, though, and knew more about the game of fate and chance than that caller. I knew the odds for and against getting struck down by lightning or catching the Asian flu. I was aware of my chances of being dealt a royal flush. Of course you don't have to be a life agent to know the odds for a flip of the coin. This is common knowledge to the simple man in the street. So I knew I had a fifty-fifty chance of getting rich if this fellow wasn't calling from the pay phone down at the nut farm. Which sure crossed my mind at the time."

Here Dean paused for breath, sipping cold coffee and addressing stern looks at the waitress, who found something more important to do. Dean appeared to study Doug with great interest, one eye brighter and more able than the other. There was determination there, a fierce and stubborn will that broke through the liquid glaze of desperation. Having come this far, the eyes reached out and tried to laser Doug to the booth, to keep him from fleeing before the story was half done, something which had happened more than once.

In the fall of 1956, just out of the army on a lark seeking work back east, Doug stayed at the Royalton Hotel in New York, a seedy but respectable hotel that catered to literary and theatrical type persons, usually those getting along in years. Late at night through the walls of his dreary room, Doug could hear old ladies practicing lines for plays that closed in the spring of 1938. In the elevator, he rode down with Carl Sandburg himself, the poet in a worn red plaid logger's shirt, washed so many times the flannel was slick and the pattern nearly gone, a checkered coat of some color that didn't match, ill-fitting trousers and a maroon tie patterned with circles and squares. Every item seemed carefully mismatched, each clashing perfectly with the other, as if the coat, the tie, the trousers and the worn work shoes were a single item the man put on and zipped up every morning, ready for a day of herding goats or writing a poem. Doug wondered if he did these things on alternating days, or whenever he happened to feel like one or the other. He meant to look it up but never did. Now studying James McArthur Hill Dean across the booth, he thought the man resembled Sandburg himself, if the poet had been crazed or alcoholic, or wasted on stupefying drugs, and if Dean had been somewhat better dressed. The thought passed quickly, Dean looking more and more like a former career agent for the Prudential Life company, a man whose thread had begun to unravel in El Paso and was now approaching the dreary speed of light.

"As you more than likely guessed," Dean went on, "being a man of rare perception which I saw right off the bat, the very next day I got a nine by twelve Kraft manila envelope in the mail, delivery being more reliable at the time. Inside were three-hundred twenty dollar bills. That's six-thousand bucks you can work it in your head. Well you could've knocked me over with a stick. That fellow might've been a loon, but he was a loon as good as his word. I took one of those bills at once to a bank I chose at random, telling the girl at the window I ran a hardware store. Well, that twenty was real as rain. I had to figure now what to do with this money chance had tossed in my lap. Six grand was worth a lot more in those days than it is now. I wasn't about to put it in a bank I'll tell you that. Those bastards at the IRS would've cut 'em out a slice and wanted to know if I had some more. I sure didn't tell my wife Mavis. She'd 've bragged to her sister Dorthea and her mother. Neither of those women thought me much of a catch. Even when Mavis and me were courting, her mother who's a former lady speedboat racer from Sarasota, Florida, thought an insurance man was dull as toast. I guess the old lady's dead for some time. I doubt anyone's crying over that except Mavis and Dorthea and that *frijole* greaser used to drive up Thursdays from Esperanza. I can't recall that Mexican's name. It might have been Juan I don't know."

"So what did you do with the money?" Doug said. He could see Dean's mind tended to wander.

Dean's good eye backed up and found Doug. "Goddamn it I'm coming to that now. I can see what's in your head don't think I can't. You figure this agent for the Prudential Life's got no more imagination than a dog. That he'll sew good fortune in a mattress and let it sit. Well there's more to a man than what he seems I'll tell you that. What I did was take the six-thousand bucks and divide it into threes. Two I put in real estate deals buying so-called useless land east of town. Two I put in a failing cactus farm, and the last two I invested in smuggling Cadillac convertibles into Mexico proper. You might not know it but a man meets all kinds of folks in the process of selling cheap term. To make a long story short, in eighteen months that worthless real estate flat tripled becoming prime apartment land. The cactus farm doubled and I sold out fast. Put the profits in a frozen jalapeño confection which catered to the Mexican trade. Boy, those folks'll eat anything on a stick. The car smuggling business got too hot to handle. I put the money in a DC-3 that made unscheduled hops down south. We took in color TV's and *Playboy* magazines, and brought out prime marijuana by the bale. By 1969 that six-thousand bucks was a tidy seven mil. Of course I sold little insurance at the time. I caught hell from Prudential Life. Mavis and her sister and that speedboat whiz didn't know what I was up to you can bet. All they could see was I was gone most of the time and bringing in ninety bucks a month.

"By 1971 I'd cut my ties with illegal enterprise. Your dope operation draws unsavory folk I'll tell you that. Taking funds out a little at a time, I put money into leasing tanker ships. Two years later I was worth some eight-hundred million at a guess. I don't mind saying I earned fourteen grand selling a little health and life. Well I figured enough was enough. I pulled out my assets through dummy corporations. Put my money in international banks set up for hiding taxable funds. I wrote a suicide note and left a trust fund for the kids. Not a cent for Mavis but I'd guess she got her hands on some. I laundered that money real good. Those IRS turkey buzzards couldn't tell it wasn't straight. I left El Paso disguised as a Mexican fruit picker. Hitchhiked to Fort Stockton and then Odessa where I bought respectable clothes and a new Buick. This left me some sixty-one grand in cash to see me through the first phase of my disappearance. My plan was to drive on to Dallas and fly to London, using the real passport of a Scottish textile merchant. From there I'd vanish for good and pursue fun and hijinks in the south of France. Well I got it in my head to cut down south of Dallas to Ellis County where I was born. That was the worst idea I ever had. The coin of fate come down tails and hit me hard. Driving up 35 I came across a young lady stalled out by the side of the road in a red Datsun two-door car. I guess it was a fool thing to do, considering the amount of cash on my person at the time. But this girl was young and pretty as a peach. I'm talking here your movie star magazine pretty. Why legs up to here all tan the color of honey in a jar. After a lifetime of Mavis I was taken with her charms. I'd say those shorts were abbreviated at best. That and half a T-shirt which didn't begin to hide the biggest free-standing whompers I ever saw. This shirt was cut off and revealed a fetching ribcage and a tummy flat as a plate. The shirt pictured the emblem of Texas Tech University in Lubbock. The girl told me she was a student taking a split major in art and veterinary medicine.

"The last I recall of that day was peering under the girl's hood while sneaking a quick peek at her crotch. I was reminded quite clearly of baby ducks. I woke up shortly before dawn the next day in a thicket of mesquite off the road. I was wearing those Sears boxer shorts and nothing else. My head hurt like blazes. I guess she struck me with a tire iron or some other handy tool. I tried without luck to wave down passing cars. Those drivers had a lot more sense than I'd shown myself. The Texas Highway Patrol picked me up and drove me on into Ennis. My scalp required twenty-two stitches. I was told I was lucky to be alive. The police asked a great many questions. Who was I and what exactly happened. I told them I didn't know and learned to my great alarm this was true. It was gone, the whole thing. My mind wiped clean as a slate. This is a frightening moment in your life I'll tell you that. The doctors said memory loss was likely, considering the severity of the blow. The cops said they'd do everything they could. I was given a pair of used blue jeans and a Morris the Cat shirt. An intern contributed old Nikes. I stayed in Ennis three days. I started having bad dreams. I woke up sweating and flat scared. Who was I? Suppose I'd committed some crime and they found out? I hitched out of town the next night. In Wichita Falls I got a job loading trucks at a Pepsi-Cola plant. For a while I was content. It didn't seem too bad not having any past. There might be something there I didn't even want to know. Nine months later I woke abruptly in the night. It all came back to me at once. I laughed out loud when I remembered. There I was making three-fifty an hour and living in the YMCA. Why I wasn't a bum at all. I didn't have to do this all my life. I had seven-hundred and thirty-six million stashed away in my international accounts."

Dean paused to look at Doug. “I don’t want to presume on your kindness, but some more hot coffee would be welcome. If you can see your way clear maybe a slice of that pie.”

Doug signalled the waitress who reluctantly filled the order. Dean finished off the dish in record time.

“I finally remembered it all,” Dean continued. “Every minute of my life. Every policy I ever sold, every ounce of Mexican dope. I remembered my fourth grade teacher who was Ernestine Phapes. I recalled the whole thing except the money. I don’t know where it is, not a dime. I can’t remember a thing. I’ve gone to the library a couple of hundred times. It doesn’t do me any good. Name a Swiss bank or one down in the Caymans I’ll give you the phone and address. I don’t recall a single account or a number to go with it. I can’t even prove I’m James McArthur Hill Dean. I could go back and throw myself on the mercy of Mavis Lee but what’s the point?”

Doug waited. It appeared Dean was through. “And all this really happened?” he said, “Boy is that something.”

Dean blinked at him. “What do you mean did it happen? You got the ruination of my life. What the fuck you want for coffee and pie. I don’t have to put up with any of this. I don’t need the aggravation.”

Doug realized he’d offended Dean in some way. He stood quickly and left a five dollar bill on the table. Dean made no move to take it. He seemed to be into labored breathing.

“You didn’t have to listen to any of that,” the waitress told him as he paid his check. “That was your idea and not mine.”

“It’s okay,” Doug said.

“You taken with one of these oil paintings or not?”

“I don’t guess so now.”

“I favor the one with the deer. There’s something wrong with them ducks.”

There seems to be a lesson in Dean's story. Doug can't put his finger right on it. Don't pick up pretty girls on the road, maybe that. Simple but sound advice. During the story, it occurred to Doug that maybe he and Dean had numbered accounts in the same bank. Wouldn't that be something? It was certainly a small world. Maybe his illegal funds were lying dormant next to Dean's.

In that indecisive moment when day and night can't decide exactly what they want to do, Doug reaches the outskirts of Austin having left 290 for no reason, angling slightly south to 71 past Bastrop and the dead snake loop of the Colorado. He'd intended to pass Austin altogether, shunning this town that had sold its fun hippie dog charm and indifference for a high tech pottage that didn't taste that good when it arrived. The freckle-faced girl next door who liked to screw Andy Hardy just for fun and sweet release on a hot locust day in that black and white forever soft Saturday afternoon on is now selling it in the street. And Andy coming back to town later, red nose and bow tie and sleeveless sweater, cries out in that beloved froggy voice, "Holy fucking Toledo, Polly, what have you done to yourself!"

Doug can't forgive this town and wants no part of it now. He can't tolerate the blatant dismissal of the past. People can't see the damage to the universal mind when an ice cream parlor disappears, when Krazy Kat mildews in the attic and a Lionel caboose goes to rust. He is fearfully aware that he's racing desperately backwards through his life, fleeing Mr. Present and his ugly pal Future. He knows this pair is tailgating him all the way, stuffing Mays and Septembers down their gullets faster than he can possibly bring them back. What do they care? They've got all the time there is to cover yesterday in dog shit and plastic. It's all fading so quickly he isn't certain any more he can catch it. The Green Hornet works in a hardware store in Columbus, Ohio. Kato's an aging fag waiter. There isn't a cinnamon square left in all the world.

There might be some connection between Doug's dismal flight and that of James McArthur Hill Dean. If there is, Doug hopes he won't find it. They both fled a woman, a way of life. Dean searching for a lost better tomorrow, Doug going the other way. And each to the oddsmakers' delight have secret numbered accounts that will likely remain secret for altogether different reasons. Similarities keep popping into his head; Doug looks for opposites to cancel them out.

Driving through the night, he reflects on unanswered questions. Was the girl in the Datsun acting alone? Did she deliver the blow requiring twenty-two stitches, or was this a confederates's work? How did she spend the money? What did she do with the passport naming Dean a Scottish textile merchant? Someone had to drive the Buick and who was that? These and other questions. Doug isn't fond of stories that leave a lot of things out. They aren't really stories until they're done. Books end up this way, people drifting off and you never get to know what they do. If he knew Dean's mother-in-law's name, he'd look her up. There would be a written account of various meets. Speedboat racing is an accepted sporting event.

Down 71 into Austin, safe in the dull romantic hum of highway traffic. Headlight comets whining by in the sultry dark, there and suddenly gone, sucking air and laying silence, leaving Doug alone and snug going nowhere really at all. The red agate eyes of mean farmhouse dogs disappear, giving way to bad motels and 7-Elevens, franchise chicken and stores with muffler trophies on display. All this passing in a pink electric blur, a wash of windshield color swept away.

Doug sees all this but he doesn't. What he sees is the small shadow figure far ahead in the lights of other cars, standing by the road backpack on the ground, arm out in a haphazard semi-legal poke. The figure is indistinct but he's certain it's a girl, lean and bare-legged in cutoff denim jeans. He steps on the gas to pass, to reach her as fast as he can. A little flutter starts in his belly and sends whisker electric charges all over, surges without a label. The Dean story sets him up with an easy-to-read moral. *Twilight Zone* music up and out. His lights hit the girl and wash her out in pure white. He sees her and knows her at once in an adrenal rush of cardiac delight. He can't believe his eyes, but there isn't time to think. He jerks the wheel and hits the brakes. The car leaves asphalt and skips over gravel. The rear end slides to the right churning dust. He opens the passenger door and there she is. She peers in squinty-eyed and Doug grins at her like a kid, taking pleasure in her face as she remembers.

"Oh wow what a really neat car," she says, and slides in beside him. "You're Royce's friend, right? Well I'll be."

“Tug Hoower,” he says, too stricken to find his tongue. She fiddles with the backpack, trying to keep it on her lap and close the door. His throat swells just short of closing. He tries to breathe and can’t. He is touched so deeply by her presence tears begin to blur his eyes. He rubs his face on his sleeve. She’s here. Right next to him. His highschool carhop queen of all time, his skinny little apple-tit charmer. Not lost forever at Mary Anne’s but right here.

THE HEREAFTER GANG

In Fort Worth Doug met an elegant lady in a purple jersey dress. This was at a cocktail party at the River Crest Country Club. He was holding down a marginal job, and had a borderline invitation to attend. He and Lindy had been divorced for some time. He was confident and lazy, getting so much fucking it was fast becoming a social obligation. The girl brought jaded hormones alive with a single glance. He was taken by her lean good looks, the fine bones of her face, the studied indifference of her stance. She reminded him of Candice Bergen when she smiled. He went to her at once, cutting her quickly from a herd of local dandies equally taken by her charms. She accepted his attentions, pleased he'd managed to cleverly sweep her away. He loved her classic nose. Her tan was plainly imported, the season then in Texas being winter. She had the tight glowing skin that comes from stress-free living and daily tennis. He knew she was Fort Worth rich, which differs from the gaudy flamboyance of Houston or Dallas wealth. Fort Worth rich is more subtle and restrained. The wealthy feel uneasy and out of place in a city that won't shake its fine cowtown shitkicker image. Culture arrives daily by the barrel, but Fort Worth remains lazy and easygoing with its barbecue stands and brick streets, and colored folks who haven't yet heard they've been promoted past Negro up to Black.

The girl took him to her house in Westover Hills, a home set back in tall trees behind a white brick wall freshly aged, past an iron gate to a graveled drive. In the hall she kicked Italian shoes aside, skidding them over the parquet floor, offered a whiskey kiss and gave him glasses and wine to carry and shuffled him off to bed.

In the early morning hours they traded lives, Doug finding hers more interesting than his own. The rich doctor husband had recently left her. Run off with the real estate cutie who sold them the house. She had money of her own. Trusts and pieces of this and that, financial convolutions he didn't begin to understand. Except there was clearly plenty of it. Plus the house and half the doctor's wealth, Texas being a community property state. Doug met a well-mannered seven-year-old boy, a Great Dane and an alley cat, all whisked away by a protective Aunt Jemima who gave Doug a jaundiced eye. She knew her own duties in this house and had no trouble guessing his.

And in a week he knew all this could be his, the house and the money, the girl with slatey eyes who asked nothing of him but himself. She found it a constant wonder that he was kind, that he never flew into a rage and blackened her eye. That he didn't want her to screw the Great Dane. Doug figured the doctor was an asshole beyond belief. If he opened a door or brought her a daisy she started to cry. All this and money too. She knew he didn't have a dime and never would. She didn't care. She loved him or something close to it, and he was half in love with her. He was honest enough to know he'd feel the same if he'd found her serving up his Big Mac. She was a honey and a half. It was a perfect movie script with a happy ending. Doug, poor but kind and giving. The girl, rich beyond his dreams, vulnerable and soft as silly putty. Could they find happiness together? Well sure they could. And this scared the hell out of Doug, and saddened him as well. He knew he'd make a lousy Cinderella. Rich food and contentment would take their toll. Hanging onto the past was all he had; it took a lot of effort to handle that, to keep from sliding into the present. The only weapons he had were uncertainty and chance. Take those away and there'd be nothing left at all. A life with this girl would defeat him. Every day secure, every tomorrow to his liking. He was already falling into the pattern. It wasn't hard to do. Honey, let's you and me jet off to Paris—and hey, I need a new cashmere jock. And soon he'd start thinking that today's just dandy and the future's the place to be. Jack Benny and Joe Palooka would fade quietly into the rich and heavy drapes.

Only what would happen first is he'd spot some mean-eyed Alabama girl with hipbones lean as handlebars. Get pussy-whiskey drunk and wake up in a mobile home, trying to remember the name of his first dog. He'd find his way back, to the fine-limbed girl and the buttered *croissants* and the well-mannered kid and the Aunt Jemima SS trooper. But he'd go out and do it all again. The girl would start finding Willie Nelson among the Bach. Red hots in the crystal candy dish. He'd start staying home from charity balls and civic events, lost over blue French skies with Werner Voss. Playing out a hand with the Earps, waiting for the Clantons to ride in. In the end he'd be just as big an asshole as the runaway doctor himself. Only nicer. And the hurt would be worse for her because he was. He couldn't do that. Not to her and not to him.

The final parting was full of lies he made up to break her heart, to make her throw him out of the house and out of her life. She didn't believe him for a minute. There was something else to it, something he wouldn't tell her. She started crying and wouldn't stop. He hadn't wanted it to happen like this. He knew he was foolish to think there might be an easy way out. In the end he simply left. He'd run out of ways to convince her he was a shit. But he'd managed to break her heart and his too.

And some dreary months after that, winding his way south the hard way through Abilene and Waco and Austin down to Houston, through neighborhood bars named The Office and Outa Town, cavorting with the slap-happy afternoon over-forty drunks, he met Erlene. He was more or less charmed with her at once. A whonker-jawed whiney-voice girl, squirrel-eyed and pleasantly stewed. He was in some awe of her legs. No big news to her, he wasn't the first. She confided she was a former Kilgore Rangerette kicker. She tried to stay in shape, which, you know, more girls ought to do, don't you think? Doug said he did. He liked her squinty face and wide mouth and wondered what she was doing in this beery home for losers. The people in here sang songs. *Red Sails in the Sunset.* Old ladies in pedal pushers, cigarette sopranos in sometime harmony with dead-eyed salesmen in white shoes and checkered pants, men looking for an afternoon romp. with anyone who'd promise not to fart in the car. A sad barometer of just how far he'd fallen, Doug decided.

A whiskey-fogged path from the Fort Worth sweetie to swamp city. With throw-up stops in between. No money and no place to go. A drifter on the jukebox trail. He'd left the job in Fort Worth never even going back, not picking up his check. Just hitching out fast fleeing the sleepy-eyed lady, the *aprês* breakfast champagne fuck on clean sheets, running before he could change his mind.

Erlene, looking cheerleader-seventeen instead of maybe twenty-four, whisked him off to her apartment for a bath and a hot meal and into her healing arms. He was struck by her beauty, her tawny animal grace. He cried in relief as he took her. She accepted his remorse, let him pump her full of regret. He didn't tell her it wasn't for her and if she guessed she didn't say.

She understood. She knew a man could get down on his luck. She was a legal secretary and she'd put a little aside. He could work things out, no hurry. When he felt more fit she had a friend in the ad business, a job wouldn't be any problem. Alarms should have sounded but they didn't. He was simply too frazzled at the edges to stop and listen, too glassy eyed and dizzy at the sight of this long-legged cutie playing *Stars and Stripes Forever* on his horn. Why me? he wondered, when she could easily find a three-piece lawyer on the loose, a task that ought to take her maybe two quick shots below the belt. He hadn't yet heard of Otta Gee, and wouldn't for some time. He didn't know the Lamprey women had a nasty salvage fetish. That they liked junkyards a lot better than a flashy showroom floor. Preferred rebuilts to your factory fresh goods. Believed the customized male gave better, more grateful service.

Another scuzzy job was the last thing he wanted. That and another wife. He wanted Edgar Bergen and Charlie McCarthy. Waxahachie boyhood nights and Montana outlaw pals. But he was too tired to protest, too lonely for his Fort Worth woman. This fine silky girl Erlene was understanding. She went to the pound and helped him find a kitty. This sly and generous act totally disarmed him, effectively sealed his fate. Why not give reality another chance? It might be fun with Erlene. As promised, she got him a do-nothing, fat-money job, sensing Doug's needs almost better than Doug himself. She quit her own job the next day, celebrating the big event with a fun oral encounter with Ham Bayliss, the dog-faced shrink. Doug didn't know about Ham and Stew Geeter and the rest, or that Pastor Jack was waiting in the wings. When he started to guess the truth he wasn't surprised. He'd already begun to roam. Secretaries and waitresses, and wives in Erlene's circle of friends. Yet they cared for each other, and often preferred carnal joy at home. When he thought about the Fort Worth sweetie—and he did—he decided they might have made it. Money wasn't everything, too little or too much. He missed her a lot, and cried when he remembered the good times. She wasn't a country girl or so it seemed, and he wondered more than once about that. There was something there that kept her in his mind, and he guessed she had a hillbilly soul. He wondered if he had it to do again what he'd do, and wasn't sure he wanted to know.

"Sue Jean," the girl said, "I don't much like just Sue it hasn't got a ring to it. Okay if I toss this stuff in the back?"

"Just don't hit the cat," Doug said, "she's back there digging through the floor."

"Oh, yeah?" She liked the idea of the cat, stretched over the seat and in the dark tried to coax Mousebreath to the surface. And Doug watched the cutoffs hike up to reveal a dazzling arc of bottom. He marveled at the point where bony ankles met her feet, imagined the high arch, the sweet hidden little toes. Oh Lord, those little toes.

"We going on or what?" she wanted to know.

"Do what?" Doug said.

"We going to drive or sit? I mean, I don't care, man, whatever."

Doug tried to pull himself together. Driving seemed a complex operation. She was an assault upon his senses. The smells of her filled the car. He couldn't breathe without drawing some part of her into himself. Each scent mingled with another but he could easily sort them out. He knew one molecule from another, an uncanny sense developed over the years, possibly heightened by regular soil immersion. In an instant he discovered and set aside the more obvious tastes and smells. Pepsi Cola. Salem cigarettes. Tom's peanut butter crackers. Lipstick. Gingersnaps. My Sin. Cheeseburger. Cedar pollen. Stale potato chips. Zest, Crest and catsup. Her hair slightly wet, acid perspiration on her neck. The crown of her head dry, musty like cobwebs in an attic. And the skin of this teenage cutie! A melody of tastes to be discovered. Sun on her shoulder, a ghost from the summer day. Apricots in the hollow of her arm. Her thighs, if he could touch them with his tongue, dry and musky as lizard breath. On her cheeks a touch of parsley and 7-Up. Dizzied already by these delights, he raced to the ultimate sensory prize and was staggered by his find. Between those legs was a treasure that knocked him silly. Gulf Coast oysters and the tangy taste of Sprite. Snickers and cherry pie. Wintergreen Certs and the aftertaste of rain. Why there's a nest of baby bunnies in this girl!

Doug's sensory apparatus was very close to overload. He turned his attention back to traffic. The girl lit a ciggie and passed it on. He drew in smoke to clear his head. Out of the corner of his eye he saw her slumped in the seat, toes curled around the dash. Lazy and unconcerned. In the dark her legs the color of onion soup.

"Well I'm glad you picked me up when you did," Sue Jean said. "You ought 've seen the guy took me out of town. I'm not hardly in the car he says do it while I drive. Well I am not on the *Circus of Stars,* I said. Just what do you think this is?"

"Right," Doug said.

"We going to pass the capitol or what?"

"You want to see it?"

"I don't know, do I?"

Doug turned off Airport Boulevard and tried to circle back, got lost in East Austin and Mexican homes and bars, finally made his way back the way he'd come, across the river and back south, found Riverside by luck and 35. Sue Jean scooted close, girl breath on his arm.

"That's it, huh?"

"That pink-colored dome lit up."

"Hey, there's all the college and stuff. I just bet they're having fun."

"I bet they are too."

"My Lord, there's the tower where the guy shot everyone dead. I read he talked with the devil and wouldn't keep himself clean."

"I knew a friend saw it happen."

"You didn't."

"He was right there going to school."

Sue Jean digested this. She studied the lights and buildings until there was nothing to hold her interest. She folded her legs in the seat and leaned in against the door. In a moment Doug dared a look and saw she'd gone to sleep. She had kicked her moccasins off. A shapely little foot touched his leg. He longed to hold it but turned his attention to the road. So far, the trip wasn't going badly at all. He was doing a better job of running away than James McArthur Hill Dean. He didn't have as much money, but then he sure hadn't lost as much, either. And he had the girl beside him, sleeping as he drove through the night. She didn't appear to be thinking about hitting him in the head. Oh what a little honey. He wished old Royce could see him now.

Sam Bass is buried in Round Rock, Texas, which is eighteen miles north of Austin on Highway 35. Along with Joel Collins, Jack Davis, Jim Berry, Tom Nixon and Bill Heffridge, Sam stole $60,000 from the Union Pacific Express at Big Springs near Ogallala, in Nebraska Territory. This was in 1877. Collins and Heffridge were later shot down by the law on the Kansas prairie. Berry was killed in Missouri. Davis wisely left for points south, and Tom Nixon remained at large. Bass was shot in Round Rock in 1878 by Texas Rangers. He died at two minutes to four on July the twenty-first. If it hadn't been dark Doug would have stopped to look at the grave. He understood the original stone had been chipped away by tourists.

The summer night was dark, made of no more substance than the air, pressing in so close Doug imagined that the car stood perfectly still. On either side, clever machines cranked the roadside along for his amusement, sending billboards and fences swiftly by. The highway was the ash-gray color of the moon. There were sleepy towns and fat watertowers, underpasses with the aerosol names of local teams. There was PEACE and FUCK YOU and JESUS LOVES. And he wondered if he drove enough roads through Texas he would find some angry warning from Dean: NEVER HELP GIRLS WITH BIG TITS! Had Dean spread his wrath in this manner, or did he keep all the poison to himself?

At Georgetown they had a candle factory you could see from 35. You could go in and buy candles and watch them make them right there. He'd always wanted to do this and hadn't. Erlene didn't ever like to stop. Erlene wasn't big on snake farms and peach stands and quilts. So they always drove by. Alone sometimes, searching for rich and freshly tilled soil, he stopped for honey in Mason jars, country-made honey dark as syrup. He looked at plastic armadillos, armadillo ashtrays, armadillos made of grainy brown sugar. Once he brought a rattlesnake ashtray home. It looked as real as it could be. It disappeared in a couple of days and he knew Erlene had tossed it out. He stopped at cafes where the owner had drawn burgers on the window. Emerald-green lettuce and fire engine red tomatoes. A sign at the Georgetown exit said Inner Space Caverns. He'd never been there either. He used to stop for cider sold in fruit jars and jugs, for cantaloupes and melons. All this without Erlene or before they met. He liked to talk to the fresh-faced girls who ran the stands.

He thought about the caves. This part of Texas was nearly hollow, honeycombed with limestone caverns. Blind salamanders and fish lived there in the dark. And what else? Maybe blind armadillos with pearly shells.

The tires changed pitch as he crossed the iron bridge over the North San Gabriel River. He knew how it looked in the light, block-shaped cliffs of gray stone covered with indistinct brush. Mousebreath came out of hiding, crouched on Doug's shoulder and dug in his back for balance. She studied the interesting stranger, then sprang down and sniffed the girl's crotch and curled up behind her legs, finding the scent as appealing as Doug. Cats can do anything they want.

THE HEREAFTER GANG

When he drives the long highways he wonders about the sad abandoned ventures along the road. There are hundreds of these slap-hazard buildings of rusted tin and silvered wood, buildings made of cement blocks on weekends and after work, walls painted Sears red or yellow and a window patched up with masking tape. The man tells the woman it'll work. They're drinking iced tea at the kitchen table and he brings out the Big Chief tablet where he's got all the answers written out. He's got it figured in black and white. It's all in the numbers he tells her, number and location is where it's at. The Shell station's right there and you got to get off anyway, right? Now don't even count the people getting off the interstate or hauling a boat up to the lake. Hell just stand out there and count 'em like I did, honey. Not everyone's going to stop but they don't all have to, that's the thing. You got any idea how much we make, we get one out of three hundred cars that passes by? It's the odds is what it is, this whole thing's the odds, that's business. And the woman mutters something about all that money for a barbecue — fruit stand — antique — smoked ham — snow cone — fireworks — kiddie ride business by the road and wonders why he's asking her at all, she can see in his face he's going to do it.

And Doug driving north through the night passes the boarded-up dreams with the sweet-legged girl sleeping beside him, and he sees far off the tight cluster of dark trees against the sky, the land cleared for planting on either side. A single square of light is nearly lost in the hackberries and cedars, and he builds the house in his head, the boxy shape, the narrow stairs, the high-ceilinged wallpaper rooms. The window belongs to the kitchen. The man tells the woman he hates the farm. Farming is going to shit. The government's made it hard to keep your head above water and burritos are the answer. Burritos will set us free. The woman, drinking bourbon from a Mickey Mouse glass, is made of stronger stuff than he imagined. She looks at him with eyes made of K-Mart years and second liens and says not with my egg money, motherfucker. The man sees at once where this is going, and never brings it up again.

Doug knew the names of every town off 35. He liked to recite them like a poem, putting accents where they belonged. Andice, Wier, Schwertner—Jonah, Liberty Hill. A poultry truck had run off the road, just short of Exit 279. Run off the road and turned over. No one was hurt except the chickens, squashed on the road and running loose in jerky despair. Four-, maybe five-hundred chickens. The Mexican driver stared at his overturned truck, hands deep in hip pockets. There didn't seem an answer to this dilemma, but he had to give it a try.

Sue Jean woke and stretched, punching the car lighter before her eyes were fully open.

"Hey, where are we?" she wanted to know.

"Past Prairie Dell south of Salado."

"Well shit. I guess I know 'bout everything now."

"North of Austin a ways," Doug said. "You didn't sleep real long. Up ahead we got Belton and Temple and Waco."

"I heard of that one," she said.

This seemed to satisfy her. A name she knew. She scratched the cat under the jaw and puffed her ciggie. Mousebreath appeared content. Sue Jean wriggled her toes on the dash. Doug stirred uneasily at the sight. He'd hoped she'd stay asleep. She could sleep and he could drive and there'd be nothing to resolve. That was the last thing he wanted to do. Resolve something that had to do with her. Talk to her and say something wrong, scare the little darling off. He wanted her right there. He was willing to do whatever it took to keep her. Which at the moment he felt was nothing. Drive and don't rock the boat. Don't do something funny like stopping. He'd have to get gas. But that wasn't like pulling into the Dirty Sheet Motel with some lame excuse she'd see through in a minute. Like he had to get some sleep. Why she'd bolt like a rabbit.

Of course he'd run about fifteen fantasies through his head the minute she got in the car. All he could handle without breaking out in a sweat. He'd tried to put that stuff out of his mind because girls knew right what you were thinking. Especially if you thought about *that.*

The thing was, he knew just having her there was enough. He felt this thought coming on and when it did it hit him hard. Lord, this cookie had shaken him up good. Driving with her in the dark was a first-class porno hit.

"You work somewhere or what?" said Sue Jean.

"I did, I don't do it anymore.

"I bet you're running away from your old lady."

"You don't know if I am or not."

Sue Jean laughed. A cocky little grin like boy I got something on you. He felt this brought them close together. Her toes needed constant attention on the dash.

"I am putting an old lifestyle behind is what I'm doing," Doug said. "Some of that has to do with my wife. There's more to it than that."

"What's your old lady like?"

"I guess she's a very nice person.

"So that's why you're splitting up."

"Things happen in your average marriage today. They've got figures on that."

"My folks split when I was a kid."

"I'm sorry to hear it."

"He was an asshole and a half you don't have to be sorry about that."

"He might've had some reason you don't know."

"I don't want to hear what it is."

"There's two sides to every picture I know that."

"I bet she caught you fucking around."

Doug laughed to cover his irritation. "You shouldn't say something like that it isn't polite."

"Well ex-*cuse* me. I *heard* somewhere guys like to play around."

"That doesn't mean you have talk about it."

"This fella teaches social science tried to get me to sit on a baked potato. He said not many girls'd do it. I said I sure as hell wouldn't either."

"I never heard such a thing."

"You think I'm nosey or what?"

"You are a little."

"You want me to stop asking questions?"

"I don't guess." He did, but he didn't want to seem unfriendly. He'd tell her whatever she wanted to keep her happy, or just make something up as he went along. He didn't feel this kind of talk would earn him points. Each question just added to her list of adult failures, the kind of crap she expected to hear.

She wanted to know what he did, or what he'd done before he stopped. He told her as little as he could. She thought it was real exciting. She'd watched TV and seen girls gain prestige and money overnight in spite of having great tits. Writing zippy campaigns that set clients on their heels.

"Well I don't know why you didn't like that."

"Well I didn't like it at all."

"So you're going to do what?"

"I guess whatever I want."

"You're starting to sound like Royce."

"Maybe I am." This pleased Doug a lot.

"You just might run off then figure you want to get it all back. I don't guess you thought about that."

Doug was a little startled hearing this from a girl scarcely into mini pads. "Listen, I know what I want to do. And I'm not going to want to go back."

"Okay so don't." She snubbed her ciggie in the tray, taking time with this simple act. "Look, you want to pull off somewhere a minute, that okay?"

Vivid picture of her squatting off the trail. Doug keeps an eye out for Comanches. "I'll try and find a gas station ahead."

"I don't want to pee I want to talk. Just stop somewhere, all right?"

Doug felt alarmed. Talk about what? This smacked of resolution. Maybe she'd open the door and run. He wanted no part of this at all.

The Salado exit was just ahead and he pulled off and turned to the left, crossing the bridge over 35 to the other side. The access road marked the ass end of town, a dismal wipeout left behind when progress found a new direction. Headlights swung about and captured a spectral sight. Gas pumps pulled out by the roots, nerve endings left exposed. A moonscape drive jackhammered half across before someone discovered what a gut-shaking job he'd undertaken. Windows all gone, concrete and white tile facing ankle deep. No burrito sales here. Past this to a stubble field of corn, a three-day beard on the earth. Off the road a stark brick chimney and dead trees. Doug turned past darkened homes, surprised to find a TV ghost in one or two. Turned again and found a two-story red brick building, a cartoon schoolhouse warped and too high for proper dimension. Boarded windows and a massive old-fashioned fire slide, like the one he'd had at Lincoln Elementary, clinging to a wall by rusted bolts as big as skillets. He drove into the yard under thick-holed oaks, acorns snapping beneath the tires. He turned off the key and doused the lights.

"You got a weird idea of pulling off the road," Sue Jean said.

"I went to a school looked just like this," Doug said. "Well I'll be."

The building seemed forbidding. Ghostly teachers in the halls chanting exports of Argentina. He rolled down the window. The night smelled of some kind of flower. Sue Jean lit a ciggie. Folding her legs took time. Her skin seemed pale, the tan filtered out by streetlights down the block. The fine hairs on her arms a coating of dust. She faced him with hands folded on her knees.

"Listen, I figure we ought to talk."

"That's fine with me."

"That's a fib and you know it. It's not either fine with you."

"Well I'm not accustomed to being told I'm a liar."

"Well I guess I know if you don't want to stop and talk."

"I don't see how you can say what another person's thinking."

"I'm not your Maid Marion on the cable TV been hidin' in the woods. I know what's what when I see it."

"Well you sure think you do."

"You never even asked where I was going. You pick me up and off we go."

"I didn't see the sense of doing that. If you were going the other way, I guess you'd stood on the other side. That's what I'd do I was going the other way.

"I see you'll do one of your jokes to throw me off."

"I didn't think I did a joke."

"I guess I know why you picked me up."

"You ought to get a gypsy suit for this act."

"There goes another of those jokes. What I know is you been thinking about me all night. So don't you say you haven't. Well I don't care if you do it's fine with me. You ought to think about that instead of how old I am and if the cops are going to fall out of a tree."

"Well all right. Just how old are you?" Doug felt hot around the ears.

"Fifteen sound good? How 'bout twenty-two?" Sue Jean laughed. "Listen, don't you kid around with me. I pull my pants down right here and say I'm eight you'll do what? Throw me out of the car?"

She leaned in quickly, stretching across the seat with lanky grace, turning her head to plant a fresh young kiss on his mouth, a highschool hot night kiss that left Doug electrified.

"I bet you'd 've drove all night and not said a thing at all. You're a sweetie I'll say that." She scooted down in the seat and lit up. Assumed the toes curled driving stance. A set of the female mouth that signaled decision.

"I'm short on ciggies. We ought to get some burgers and stuff to go. I'd like a place has got a tub. A shower's like it's raining inside you ask me."

"Right," Doug said, "that's what we'll do. Ciggies and a tub. No problem."

There were manual acts to do like turning keys and flipping lights. This should have helped him get his psychic motor running straight again. Nothing helped at all. There was a two-second lag between himself and current events. Driving seemed a grace he couldn't handle. He didn't imagine any of this would happen. Something else might but this wouldn't. A tire tool waiting in the wings. You don't get what you want you get something else instead. Carhop cuties don't ever come across. James McArthur Hill Dean got twenty-two stitches in his head. Sam Bass was gunned down by the Rangers.

THE HEREAFTER GANG

Someone has hosed down the hot parking lot and the asphalt steams off the day, reflecting warps of neon pink and green. Doug stands in the room the door ajar, skulking like a thief in the dark. Imminent disaster is in the air. He knows where the SWAT team will disperse. He doesn't know where he is, hasn't the slightest idea of the name of this Ramada-Western-Hilton-Travelers Inn. There might be matches in the room, an ashtray with identifying marks. Sue Jean comes quickly out of the night and gives him a start. She slips inside and shuts the door and snaps the lights, holds the zipper bag in two fingers like a teacup at a party, creeps across the room with exaggerated stealth, a cartoon burglar on the prowl. She gets the giggles and can't stop. Jesus, what does he do now? Whatever it is, it's wrong, he knows that. She's seen maybe what? Some upstanding highschool cock white as snow. A factory fresh weenie. What happens when she sees this bent and purple club, this prewar battle-scarred torpedo that has dented more hulls than he can count? He is startled by her appearance. He's only seen her in the light once before, at Mary Anne's. He figured sixteen, seventeen tops. Now he's certain she's maybe twelve. He is struck with shame and remorse, prepubescent lust. What does he do next? How does he even start with this sweet little cookie of his dreams?

While he desperately tries to work this out, the cookie starts without him. Simply kicks old moccasins off her feet, sheds the T-shirt like a snake, hops out of her pants cute as a bug leaving a ragged girl trail across the room. He can't absorb this splendid sight, a belly button, a gawky knee, tits round as tennis balls. She finds the sack of goodies where she's dropped them by the door, flips the TV and plops down cross-legged on the bed, lights a ciggie, dips burgers, fries, onion rings, and brownies from the sack, lines them in a circle around her legs, all this to Doug a single act.

His heart swells and tears sting his eyes. Oh Lord, this sweetie is everything he's dared to hope she'd be. She's a teenage honey, self-centered and indifferent to his wants, to anything at all but her own simple needs. She's forgotten he exists. Her eyes narrow with sudden interest. She cocks her head to gain a fuller understanding of the shampoo commercial on the tube. Her body rocks slightly to the music. The little toes never stop. She can spread them like a monkey, grasp onion rings at will. She slides one hand to her cheek and keeps going, lets fingers spill color-streaked hair while they cross the top of her head to the other side. She holds this position, forgetting the hand is there. Doug is overtaken with emotion. This sweet and childish gesture unaware, this wanton and endearing innocent act. He can't take his eyes off this graceless little ferret. He can't move from where he stands. He is taken by a knobby collarbone. A single drop of mayonnaise rests like a pearl on her breast. And Jesus, what's that, a fuzzy caterpillar, nudging the very spot where her heels cross together. As she stretches one hand to get a smoke the creature parts, and there's a Del Monte Cling Peach in Lite Syrup with a smile!

This is more than Doug can bear. Berserker genes have been waiting in the wings. A sly and subtle approach goes by the wind. He launches himself at the sweetie, upending her and setting her asqueal as junkfood scatters into orbit. Oh, the moment when his mouth meets silky resistance, slips quickly through duckfuzz tickle and plunges on. He knows at once he's found the switch that sets teenage gears into motion. His cookie machine bucks and nearly throws him, mutters some plea about a shower, nonsense that Doug can scarcely hear. He's already drunk on hillbilly wine; he'd as soon mix Glenlivet and Sprite as scrub his baby doll clean.

Doug invents bold games for the occasion. Sue Jean listens wide-eyed, teeth against her lips at such wonders, then complies with cute reluctance he finds appealing. Then cautiously at first, she suggests with a sly look well what if you did this or did that? Escalation comes quickly and Doug's sometime fantasy, a backseat romp in a '49 Chevy, hot and heavy groping then a root beer float, moves at warp speed to a fullscale belly knocker Pillsbury fuckoff spree. Sue Jean loves Drugstore Debbie and the Pharmaceutical Rep, a favorite of Janet Dauber the dentist's wife on Thursday afternoons. She offers two sweet vanilla cones, and in return from generous Doug there is a catsup banana split. He closes his eyes and counts to ten while she hides the Milk Duds, as if he doesn't know where, this sly and foxy girl. Oh, this charmer has stabbed his heart! She's even more clever than he imagined, inventing on her own the classic onion ring toss, retrieving crispy winners like a pro. He mounts her on pillows, exhausting the bed's supply and jerking extras from the closet, working in a frenzy folding every quilt and blanket, pulling cushions off the chairs in a grim determined effort to build the tallest pussy mountain ever known. She is lost in springy down, a teeny-burger to go. The tower topples at the first touch of his lips and sends them laughing to the floor.

This girl is loving without a fault, cranky and understanding, oblivious to his needs, petty and stubborn and insufferable to the core, all the traits he cherishes in his heart. He loves her with sweet addiction, is staggered by her total disregard. And just when he thinks he's seen all she has to offer, she stuns him with a pout he can't recall, a flat-eyed and slack-jawed stare, a gray-eyed glance full of hillbilly doubt generations in the making, a tilt to the girl-child breasts he hasn't seen, a hollow at her back where the gaunt vertebrae come together in a graceless altogether lovely slouch. And why should he be so surprised that he's only scratched the surface, that there's clearly no end to his cookie's magic charms? He knew the first time he saw her she was absolutely tops, the culmination of a million little backwater dreary-eyed girls, his number one highschool dream!

And if there's a moment of special magic in this night that lasts forever, a pearl he can set aside and name as sweet perfection, it's the time when she sits astride his thighs, rocking on his loins in passive rhythm, a girl who put a quarter in the tarnished plastic horsey at the fair. While she rides at this slow and easy pace, those dishwater Appalachian eyes half obscured in a tumble of packing hair, she takes the time to smoke her ciggie and sip a Sunkist Orange and watch the tube with some concern. Doug can't see the picture, but he knows *The Poseidon Adventure* well. Ernest Borgnine emotes, turning each simple line into cardiac arrest, eyes bulging in froggy constipation. And Doug, clearly sensing where his own scenario will take him, projects a mental time and distance line from his sweetie's motive oyster to the TV and back, triangulates an answer and confirms he and Ernie and maybe the hapless vessel too will climax all at once. And when it happens, when he reaches the Krakatoa of his career, nearly spears this sweetie through the lungs, drops his primary booster and fires again, he knows with warm assurance she's the carhop queen of all time. Her eyes are on the screen with rapt attention, lips mouthing everybody's lines while her thighs rock Doug through his frenzy, scarcely missing a beat. At the same time, her mouth opens slightly revealing Hershey bar teeth, and she mutters a little Oh! in acknowledgement of his feat; either that or childish wonder that Shelly Winters has a breast stroke that rivals Orca the whale.

And through this long delight, Mousebreath wanders beneath the bed and cushionless chairs, sniffs at mounds of clothing, the familiar and the strange, stalks the alien terrain, slithers across the carpet veldt consuming burger bites and fries, exotic onion rings and candy wrappers, bits of double-chocolate brownie, finally retches this mess in the tub and staggers into restless sleep, disgusted with herself and trips in cars, with Doug's new friend, and most of all with Doug himself.

THE HEREAFTER GANG

Morning found two different people. He called her Sue Jean with easy assurance. It was safe to use her name. They shared a small history and looks passed between them. Doug felt an urgent need to touch, to prove no intimacy too outrageous to try again. He still had her taste in his mouth, he didn't want it to ever go away.

Doug learned they'd spent the night in Temple, Texas. They were dressed and on the road by noon, after sweet reruns of the night before. They passed a plaster bull made African elephant size, a thick-bodied Hereford with short legs and a cock a yard long, testicles the size of basketballs. Sue Jean said boy that dude could show a girl a good time. This and other pranks. Love play to the other side of town where Doug found a good café. Fried ham and waffles, scrambled eggs and orange juice and coffee. Sue Jean's hair washed and clean, the color of toast and marmalade, two springy pony tails that made her look at least eleven. This pleased Doug, and caused him some alarm. The truck drivers and farmers with their Miller's gimme caps hadn't missed his little charmer, who'd pranced inside like a teenage hooker on patrol. These boys knew paradise and prison lay beneath her faded jeans. According to the rules, she was still baby sister Bobbie Lou, and not fair game for several years. Doug knew these men from younger days, and later in shitkicker bars. He knew their rigid code drawn from the First Baptist Church and the lyrics of country songs. Their faces were weathered red as angry sores, plowed with spider comets and bursting stars. Only fags and city people got tans below the neck. Their lips were cracked blue, eyes the shade of frozen pipe. Big hands with sausage fingers unfit for nine irons or tennis fun. Every man there had smashed a horny nail black changing tires. When the hands weren't in use they didn't fidget or move around; they rested like tools on the shelf. Their hostile eyes told Doug he'd better be this honey's daddy or close kin. And Sue Jean, up to mischief or unconcerned, slid close up to Doug and whispered how'bout if I give it a little yank?"

Doug ate as quickly as he could, bolting down food like a dog. He didn't look at Sue Jean until they were outside and back in the car.

"I wish you wouldn't do that again," he said.

"I'm concerned about the way you eat. It doesn't look like you're used to sitting up."

"Sue Jean, those boys carry automatic weapons in their trucks. And you might try to walk different too."

"Well just bite my head off. I don't care for that early in the day."

"I'm not mad at all I'm just saying."

"You ought to learn to take a joke."

"Getting shot by truckers isn't any joke to me."

"You sure did gobble that food. That was something else to watch." Sue Jean lost her pout and laughed. Doug felt relieved. He wanted her happy at all times. She looked so good in bright light he wanted to stop right there and throw her down. She really had him on a run. He'd robbed the candy store blind and he was driving on a jelly bean high. Oh, you little sweetie. He started looking for dirt roads. Now what would she think of that? Maybe she'd like it fine or maybe not.

"I had a cousin in Hobbs, New Mexico, ate everything she could," Sue Jean said. "I mean that girl could eat. Wouldn't any man give her a second look. She didn't care long as Hershey didn't stop making bars. Her folks took her to one fat clinic after another and it didn't help at all. That girl could clean out a 7-Eleven. She finally got a doctor set her to watching that *Love Connection* show. Well, that turned her right around. She'd watch those girls getting dates and start thinking it was her. I bet she lost two-hundred pounds. Married a man had a good career in siding. She doesn't miss that show. They better not take it off."

"I've seen that thing," Doug said. "You can't tell what they're going to do."

"I guess wrong every time," Sue Jean said. "I think some date'll work out and it goes to shit."

"I figure they kinda make things up."

"They do no such thing." Sue Jean looked disappointed in Doug. "That show is taped before a *live* audience, in case you didn't know. They can't make things up you do that."

"Well I've seen this couple, a lot of times they'll say they just kissed goodnight and went home. You can sure tell they didn't. Some of 'em spent all night but they can't come right out and say it. They could if it was cable."

"Maybe. I don't know if they do or not." Sue Jean wasn't happy she hadn't thought of that herself. Doug could tell by the way she frowned and sucked her ciggie till it hollowed out her cheeks.

A sign said Waco was 35 miles, Dallas 131. A little further on Doug spotted his favorite highway sign which read:

HOSPITAL

CAMPING

He pictured this rattletrap bus painted white, bizarre picnickers tumbling head over heels out the door like a Monty Python show, bandaged heads and plaster casts and all that, running for the cement tables under the trees in a fastframe slapstick gait.

"How much money you got?" Sue Jean wanted to know. "You mind me asking that?"

A quick and startling image. Doug at eighty-three conning strangers out of coffee and peach pie. "Why, you going to rob me and throw me in the ditch?"

"Sure. I got this big .44 in my pants."

"That isn't all you got either."

"Serious now."

"Six or seven hundred dollars."

"Ho-ly shit. We'll dry up about Nebraska."

Doug wanted to shout. That wonderful word *we.* They were in this together. He hasn't dared say it out loud. Now she's said it herself it's all right.

"Well I've got forty-two bucks if it'll help," Sue Jean said.

"You hold onto that. We'll be just fine."

"You didn't give running off a lot of thought."

"I guess not."

"I saved me up five-hundred dollars last summer selling cookies door to door. Mostly guys in those singles complexes. Why'd you take off half broke?"

"It's kind of complicated."

"Oh well I'm likely too little to understand. Don't you go to any trouble."

"Now it isn't that at all. Sue Jean, you look at me."

"I guess I can hear you just fine."

"I don't have any money because Erlene beat me to the punch."

He had her attention now. "Another guy, right?"

"That's about it."

"Oh brother." She lit another ciggie. "Your face is all red, you know that?"

"I don't like things make me look stupid."

"'Cause she did it first."

"I guess so."

Sue Jean worked a tooth with her finger, dislodging bits of ham. "You can't get bread out of the bank and Erlene's offed your plastic. So what you going to do?"

"Get work somewhere."

"That advertising stuff."

"Listen, not anything like it I'll tell you that. I'm thinking a store in some town. It's not going to be your big city. You want to know the truth?"

"What's that?"

"I don't want a job at all."

Sue Jean laughed. "That isn't a big surprise."

"You ever think of something you want to do?" He almost said when you grow up.

"Huh-unh. I'm kinda like you."

"Me and Royce."

"Yeah, Royce." She grinned at his name. "I guess old Royce has turned over 'bout two-thousand jobs."

Thinking about Royce somehow brought them both to silence. He was a comforting link between them as the dry summer miles rolled by revealing Troy and Moody and Lorena, and places they couldn't see stretching out on either side, towns in small type on secondary roads. Doug wanted to turn off and see them all. Sunrise and Highbank, Westphalia, Rose Bud and Ben Hur. Mountain, and maybe four miles south of that, Mound. Two miles further on, Flat. Someone had a way with topographics. The more he drove, the more he seemed to know what he was after. He wasn't sure at all what it was or what he'd do when he found it. He knew, though. He felt it coming. The now was rapidly falling away, running his film backwards at an easygoing pace, the soundtrack a tinny little Nepalese beat. The torn calendar squares leaped back into the frame, pressed themselves neatly into place putting Doug days right where they belonged. It worked in the movies and it worked for him too. He could feel a strong wind at his back. God, how he loved the little two-bit towns and empty stretches in between. His heart swelled with feeling for dirt roads and rusty barns, greasy cafes and town squares, hardware stores and dusty smells. Now everything he saw had a special light of its own, a red-tailed hawk on a wire fence, a lone cedar tree off the road. A sign shot full of holes suddenly seemed a thing of wonder. The brightness hurt his eyes; the earth seemed cleansed, fresh and vivid after a rain, each image perfectly etched, a spectacular special effect. He wondered with alarm if the drugs might be acting up again. No, absolutely not. There was real magic here and he knew it for what it was. He had felt this way before, in the moist embrace of hot and healing soil, that sense of being nowhere at all but simply there, sending filaments of himself through the earth and the sandy beds of creeks, into the mushy nests of mice, the vaults of trees, chasing a bright vein of mica through a hill. He has found dead Comanches, the bones of Stegosaurus, tickled the bellies of moles and coral snakes, circled the pale roots through cold wet pipes and followed plumbing to a house, watched a farmer's wife make fudge through a cracked linoleum floor, peeked up her dress and kissed her toes.

And now, for an instant, he lived this sensation once again, driving through the hot afternoon with his sweetie at his side, and he wondered if she was part of the magic too. This out-of-Doug experience passed at once, but it left him with the sharp taste of Waxahachie dirt in his mouth, and for no apparent reason, a chickburger eaten at Veazey's marble soda fountain in 1942. Jack Hamper now dead was likely there, they went everywhere together. Jack's mother served Velveeta cheese and crushed olives on white Wonder Bread, made this every Tuesday for the ladies who come for bridge, pressed bite-size snacks from diamond, heart, club and spade cookie cutters. Before that, before Doug moved to Oklahoma and met Jack, he stood on a chair and watched his mother circle vienna sausage and crackers on a tray for aunts and cousins who came to visit. Fans on the floor made the sleepy sound of bees. He threw up Milk Duds for days when he was ten. This after a Saturday matinee at the Ritz Theater on Thirteenth, two blocks from where they lived in Oklahoma City. *Dr. Cyclops* was the movie. In color. The doctor shrank people down until they were only inches high. They had to run from a cat. In a scene Doug never forgot, Dr. Cyclops grabbed a man by the throat and smashed his head through a purple radium tube. The tube throbbed and the head turned into a skull before your eyes. The doctor had a slick bald head, and wore glasses that made his eyes bug out.

Time's a big gyp, thought Doug. By the time you know what's good enough to keep it's in the trash and it's hell to get it back. Find a girl in a swimsuit ad in Cosmopolitan magazine. Hold two fingers just right and she's naked as she can be. When a cat pees on the rug, it's better to find it barefoot than in a sock. People you see in dreams, no one you've ever seen before. Who are they and where do they live? Hamburgers used to be five cents. Tums spelled backwards is SMUT. Dial spelled backwards is LAID. Maybe there's a moral in that. Or maybe not.

Waco behind now and Hillsboro ahead. New and interesting names peppered about, like Irene, Osceola, Maypearl. Leroy, Mount Calm, China Spring and Frost. Doug told Sue Jean things he might want to do. Like growing strawberries and selling them by the road. Doing something nice with wood.

"I'm not talking your tables and chairs," Doug said. "Maybe something you wouldn't have to saw a whole lot. I'm thinking boxes right off. Boxes'd be good."

Sue Jean showed him one of her squinty looks. "Well who's going to buy an ol' box? I'd like to know that."

"Lots of people would. Why I see a ready market."

"Making those boxes."

"People got to put things away, Sue Jean. Boxes are good to have." Doug lost interest in this idea at once, but didn't know how to stop. "What I'd do is make a couple of different sizes then paint 'em up nice. One set'd be red and yellow, the other in your basic greens and blues. Boy I can see a hundred and one uses right off."

"I'll throw up I even smell that paint. You just say paint to me I toss everything I got."

"Well then you'd be in some different end of the operation."

"Like what?"

"I don't know. Something else."

"I'm surprised nobody thought of this before. I'm riding with the man invented the box."

"I didn't say that. I didn't say I invented it, now did I? Where I see you is in sales."

"I'd be a lot better in cookies. I can't see charmin' some dude into a box."

Doug was sorry he'd brought it up. Boxes were nice to think about but that was about it. What he liked was the smell of freshly cut wood and the racket a big ripsaw makes. He remembered that from his father's lumber yard.

"Fruit might be the thing for us," Doug said. "Strawberries and peaches. Lord, we used to buy peaches every time we turned around. And melons and tomatoes. City people go for those little wood crates."

"Where we going to grow this stuff?"

"You need a little piece of land. Not all that much if the soil's good. I expect you'd be surprised what you can grow in a patch of dirt."

"We better stop and do it quick," Sue Jean said.

"Do what?"

"Buy that land before we run out of money."

Doug loved this practical side to his sweetie. "Sue Jean, I didn't mean we'd do that today. We'll have to do something else first."

"Well I guess I knew that. You didn't have to tell me."

"I didn't mean you didn't know it, I just said it."

"I'm not sure of that fruit."

"It's just an idea."

"What me and this girlfriend did was buy Pillsbury cookies and bake 'em up. The kind they got wrapped like sausage. You can get a whole lot you slice them thin. Francine'd wear a blouse down to here. We said our mom was crippled in a Abilene car mishap. That girl was born with a 48-D. I never saw the like."

"Well cookies might be all right."

"We oughta hire Francine in the shop. That girl can sure push a brownie."

"Well you see? That's what I mean about getting an idea and talking it out," Doug said, warming to a subject he understood. "A lot of people wouldn't, they'd turn up their noses at something new. Everybody's got this thing you got to do what they like to do. If you're a guy like me grew up when I did it's some job in a office. You sit and look up at this light, I don't know if you ever saw 'em. It's got these grills like an icetray without any bottom. You know what you think you look up? I'm a lettuce. A lettuce or a celery on the shelf."

Sue Jean laughed at that.

"No I mean it," Doug said. "That's what you think. You're just sitting on this shelf."

"So why'd you do it?"

"'Cause that's what you did. See, having your personal lifestyle choice is real new. We didn't do any of that."

Sue Jean wanted to know about his parents. He told her his mother was dead and that his father was in a home. That his dad used to run a lumber yard and sell land in Waxahachie, a town they'd be coming to soon. He had a quick mental picture of his folks still there, of stopping off and introducing Sue Jean. Hi mom and dad, I've shucked Erlene and I'm humping this teenage sweetie on the road, what do you think? Highway 35 forked left to Fort Worth, right to Waxahachie and Dallas. Doug turned right and glanced back at the other road, saw the sad blue eyes of his Fort Worth honey in the mirror. He hadn't been to Fort Worth since he'd left her; he knew if he did he'd have to see her and that wouldn't work at all. She probably had another doctor by now. He likely hit her from time to time. People tend to fuck up the same way if they can.

Sue Jean teased the cat with an empty ciggie pack on a string. Mousebreath tired of this quickly and went back to digging out through the floor. Sue Jean had affection left over, and scooted close to Doug.

"You've made out with a lot of women, huh?" This right out of left field.

"I've had some good relationships is the way I'd put it."

"Yeah I bet."

"Well the way you put it doesn't make it sound nice."

"So how many?"

"Just listen to you." He tried to laugh it off.

"No, now come on." She pounded his leg with a little fist, her face screwed up in a look he couldn't resist.

"I don't know how many," Doug said. "You're not supposed to count."

"Well just guess."

"Four thousand and six."

"Oh well sure."

"Four thousand and seven."

"The seven's me, right? You countin' each fuck or each girl? How many really?" Her eyes told him she wasn't sure if he meant this or not. Doug knew how many, and wondered what she'd like to hear.

"Tell me, I'll maybe do somethin' nice," Sue Jean said.

"Like what?"

"Something you'll like. You got to say what."

Oh, what a sly and foxy look. He'd run this honey through a six-ring circus, but that look got his head working fast. Sweet Jesus, fantasy six-oh-two. The picture hit him hard and gave him the shakes.

"W-would you take off your pants while we're driving?" He blurted out the words before his throat closed for good.

"Well aren't you a smarty." Her eyes sparked with mischief. Doug held his breath as she skinned out of cutoffs and undies, slipped them past her feet with the same unconcern as lighting a ciggie. She leaned back and propped her feet on the dash, playing minor classics with her toes, this motion pulling the T-shirt up for a belly button peek. Doug was stricken by the sight. He felt as if he'd never seen her before, the sun bright and waxy on her skin like highlights in a girly magazine. That trick of making a hollow, a concave nest of belly muscle, that was something only a skinny little honey could perform. He longed to drink from the bowl between her ribs and the sharp horns of her hips. And Lord, that pouty package of goodies poking right up at the sky, that golden line of furze, the last strip of grass you missed with the Lawn Boy mower!

And all this while he was conscious of the eighteen-wheeler moving up, the cab high as a second story window, the truck coming fast with a whine of singing tires. The words in his head said tell her to cover up but he knew he'd never do it. He felt the quick thrill, the hot pleasure of what would happen next. Saw the girl out of the corner of his eye, the truck edging up on the right and knew the driver could see all he wanted to see. Sue Jean turned to Doug with a look he couldn't define. He reached out with one hand and tore the T-shirt over her head. He felt total desperation was in control. She reached up to help, tossed the shirt in the back with a grin maybe a thousand years old. The trucker gave a blast on the horn that shook the car. Sue Jean raised her hand and gave him a finger.

Doug gripped the wheel and jerked the car off the road, squealed through an exit to the access road and the first dirt road he could find. The car churned dust; Doug found a spot and braked to a sliding stop. The cloud he'd made caught up and coated the car. The stunted oaks on either side were ocher-red, each leaf heavy with summer dust, everything the color of red brick. Sunflowers fat with thick sandpaper leaves, road weeds choked with painted rust, the land bone dry and the air sullen hot, the locusts too weary to make a sound. Doug dropped his hands and watched them shake. His heart slammed hard against his chest. Sue Jean got out and stood naked in the road, stood there taking in the sights like they'd reached Yosemite National Park.

"Oh Jesus," Doug cried, "you crazy goddamn little sweetie!" He stumbled out of the car caught his knee on the bumper, howled and fell to the road, scrambled around and picked himself up. Grabbed Sue Jean and flipped her ass-end up like an IHOP pancake to go. He took her this way, slapping her body hard against the ground, threw himself at her until her legs gave way and knocked her flat. Doug collapsed on her back; the collision brought them both to pleasure at once. Either that or some internal mishap, he couldn't tell for sure. He checked Sue Jean to see. Found that hillbilly whonker-jaw smile and didn't know any more than he did. God how he loved her disregard, her total preoccupation with herself! She was everything he'd hoped for, everything he'd dreamed, his harebrained scrawny little carhop queen.

Doug's legs nearly toppled when he stood. Red dust was thick in the air. The car was coated solid and seemed a basic part of the road. Both he and Sue Jean were kinky Celts. Sue Jean walked naked down the road, a post-rape ciggie hanging loosely in her mouth. She had Mousebreath on a leash. This was her personal job, taking Mousebreath out at every stop, watching the cat collapse and dig in prepared to hold out forever. Sue Jean just as stubborn and completely unconcerned, happy to walk around dragging a furball in her tracks.

"You going to turn around or what?" she wanted to know.

"I'll find a good place down the road," Doug said.

"Good. I'm not much into camping out."

"We're not camping out, Sue Jean."

"Listen. This ol' cat isn't about to take a shit."

"Not if she can help it."

"Bad, bad cat!" Sue Jean squatted down in the road and shook a finger in Mousebreath's face. "You are gonna flat out explode, you little fucker. You know what I'd like? I'd like a big Dairy Queen chicken-fried steak and a double chocolate Coke."

"Sounds good to me." Doug said.

"Not all your DQ's can make a onion ring right. If the salt won't stick, well that's it. You like the straight fries best or the ones curl up like a spring?"

"I like the curlies you can find 'em."

"Did I come or what?"

"I don't know."

"I guess I did."

"Fine," Doug said.

Getting dressed was a chore. Nothing short of a bath was going to help. Doug got the Mercedes started and turned the air up high. Rommel leads the Afrika Korps out of the desert storm. The windshield was coated with dust. The wipers squeaked dry leaving Japanese fans. Doug looked at Sue Jean and saw a small part of his life on a sun-brown leg. It looked as if a fish had darted by and dropped a scale. Trail of the mad drifter. Jesus, what a day.

THE HEREAFTER GANG

Full of Dairy Queen chicken fried steak and onion rings at Italy, Texas, where his dad used to bring him to watch the lumber-yard-real estate team, the Hoover Wolverines, play softball on Saturday summer nights. They played against rival lumber yards and teams from hardware stores and John Deere tractor dealers, teams from Ennis and Palmer and Ferris. The men who worked for Doug's father knew they'd damn well better make a double base hit or regret it Monday morning. After the game, Doug's father would always treat him to a hot dog and a drink. Doug had to choose between a Nehi Orange and Grapette. An agonizing decision. He seldom slept Friday nights before a game. He loved Grapette but the Nehi Orange was much bigger. Grapette came in tiny little bottles you could finish in two gulps. He knew what he wanted which was two Grapettes. He had more sense than that. His dad would blow a fuse whether the Hoover Wolverines won or not. Jesus Christ, you want *two?* Why there's kids in Europe'd likely give their left nut for just one. I don't even think they make it, you want to know. What do you think of that, Greedy Gus? So Doug didn't ask. He got a Nehi Orange and hated his father for a week.

He drinks a Coke at the DQ, which isn't like a Grapette at all. They don't make it anymore, or if they do he can't find it anywhere. He loves to watch his sweetie eat. She can't seem to get enough. Fries with the chicken fried steak, a double order of onion rings and dessert after that. The DQ has desserts of all kinds. Frozen bananas dipped in chocolate coated with nuts. You can buy popular brands of candy bars and have them ground up in an ice cream treat. Sue Jean tries a Heath Bar and a Snickers. The waitress says she isn't supposed to do two kinds, the store's got a policy on that. Doug slips her an extra buck. Sue Jean gives him a hug. He wonders if he can feed this little honey very long.

He thinks about Popsicles and Eskimo Pies. The ice cream man coming down Fifteenth and he and Jack Hamper there with nickels in their hands.

They went to Lincoln Elementary and Harding Junior High, and then Classen High together, and off to the same college after that. And Jack Hamper said fuck advanced ROTC, and they shipped him to Korea then back to Oklahoma in a box. Jack's mother quit going to the Chinese Palace Thursday nights and took to drink. Ladies stopped coming to play bridge. Her bids didn't make any sense. Doug's great-grandfather barely missed the Civil War. Grandpa Hoover was too young for Number One, his father too old for Number Two. Doug got in ROTC, and sat out Korea in the States. He thinks about this. How his family's managed to miss all the wars, and still produce a credible number of casualties on their own. Shell-shock victims of hazardous peacetime living. The socially disabled, the functionally inept.

He remembers Jack Hamper went out for sports. That was the only thing they didn't do together. Doug's father bought him a Sears fielder's mitt, nagged him every day to use it. Doug was too skinny and he wondered why his dad didn't know it. Maybe he did. Maybe he didn't want to think about how the kids at school always picked Doug last. He'd swing at most anything at all. Easy Out Hoover, and he finally got tired of hearing that. Making airplane models was more fun. Reading *Plastic Man* comics and *Captain Marvel.* A bread and jelly sandwich on the screened-in porch. If he got too bored he'd watch the dog eat peanut butter.

Hunt Mackley lived two doors down from Jack. His family took their clothes off the minute they walked in the house. They were hardshell nudists, maybe the only ones in Oklahoma City at the time. Hunt was allowed to play with other boys, but no mother would let their kid go in the Mackley house. Once Hunt showed Jack and Doug the family's naked Christmas card. All the Mackleys stood in a row and grinned. Mom and Dad and Hunt and his little sister and the cat. Mr. Mackley wore a Santa Claus hat and smoked a pipe. The postal inspectors made them stop sending cards. The Mackleys promptly moved to Atascadero, California.

Doug's father didn't like his wife's clothes. He didn't know beans about the subject but he knew the stuff he liked. He got fashion ideas from the funnies. Every Sunday morning he'd get off by himself and figure what new trends were coming up. "Boy, that Dragon Lady sure looks smart," he might say. He'd study some skimpy little number Wilma Deering slipped on to run to the Piggly Wiggly on Mars. "Don't tell me Buck Rogers isn't puttin' it to ol' Wilma now and then," he'd mutter half to himself. "He's looney if he don't." He thought Dale Arden had the best legs in the business. That Flash Gordon was getting some of that. So did Doug, but he came to this conclusion on his own. It didn't bother Doug's father that you couldn't stuff a Mary Worth body in a Brenda Starr dress. He'd circle the panels he liked and leave them lying by the mop or on the stove where his wife couldn't miss taking a look. Doug's mother didn't take to this at all. She let it go a while, then started dropping sartorial hints of her own. Mandrake the Magician in a silk maroon sock. Dick Tracy on a godawful tie she couldn't stand. Doug's father felt betrayed. He sulked around the house. "You don't listen to a soul but that godamn sister of yours," he'd say. "That woman wears clothes come out of a tree. Just look at that thing you're wearin' now. Why, they'd chase you out of Wichita Falls. You'd look right good in this outfit Blondie's got on."

Doug's mother listened. When he finished she walked up and stabbed a finger through his heart. "Now you listen to me," she said. "Don't you give me any funny papers again. Not ever. A man buys his skivies at the hardware store hasn't got room to talk. A pig can read your *Esquire* magazine all day long, and he isn't going to be Walter Pidgeon when he's done. You're no better'n that pig so I doubt you'll make it either. So you just leave me the hell alone. I dress to fit the company I'm in and I reckon that says a lot."

After that Doug's father kept the funnies to himself. Doug discovered you could trace Dale Arden and make it look like she wasn't wearing a thing.

He remembers how he felt when he heard Jack Hamper had been killed. He wonders what Erlene's doing now. Maybe humping Pastor Jack. What do preachers think about when they fuck? Do they think it's all right? He hopes Sarah Dee gets married and keeps her job. He hopes Annie's safe in a shitkicker bar. God bless Jack Armstrong, Billy and Betty and Uncle Jim. He remembers a man who worked for a big publisher in New York. He collected words that writers cut out of what they wrote. He tried to find some reason why they did. The words they cut out seemed much like the ones they left in.

Amos Fevre got tipsy at an office Christmas party. He confided in Doug he'd seen a former Miss Nevada trim red pubic hairs in a sink. Every grandmother's porch is painted gray. A checkout girl knows you're looking down her blouse. TAB spelled backwards is BAT. TIME spelled backwards is EMIT. Doug isn't sure God knows what he's doing all the time.

Doug found a shabby motel not far from the Dairy Queen, a place with a desolate pool where the water line had sunk to half a foot of black muck and happy frogs. The rawboned lady at the desk didn't like his dusty looks. Something was funny if he wanted to stop here. She didn't much care for Sue Jean and the Nazi car. Doug said they just wanted a shower and maybe hose down the car. "That'll be a extra dollar for the hose," she told Doug. "Water don't grow on trees." Hijinks for certain, she knew that. Maybe an antichrist cult on the side. Pastor Jack on the TV had told her how to look for signs. That mean-eyed cat topped it off.

He felt good, clean and back on the road. There were fine country stations beaming in out of Waco and Dallas and Fort Worth, and for once Sue Jean didn't punch in your freako rock with her toes. They'd frolicked in the shower but that was all. He wanted her again all slick and soaped up but didn't feel he had to have her. The dirt road had curbed his desperation. It was nice to just have her there smelling like Zest and onion rings. She added to the glow that overtook him with every mile. He was wrapped in a warmth he couldn't define, a magic hot afternoon that would take him anywhere he wanted to go. He was home or close to it, a farmhouse abandoned, leaning into the wind, all the windows gone and the yard choked with weeds, a dry summer field and a line of trees beyond, the promise of a creek, a gravel road and a rusty bridge, everything reached out to draw him in. In his mind he saw Hoover Bros. Real Estate & Lumber, baked white paint in wavy lines across heat-bright corrugated iron. He saw a day as hot as this, paper shades drawn, the sun filtered and condensed, the air thick with motes of gold, the lazy-eyed girl cross-legged on the bed. The very first he'd ever seen without a window in between. Hands-on instruction that had set the course of his life. Oh Lord, he was back, Waxahachie dead ahead. Back again and he hadn't learned a thing since he'd left. Everything he knew was what Cindy Nance taught him in a single afternoon. He'd spent his whole life finding out that she was right. Or half right, at least, and what's the matter with that?

Maybe that's a secret everybody ought to know, he decided. What you learn first off is flat it and you're a fool if you don't hold the line. A breakthrough in early education. He could start up a school. Soon as some kid hears talk about commerce and trade you jerk him out real quick, stick him in a room with a Waxahachie girl and set him straight. He wouldn't go into banking after that. He could get into drifting right off. And he wouldn't make the same mistakes *he'd* made, either. Cindy Nance was wrong about that. She was right about everything else but she was wrong about that. You didn't have to grow up and get a job. Work dulled your senses and took the edge off of life. Worse still, it cut right into perfectly good loving time. If he ever saw Cindy Nance again he'd let her know. She'd only showed him one great truth and not two.

Sue Jean cut into his thoughts. "If that's not a shit-eatin' grin I never saw it. I can see what's in your head don't think I can't."

"Just thinking about you," Doug said.

"Shoot you are. Your mouth's set to lie down and bark, and it sure isn't me."

"It's someone I used to know."

"Uh-huh. Number what?"

"Number one."

"Lord God. We're talking your prime-evil love. What's her name?"

"Cindy Nance."

"Was she good?"

"It's not so much her as coming back," Doug said. "It was all good here. That's how it seems to me."

"I never been anywhere but Houston. That and Mobile, Alabama, but I don't remember that."

"Why I've been there. I never heard you say Mobile, Alabama."

"You never asked. That's where my daddy took off. Mother moved to Houston and found a new asshole in a minute. Took her insurance money and sunk it in a muttonburger franchise in Port Lavaca, Texas. That was sure a dumb thing to do. Your tourists got to have those nuggets. They won't put up with sheep and fries. She got rid of him quick."

"A business won't always work out I know that."

She gave him a shifty eye. "You still thinking fruit stands or what?"

"Not a lot," Doug said.

The tables at the roadside park were slabs of native Texas stone, half a dozen tables set back from the drive that circled in from 35. There was a lot of this white and porous rock across the state and the restrooms were limestone too, and the square bins for garbage. A tattered state flag hung limp in humid air; the sky seemed dry and overexposed. Swings and a broken slide were in the open past the johns on brittle grass, ironwork lethal to the touch. Sue Jean sat on a swing and smoked her ciggie. The cat sat crouched and mad as hell, indignant at being tied to a pole. The swing was built for toddlers and Sue Jean sat bent and hunched up, knees level with her chin, dragging bare feet in the hot dusty hollow that is a natural formation under swings. Two boys maybe eight and eleven sat at her feet. They listened with great interest to what she said. When the swing came forward in its arc they peeked slyly up her shorts, hoping to learn the secret of life.

Doug sat at a table near the '39 Mercedes he had more or less stolen from Parker Symmes, a well-known proctologist in Houston, Texas. A white RV was parked close behind the car, though no other people were in the park. On the front of the RV it said "Charlie and Freida Duckman, Travelin' On." Doug drank a cold Dr Pepper in the can from the machine near the john. He had studied the map and pictures behind plastic which showed where you were and the things you'd want to see. The pictures there were formerly tourist bright but the sun had done its work, bleaching all the inks but the yellow and a faint tinge of blue. Fun in area lakes seemed uninviting. Water skiers and boaters appeared startled, snapped there in action microseconds after the bomb.

Some years before Doug would drive this way every week, by the very same spot when it was thick with twisted oaks and big pecans. He would pull off the road and take barbecue ribs in a sack and a bait bucket full of iced beer and sit out beneath the trees. Even if the day was August hot as it was now it was always cool in the shade. Squirrels and jays would come to watch. There were not as many cars on the road as there are now, and locusts made more noise than traffic. He would sit there and listen and read about Liver Eating Johnston and his hijinks among the Crows. Maybe he'd finish off the beer and get a pint of something cheap from the car. Once he wrote his name and the date and left a note in an empty pint, and set the bottle in a branch. The note asked the finder to express his random thoughts, the first thing that came into his head. No one ever answered, but it pleased Doug to find the pint there on every trip.

Then the highway department built a road off 35 and made picnic tables and johns and raised the flag, and cut down all the trees in favor of more contemporary shade, tin roofs on poles which were made incidentally by a Corsicana company—now defunct—that made a fortune selling carports in the fifties. Before he married Erlene and after Lindy, Doug went out with a girl named Jackie Mapes. She opened mail for the Texas Highway Department in Austin and sent him wildlife calendars for some time. Doug asked her why they put a park there when there were places all over with no trees. Jackie said because the spot was something point four miles from the last park down the road. Doug felt this had the sad ring of truth.

The man from the RV had been leaning against his door. When Doug waved at Sue Jean he started over. The two boys were his and he'd been waiting for some excuse. He was short and squarely built, as if he'd come out of a box and still retained the shape. He seemed in his sixties, older than Doug but not a lot, though Doug appeared a great deal younger thanks to the practice of regular soil immersion. Everything about the man was blue and brand new, blue Nikes and socks, blue shorts and blue polo shirt with an animal on the pocket. He walked as if life were full of purpose, the top half of his body well ahead of the rest, apparently gravity free. His hair, his nose, his chin, every feature seemed to buck a strong wind. Doug was reminded of the Indian on the hood of early Pontiacs.

"You almost got the symbol for the Olympics," the man announced, sliding down across from Doug. "I can fix that in a jiffy." He picked up Doug's Dr Pepper and pressed another wet circle in the stone. This act seemed to please him.

"History of the earth is right here before your eyes," he told Doug. "Ordovician limestone's what it is. These fossilized shells are dead ringers for the ones you find today on your common coastal beach. Molluscular life has made very few gains, I'm sorry to say.

"I guess not," Doug said.

"Your creationists are full of shit. This stuff here's half a billion years old, don't let anyone tell you different. What happens is your creature takes lime from the water to build a shell. When he dies those shells pile up on the ocean floor. That curly bastard there's your cephalopod. Some of those buggers had shells like an elephant's trunk. A few measured several feet long. Beat the living Jesus out of your pesky trilobites. That your car, the Mercedes? Boy what a number."

"It's not exactly mine," Doug said, wishing right away that he'd kept this to himself. "It belongs to a proctologist in Houston. He collects cars that were driven by German doctors during the war."

"Asshole diggers." The man made a face. "Who the hell'd want to do that? I'm Charlie Duckman, you likely guessed from the sign. That's our motto, me and Freida's. Travelin' On. It's a way of life with me."

Doug shook hands but avoided giving his name. "There's a lot of money in proctology," he said.

"I don't doubt it."

"They all seem to have good cars."

"Doesn't seem like decent work," Duckman said. "You wonder if those fellas wash their hands. There's things you're better off you don't know. You ever go back in the kitchen of one of your finer restaurants? I advise you not to do it. You can't say what people'll do. The papers say those boys up at SAC are into drugs. I hear top models pee in the tub."

"That wouldn't bother me."

"I don't much care for such talk."

"I went to a party at this house," Doug said. "Mostly GP's and dentists, but there were a bunch of proctologists there too. All their wives look alike. Tall stringy women, nervous as deer on opening day. They move real fast. Won't let a man get behind them for any reason."

"You make that up?"

"I'm telling you what I saw."

"Then I guess it's probably true. Nothing surprises me. Not a thing. Say, that car must be worth a pretty penny."

"It used to belong to Dr. Josef Mengele," Doug said. "I know you heard of him. It was found in a garage in a remote German town. A Quartermaster sergeant named Billy C. Russ. This was 1953. That date's fully documented. It was up on blocks in mint condition. Someone took care of that car during the war. The authorities would give a lot to know who."

"Well I'll say. Imagine that." Duckman seemed distracted. Slightly out of synch. Following a line from the Pontiac eyes, Doug could see he was taken by Sue Jean's youthful appearance. Her skin was tanned the color of clover honey, and her legs seemed remarkably long for a girl scarcely five foot three.

"Those two sprites are my grandkids," Duckman said. "We got 'em for the summer. My wife's inside the RV. I'm retired and we travel all over. We're originally from Roswell, New Mexico, and I still maintain a home there. Freida gets carsick every time I turn on the engine. She's sure a trooper."

Duckman glanced over his shoulder, though there was clearly no one around. "I'll tell you who I am, you want to know. I'm a former agent of the Federal Bureau of Investigation. I can see you're surprised, don't think anything of that. They train us so we'll blend right in. Stopping right here was no happenstance event I'll tell you that. This very spot's where the most baffling case I ever ran had its start. I can't reveal names. A man was found by state troopers. Knocked cold and stark naked, his car gone. Some cock and bull story about stopping to help a girl in distress. The locals bought this but I didn't. I saw links to bigger things. I'm convinced this fellow came from El Paso, Texas. Mixed up with cartels and the like. This boy was in with crime bosses down in Houston. Don't tell me he wasn't. Disappeared without a trace. What do you think of that?"

"That's amazing," Doug said, who truly thought it was. Earlier that week he had nearly thrown up in the back seat of Sunny D'Angelo's car. Sunny was the undisputed crime boss of Houston, and Doug knew him on a personal basis. Stranger still, he'd had coffee and peach pie not twenty-four hours before with the elusive James McArthur Hill Dean, the very man Charlie Duckman had just described. It's uncanny how things come together.

"You don't mind me saying," Duckman said, "that daughter of yours is a looker. I mean no disrespect in any way. I'll bet she's a topnotch student."

"We're on our way now to Wichita, Kansas," Doug said. "The girl's a cutup on the bass clarinet. They've got a special school for that."

"Well I'll say. I'll bet you're proud as you can be."

Doug felt this last business would throw Duckman off. There actually was such a school, which Doug's cousin had attended. The boy had gone on to sell term insurance and become a Life Member of the Million Dollar Round Table. Doug regretted this encounter with Charlie Duckman. He was certain all lawmen retired or not could get word to each other in some manner. Perhaps through a secret device no larger than a postage stamp.

"The open road's the answer," Duckman said, standing up to stretch and pop a stick of Black Jack gum in his mouth. "It suits me and Freida to a tee. Keep out of cities is my advice."

"I think I will," Doug said.

"I'd of got out sooner if I could. You don't make any money in the Bureau, that's for sure. Your New York TV folks spend more on a goddamn Pepsi commercial than I ever made in my life. You think that's fair? No, it's not. Life's moving too fast. I miss the hell out of Maggie and Jiggs. My God what a bitch. Always conking that poor little bastard with a rolling pin. I laughed out loud every time. Fella drew those bumps on his head with the stars, whoever drew that could do stars. I wonder if Kate Smith's still alive. I guess not. You want to know what was the beginning of the end, I'll tell you straight. I saw it real clear and I doubt if many did. That was the day your Tarzan movies were no longer credible in light of African politics. I better be off."

Doug watched him go, striding off with purpose. In a minute Sue Jean left her swing and picked up the cat. The boys lost interest at once. They ran back to the RV, damp thoughts implanted in their heads. Doug got the air going fast and Sue Jean dumped Mousebreath in the back.

"God is it hot," she said. "I'd say a hundred and two. The radio said it might go right through the roof." She assumed her riding position, hunched down in the seat, bare feet on the dash. She lit a Salem at once. Doug thought a beer would taste good, one of those Mexican brands if he could find it. He pulled away from the roadside park, back on 35. In the mirror Charlie Duckman checked his tires.

"Who's the funny looking dude?" Sue Jean wanted to know.

"He thinks you're a looker."

"Good for him."

"Well he had some real sound ideas, I'll say that."

"I'll bet."

"You didn't even meet him, Sue Jean."

"Those boys of his are horny little devils."

Doug thought her swing posture had made it easy for them to look, but kept this opinion to himself. "Waxahachie's not far," he told her. "We can stop if you want. I can show you right where I grew up."

"They got a good Dairy Queen, fine." Without a word she stripped the T-shirt over her head. She was sticky from the heat and for a moment seemed a moth breaking free, everything tangled, but a promise of better things. She wadded up the shirt and wiped her face and under her arms, then started on her tummy and her thighs. Doug felt a moment of desperation. Sitting there drying herself off like she just stepped out of the tub. Not a thought to all the cars whizzing by. This excited him more than screwing her to the bed and he didn't even have to guess why. He was thinking about the truck passing just before they stopped, the driver seeing Sue Jean jaybird naked, and Sue Jean knowing Doug had wanted that to happen and going right along. Boy, that was something. There didn't seem much she wouldn't do. He looked at her then and saw sweat pearling up between the fine apple tits. The urge hit him straight on. He reached over quick and wiped his hand between her breasts and licked his palm.

"You are screwy, you know that?" She gave him a squinty look but it was clear she didn't care. "I mean, you are something else, man."

"I like the way you taste," he said. "There's nothing wrong with that."

"So how do I?"

"Like sour apples."

"I do not. What'd that old guy say about me?"

"I told you. He said you were a looker."

"Who'd you say I was? I bet I know who you didn't."

"You sure are a honey." He reached over without looking and grabbed again.

"Now you just stop that, Doug." She slapped him off but laughed. "I'm all hot and dirty."

"I'm hot and dirty too and raring to jump."

"That's not what I mean and you know it." She turned in the seat and sat on her legs. She had a curious habit of looking at everything sideways, this funny little cockeyed look as if she were trying to soak up everything she saw. "Listen," she said, "what's the three dumbest things you ever did?"

"I'll have to think on that," Doug said, "I guess I've done a lot more than three." All her questions came out of left field, like they'd just popped into her head. This didn't bother him anymore, he was used to how she thought. Her mind seemed to run to numbers. What are your four favorite records? Your three favorite colors? Talking to this cutie was a challenge. She could unnerve him quick.

"Well the third dumbest thing I guess was marrying Erlene," Doug said. "That wasn't real bright. You ought to see that woman's mother. The second worst thing was getting work. I shouldn't ever of done that. I'm not real suited for your work situations. I'd just as soon been a forest ranger as messing with that advertising stuff. Bears couldn't be much more of an aggravation."

"And what's the dumbest, you think?"

"Getting mixed up with Sunny D'Angelo's got to be first," Doug said.

"You know *him?*" She showed real interest in this.

"I guess I do, all right. It wasn't my fault but you don't get credit for that. Fate'll just deal you a hand when you least expect it. You ever see a little dog run out in the street, you just let it. That's my advice."

"God I couldn't do that." Sue Jean seemed horrified at the thought.

"Then you better make sure whose dog it is."

"Now that's silly." She took Doug's hand off her breast, where he was pretending to open a safe. "You wouldn't have time to *ask,* you know? That little doggie running out in the street. There isn't any way of telling whose it is."

"Well see, that's just what I was saying."

There was more to this story, but Sue Jean didn't ask. She did this a lot, losing interest halfway through whatever was going on, a conversation or something on the tube. It didn't matter what it was. When she was through she just quit. Lighting another ciggie, she began to flip the radio from one end to the other. She found a group she liked and told Doug it was Radioactive Cabbage. Doug had never heard of them before. This went on all the time. They had no common musical ground except the no man's land of the Beatles and Janis Joplin. Doug had missed them on one end of the scale, and Sue Jean on the other. Stan Kenton and George Shearing didn't even ring a bell. He didn't bring up Tommy Dorsey. When she curled up to sleep he found some good Willie Nelson and kept it low. He watched her as he drove. Lord, how he loved to watch her sleep. She slept with her mouth half open, a straw-colored curl stuck to her cheek. A frown between her eyes, sullen even when she slept. He wanted to just stop right there and start licking her all over. Suck her little Popsicle toes. Sometimes she hit him like that. She didn't even have to be naked. My how she loved to play and frolic. Last night in the motel had been as good as it could be. And darned if they didn't do it all morning then pull off the road and do it again, both of them turned on good by the trucker.

His throat swelled at the thought. He was dazzled just being there with her. Overcome with tenderness and lust. She seemed more vulnerable, younger than ever in her sleep. He could smell her sweat from here and still taste that little Frito and Pepsi Cola cunt. He felt like he was stoned, flying overhead above the car. Not on the dope anymore, that was gone; he was stoned on the girl herself. Oh my what a sweetie. The best of a lifetime of gray-eyed, petulant little cuties. Sugary girls in cotton candy sweaters and fuzzy collars. Girls with flushed cheeks in football letter jackets that swallowed them up. Lazy, sullen, gum-chewing ciggie-smoking girls, the fun southern sweeties he'd loved all his life. Girls with dusty airbrushed skin all over, even in areas where bumps and rashes persist. Never turn a girl from Minnesota upside down. It's not a good idea. He thought about collarbones and teenage knees. He looked at her lying there asleep. Why those nipples could sit up and bark.

The road stretched out hot and black, signs pointing to Dallas and Fort Worth. Water towers and towns off the road, truck stops and places to buy hams and walnut bowls. And here I am, he thought. I don't want anything and still I want everything there is. I'd like to talk the way Jack Nicholson does. It might be fun to grow herbs. I'd like to fly just once in a Fokker. Rob a train in Springfield, Missouri. A girl sees me on the street. She finds out who I am and where I live. She sends explicit photos through the mail.

He decided he might lack depth of character or maybe not. He had lived all his life in reverse anticipation. Total noncommitment was a dedication of sorts. He couldn't really complain. The past he didn't want—Erlene and Houston and the do-nothing job at Clinton-Fevre—were far behind, the past he wanted up ahead. The inability to cope had set him free. Why, he had Parker Symmes's stolen car, his carhop queen by his side. What was the matter with that? It was clear enough now his health was fine. Sue Jean's antics would've killed him by now if his ticker was on the blink. So all that shit was part of the pharmaceutical circus. Whiskey and dope had done him in but not his heart.

He decided Charlie Duckman and James McArthur Hill Dean were a lot alike, though on opposite sides of the law. Both were out of step and didn't know it. Living on daylight zonker time. He wondered if either one knew Standard Oil had sold various petroleum products to the Germans during the war. He'd bet a dollar Charlie Duckman had a silver Lincoln Zephyr in his past.

Doug thought about this as they started back north, Waxahachie maybe twenty miles away. Life had a way of pulling loose threads together. Things didn't just happen; there was purpose and direction. That's the way it had to be. If it wasn't you wouldn't meet James McArthur Hill Dean and then Charlie Duckman, too. Or run smack into Herb Tarchek and the daughter of Cully Moon. There wasn't any way of telling how many times it happened and you didn't ever know. Fate just pulls another string and there you are. Maybe the old man at the Texaco in Temple was the South Texas god who'd fathered Erlene Lamprey Hoover. You couldn't tell. Maybe Sue Jean's second dad wandered down to El Paso where he talked the former speedboat whiz into rattlesnake nuggets on a stick. Well why not? Doug was taken with the wonder of it all. God has the shop working smooth. The universe is sound as a new watch and that's a good thing to know.

Sunny D'Angelo had told him about a dope dealer who put big piranhas in a hundred-gallon tank, then hid a lot of coke beneath the gravel. Sunny said the guy saw this in a movie. This was the first place the narcs looked, since they'd seen the movie, too. They threw a white marble ashtray from Italy at the tank and those fish went snapping around on the rug. One agent suffered a nasty bite on the leg.

Sunny probably knew he'd run off. Sunny knew everything he really wanted to know, mostly before it happened. He thought about Audio Visual Annie Tonklin, and wondered where she was. On a bus somewhere or in a shitkicker bar. He hoped she was doing real fine.

He watched familiar miles roll by. The signs for cafés and auto parts stores had names he knew. He went to school with Darby Kane, window peeked at Mac Pearly's cousin, Lorna Toon. The '38 Ford had been sitting in that field since he was a kid. Harrow Rick's father hit a truck full of black cotton pickers head on. Harrow's old man was killed outright in the crash and the cotton pickers didn't get a scratch. A Pepsi truck edged up behind and Doug moved to let it pass. A blue Camaro with the left light gone came into view. Doug saw it was Erlene and Pastor Jack. The message didn't register at once. Life seemed to contract and pull him back. This seemed a violation of his rights. He jammed his foot hard and speeded up.

Sue Jean opened her eyes looking cross. "What's up?" she wanted to know.

"I'm being pursued is what's up," Doug said. "I don't need any of this." Sue Jean turned around to look. "I just bet that's the little woman."

"I'll bet it is, too."

"I better get on a shirt."

"I don't think that'll help."

"Well she can't do anything at all," Sue Jean said. "You can do whatever you want. You don't have to listen to her."

Doug wasn't sure what to do. He hadn't considered this. They'd have to stop for gas sometime and there'd be a confrontation. He'd likely knock that preacher on his ass.

"I'm going to keep on driving," he said. "I don't want to discuss any of this. She's sure got nerve bringing him."

A pickup truck was pulled off on the shoulder just ahead. The truck had Wyoming plates. Cole Younger was changing a tire. He waved at Doug. Jesus sat on the fender drinking a Tab. Doug felt alarmed and strangely detached. The dope was kicking in again.

"What's the matter with you?" Sue Jean said.

"I don't know," Doug said. "I never know what's the matter. That's the problem."

"Stay cool is what I'd do," Sue Jean said.

"Well that's sure good advice."

"I'll ask you not to snap at me. I'm not to blame for this."

"I didn't say you were. Did I say you were?" Doug kept his eyes on the mirror. He passed a line of cars, and saw Erlene whip smartly out of traffic on his tail. That Camaro had pickup on the road. "Jesus, this is past my understanding. I'd like to know what came over that woman. I'll bet that TV preacher's behind it. Those boys'll bite you in the crotch. They won't ever let go."

"I guess she wants that seven-hundred dollars," Sue Jean said.

"She doesn't even know about that. She wants to aggravate me."

The Waxahachie exit loomed ahead. Doug waited the last minute he could then jerked the Nazi car off quick, nearly spilling Sue Jean to the floor.

"Say, I don't care for your driving," she said crossly.

"You just stay put. I can't lose that car straight out. It's rated real high." He raced through Waxahachie, through the main part of town, missing several shoppers and a dog. Cars pulled out of his way. He crossed the railroad tracks and circled back. The town had changed some but not much. He whipped through familiar streets and alleys. Now he couldn't stop and look around. Erlene had fucked that up good.

"She back there or what?"

"I don't see her any more," Sue Jean said. "Listen, you're not in that *Miami Vice* hit show. Slow down this car."

"I won't," Doug said. "She can just leave my lifestyle alone." He saw a farm road sign and headed straight for it. He felt elated. He knew the road and where it went. A car came speeding out of a cross street, coming right at him. A big white Buick with the extra chrome package. Sue Jean let out a yell. The Buick braked hard. Doug swerved around it with a two-inch clearance. He got a quick look at the driver. The man saw Doug and shook his fist. Stew Geeter and Ham Bayliss. Doug stared and nearly hit a 7-Eleven.

"Lord what's the matter with you," Sue Jean said. "I saw my whole life pass by."

"I got a high-priced cardiac cutter on my tail," Doug said, "that's what. Him and a dog-faced shrink. Erlene's got a paramour army on the road. I'd like to know where those two get off."

"Well you're driving a stolen car, I know that."

"A doctor's not your highway patrol. They can't make a legal arrest."

"They could do that citizen thing. They might be in the right."

"They better not try it. This car's got prewar steel from the Saar. I'll knock that Buick flat." He checked out the car in the mirror. Ham Bayliss was backing off and starting up in an effort to get the Buick headed straight. Doug left asphalt and hit the gravel road.

"You know where you're going or what?" Sue Jean said.

"You just watch. Doctors can't handle a gravel road and I doubt Erlene can either." He looked and saw Ham was on his way. Another car pulled up behind, passing the Buick quick. Erlene's blue Camaro, chewing up gravel and laying dust. This doesn't make a lick of sense, thought Doug. A car chase from Waxahachie, Texas. What if I just stopped? What if I turned around and chased *her?* That'd give her something to think about.

Erlene raced up a car length behind. Sue Jean managed to get on a shirt. Pastor Jack shook a Bible out the window. If that book contained the whole King James it might go right through safety glass. Doug stuck his foot to the floor. The road began to twist and he gained a little room. He didn't have to slow down at all. The Nazi car was heavy as a tank and made a considerable amount of dust. Why he'd leave those suckers a mile behind. They'd wish they hadn't started this mess. The engine began to cough then seemed to catch again. Doug felt alarm. The car shook like a Mexican laundromat. Out of gas or what? He didn't have the slightest idea. He beat on the gauge which didn't seem to help. Looked up and saw the pickup coming straight at him down the road. Jesus waved and made an "ok" sign as they passed. Cole Younger fish-tailed the truck and neatly blocked the road behind.

Doug tightened his grip on the wheel. I am flat out losing it, he thought. Right now. Red Ryder'll show up next. Him and the fat little Indian kid. The engine caught once then sang like a bird.

"Sue Jean, I want you to tell me," Doug said. He looked straight ahead and not at her. "Tell me if you saw that truck, I want to know."

"Did I what?" Sue Jean punched the lighter with her foot. "Listen, you got a bad pump in this thing. I'd advise proper maintenance real quick."

Doug decided not to pursue it. Pharmaceuticals had settled in his genes or maybe not. If he was goofy he didn't care. Unhinged didn't seem much different than daily life. People at the state zany ranch likely shared his point of view.

It might help to try and think if he could. Reason seemed well out of reach. How long could a delusion block a Camaro and a Buick? Erlene might flatten Cole Younger out quick. So why not stop and have it out. Tell her he didn't like her attitude. It didn't matter but it did. She couldn't stop him but she might. He had a beat going now and Erlene could throw it off. He felt dead certain that she would. Take away his sweetie and the hot summer day. Stick him in a suit and send him out to get work. He was scared of that woman and he knew it.

Nothing seemed to be coming up behind. Doug made a curve past a falling down barn and there it was. The Phara, Texas, water tower tall as life. A big band song played in his heart. Erlene didn't know about Phara. He'd kept it to himself. She wouldn't know what to do and he'd lose her real quick. He was gone and she didn't even know it.

"Well now where are we?" Sue Jean said. "I don't guess you know."

"I'm home," Doug said.

Sue Jean looked perplexed. "I thought we just ran through it. Where you did that cop show act."

"We did. This is different."

"Well don't tell *me* anything."

"Hey, we're just fine."

"I'll bet."

"We are. Sue Jean, nothing can stop us now, we're just fine."

Two things happened at once. Something made a bad sound beneath the hood. The Nazi car rolled a few yards and stopped dead.

"Well shit," Doug said.

The second thing that happened was a pickup truck painted blue. It came down the Phara gravel road and pulled off, stopping head to head with Doug. Doug couldn't believe his eyes. Royce got out and dusted off his knees, walked up to the window and looked in.

"Royce!" Doug said, "Now if this isn't something. Hey, I told you I might start drifting."

"I see you did," Royce said. He grinned at Sue Jean and winked at Doug. "Guess you ought to be arrested on six counts of something. Be hard to say what. Man, where'd you get this fuckin' car?"

Doug didn't feel he had time to fully explain Parker Symmes. "I've got my ex-wife-to-be on my tail," he told Royce. "Her and a couple of former friends. They're driving a doctor Buick."

"Let's take a look," Royce said.

Doug got out and Royce raised up the hood. Sue Jean sat on the fender and lit a ciggie. The fat man Doug had seen at Mary Anne's jumped out of Royce's truck and headed for the brush. He seemed in desperate need.

"It's that pump," Sue Jean said. "I heard it go out. You can tell right off if it's the pump."

Doug looked nervously down the road. "If I have to I'll abandon this thing right here. I don't want to talk to her at all. I'd as soon hide out in a culvert."

"It's going to be that pump," Sue Jean said. "You wait and see.

"Well I don't have time to look for a Nazi car pump in Ellis County," Doug said.

"He's got a point," said Royce from under the hood.

"Well I'll be," Sue Jean said. "A person can't open her mouth I don't guess."

Doug searched the road again. No sign of Erlene or the Buick. Which meant the hallucination was holding strong and he was crazy as a tick. It didn't seem important if it worked.

"Sue Jean, get in and kick it over," Royce said.

Sue Jean did. The motor caught at once.

"That ought to do her for a while," Royce said. "'Course I won't guarantee it'll hold. Your Mercedes cars aren't used to bailing wire."

Doug was elated. "My God, Royce, I don't care if it does. It'll get me out of here. You flat saved my life."

"Forget it. Us drifters got to stick together. So where you headed now?"

"Couple of miles down the road. Where that Lamprey woman can't find me."

"I'll follow and make sure." Royce grinned and shook his head. "Boy, you're a cut-up I'll say that." He backed the blue pickup and turned the other way. Tapped the horn twice. The fat man waddled out of the brush hurriedly pulling up his pants. The dusty black coat caught the wind. That man's got a problem with his bowels, thought Doug, and wondered who he was and why Royce hauled him around.

"That pump's still broke," Sue Jean said. "You wait, it'll last about a mile."

"You don't fix up those pumps," Doug said. "You got to put a new one in. I doubt if that was it."

"Well thanks for that handy maintenance tip, Mr. Goodwrench. You ought to open up a Fina service station. You could sell those boxes on the side."

"What's the matter with you?"

"I know as much about cars as you, I'll tell you that. I'd like something to eat if you don't mind."

"Sue Jean, I'm in flight right now in case you didn't notice."

"Well I hope I don't faint."

"You won't faint."

"Now you don't know a thing. A girl on *Guiding Light* got a chronic sugar low and 'bout died."

Doug didn't answer. Sue Jean sat in the corner in a pout. Doug turned past the cemetery just on the edge of town. Yesterday reached out and gathered him in. His grandparents were buried right here in weedy plots under rusted marble stone. Greats and great-greats and uncles and aunts. Men in black suits and black hightop shoes, black socks thin as a woman's hose. White shirts buttoned at the top without a tie. Watch chains draped across a vest, chains attached to ivory pocket knives and watches the size and weight of river stones. Pearl-gray Stetsons set straight above the eyes, the brim out flat and the crown stained with sweat. A pink rosebud in the lapel. A Prince Albert tin in one pocket, a Morgan silver dollar in the other. Their faces farm red, never tan. There's no such thing as a tan in Phara, Texas. The women wear flower print dresses, corsets underneath hard as iron. Their hair is braided tight and bound in buns on either side. Hatpins lethal as a dagger hold a black straw firmly in place atop the head. The hat is set straight like a man's. No jaunty angles in Phara, Texas. The black straw hat is for the week. White hat, white shoes and white gloves for Sunday service at the First Methodist Church. Powder and lilac water, a bright circle of rouge for the cheeks. Pearls and a brooch handed down, brought west from Tennessee or Alabama, and Virginia before that. Back further still, from Ireland and Wales.

At night the shades drawn, the woman puts the flowered dress aside and quickly slips into a white cambric gown. Her back to the empty dressing room, she reaches under the gown and strips the armor of the day, corset and corset cover, drawers and underskirt. She sits before a mirror and a kerosene lamp and draws the many pins from her hair. The hair falls down to her waist. She brushes each side a hundred times. She thinks about the day. Her son has married a hussy from Kansas City. She works in a shop and smokes Old Gold cigarettes on the sly. The woman turns down the lamp and peeks into the other room. Her husband is safely asleep. She slips into bed, careful not to wake him. He smells of corn shucks and tobacco, dust and axle grease. She lays awake a long time. She hears a train far away, and wonders where it's going. She's been to Galveston, Texas. Weatherford and Dallas. The St. Louis Worlds Fair. She can't think of anywhere else.

Doug remembers them all, these people long dead who seemed old when he was young, people in their fifties when he was eight, people who were part of his summer days, his Easters and Christmas Eves. He remembers the great-uncles and great-aunts, pioneer mummies so old they struck terror in his heart. A visit to these survivors was an annual flagellation, a somber rite of the clan. The family would gather for this outing, arriving in great number, people Doug had never seen before, slate-eyed kinfolk in strange exotic garb, cousins with eyes a quarter-inch apart, haircuts straight out of 1386, all motored in from some rural quarter of Mars for the occasion, people who couldn't possibly be related in any way, boys his own age who spoke of livestock romance, girls who farted when they walked. Everyone packed into black Chevrolets and black Fords, then a drive to some clapboard house on the edge of desolation, some house in a field where the land had gone to seed, set amid hackberry trees with warty leaves, the porch and the roof bowed with age, the wood bare of paint for fifty years, flat gray and dry the color of mice, the yard choked with weeds and nettle, snapdragons and roses gone wild, a maze hiding rusty tractor parts and old tires, a trace of brick paths neatly laid in younger days. As the cars pulled up, scrawny pullets squawked and scattered; a pack of crazed dogs would erupt from under the house, dogs that had mange as a strong genetic trait handed down with family pride. And then the mothers, one by one, would parade their young quietly through the faded yellow halls, across the warped pine floors, beneath the dark high ceilings, and into the tomb itself. And there would be a man or maybe a woman, who could say, a paper leather husk, fragile as dried flowers under glass, a creature from *Weird Tales* part human and part rocker, wood and flesh grown together. Say hello to Uncle

Jess/Aunt Irma, mother would say, and Doug would mumble and shrink away, knowing if he looked too long, if he let those black bullet eyes draw him in, that the thing in the rocker would take possession right there, would pop into his head and take his youth, leave him stranded in that dry and hollow shell. And when the visit was all done, this pre-funereal caravan would stop along the way for ice cream, something to cut the taste of death, and mother would say now Doug, Uncle Jess/Aunt Irma's real old, and won't be here very long, that's likely the last chance you'll ever have, you remember how he/she looks. And next year they'd do it once again, and the year after that, for maybe five more years or maybe ten, one last visit fading easily into the next, this indestructible zombie still sitting right there, inhabited or not Doug couldn't say, but there it was, rocking through another somber visit, determined to escape, to steal young eyes and live again.

Now in the shadow of the silver water tower, rising like an iron castle keep above the town, the tower where a siren still sounds every noon, Doug sees one familiar sight and then another. The drugstore on the corner, the five and dime, the funeral parlor/hardware store, the grocery after that. The broad and empty streets, the high country curbs, the depot deserted forty years, the red brick buildings and tin fronts of Phara, Texas. He imagines the whoosh of fans, the dry and musty smells, the people inside passing time, peering out at searing heat, drinking the fifth Dr Pepper of the day. And then the town is gone, two main streets and that's that. Doug takes a farm road east, sees Royce and his friend are still behind. The gravel road winds through black gumbo land where Doug has found precious new life in the soil, past low Texas hills stubbed with dry summer grass, past bridges and dry creeks to the turnoff he knows in his sleep. Where he knows every rock and stunted tree. Where he's safe from Erlene and her TV preacher and her pack of doctor suitors in pursuit. She knows Waxahachie, but she doesn't know this. She can't follow him here.

"Are we there yet or what," Sue Jean wants to know.

"Close to it," Doug said. "Just right down the road."

"Well I guess you'll get around to saying where. Like I'm supposed to know."

"I thought maybe I did," Doug said. "It's my grandmother's farm. I stayed here a lot when I was a kid."

"Uh-huh."

"You'll like it, Sue Jean. There's a creek and a lot of neat stuff to do."

"And where we going to eat?"

"We'll work something out."

"Shit." Sue Jean looked at the sparse dry fields, at the lack of Dairy Queens. "Which means you don't know, right? That's what I thought."

The place was just as he remembered, the farmhouse boxy and narrow, squeezed together at the sides, the white paint peeled, the front porch running the whole length of the house, weathered gingerbread posts supporting another porch above, a porch nobody ever used. The house was set in a grove of native pecans, facing a gentle slope that led to the barn, and the road that wound past it to the creek and the iron bridge. He went through the house, through every empty room, imagined the kerosene lamps, the glass chimneys you had to clean every day, the black oilcloth on the table, the smell of the wood stove, and the cool mysterious depth of the cistern. Here in the living room his grandmother and Ellie, a black girl who lived with her family by the creek, would iron clothes and listen to *Ma Perkins* and *Stella Dallas* on the Philco radio. He could still smell the clean heat of a flatiron on the stove, see the warm orange light on the radio dial. He must have been eight or nine. A few years before that when he was six, there'd been no radio, no electricity, no phone. He was back and he felt content. His past was here. It was gone but it was here. He could see it all and bring it back to life. Cousins and aunts and uncles, farm dogs and horses and a pinto pony his grandfather kept for the kids. A chicken named Bumps that followed him like a pet. Called Bumps because he shut the screen door on it once and it could only see out of one eye. It walked with an off-center jerky chicken gait. Out back he saw the storm cellar and the iron kettle for wash, the smokehouse and the orchard, the outdoor privy. Past that the cotton fields, stretching out forever.

Now he knew he'd made it, gotten clean away, put Erlene and the present out of his life. For a moment, when the blue Camaro appeared and the white doctor Buick after that, he was certain that she had him, that he'd never get away. But the farm was sanctuary, sacred magic ground. Nothing bad had ever happened to him here, and nothing ever would.

When he came in from the back he saw Royce had everything arranged. He had extra sleeping bags in the truck, and enough pots and pans to cook a meal. After a while Royce drove back to town to get steaks and ketchup and a loaf of white bread, this and a list from Sue Jean that started off with Hostess

Twinkies and ended up much the same. The steaks were good, cooked in the fireplace where Doug had watched his grandmother bake a million potatoes under ash. Sue Jean didn't complain. Camping out was like, really great, man. She wouldn't want to do it twice, Doug knew. She liked to do a thing once but not twice. In the morning she'd be stomping around the yard, a hillbilly pout around the mouth. By noon she'd be searching the horizon for DQs and 7-Elevens. Snapping like a yard dog at everyone in sight. Generally being your A-one bitch. Lord, she was a cookie. There wasn't another like her in the world. She was plain bad news, cute as a bug. He wanted her again. Right now. Wondered if he might talk her into using one sleeping bag instead of two. It seemed like a wicked thing to do, and that meant extra fun. Doing it right here, in his grandmother's house. He'd never imagined a thing like that, stretched out in front of this very same fire, listening to Charlie McCarthy get the best of Jack Benny. It just goes to show. Hijinks will come your way, just wait around and see.

Before it got dark he walked down past the barn, along the narrow dirt road to the creek and the iron bridge. Royce went with him, and Sue Jean walked along ahead, kicking up dust in the road. The sun was low and slanting through big pecans and oaks, trees a hundred years old and maybe more. The light turned everything funny, making skin tones redder than they were. Sue Jean's bare legs looked burned, like the girl in the ad who didn't use Coppertone.

"I shot my .22 off this bridge," Doug said. "I hooked a big mossback turtle down there, along the bank. Scared the shit out of me and Ellie both. I know Ellie was with me at the time. She was the black girl who worked up at the house and she jumped as high as me and dropped her pole. We'd make peanut butter and pimiento cheese sandwiches and come down here and fish. We'd bring orange juice in a mayonnaise jar. We really had a time."

"I bet you did," Royce said.

Doug looked off to the left of the creek and saw the remains of Ellie's house, your classic North Texas 1930s nigger shack, the whole thing balanced on piles of shaky bricks. Ellie and her husband R.C. worked the farm, did whatever Doug's grandfather wanted them to do, and Ellie had a kid every time she turned around. Doug remembered the creek in winter, frozen at Christmas time like brown chocolate ice. On ahead past the creek, past the graveyard tangled high with brush, graves that had been there even before his grandmother's time, up to the fields where the corn used to grow, and another nigger shack still teetering on a bluff, the brick foundation tumbled away and the house ready to go, ready to slide down before their eyes. And he remembered it had been like that nearly fifty years before, when field hands had lived there in it, tossing old tires and daily garbage down the hill so long that the hollow was nearly full, nearly high enough to cushion any fall if the house should ever go.

And on the way back, the light nearly gone, the trees turning black and the road a phantom white, Doug felt a great warmth for Royce, a welling of the spirit, a feeling he couldn't define. It seemed so right he was there, that Royce was the friend he'd always wanted and never had, this boy he scarcely knew but seemed to know so very well. The thought hit him all at once and sent a great surge of joy through his heart, a wave of pleasure that filled his veins and overwhelmed him with emotion. He knew at once that he didn't have to look for the high lonesome, he was there. He and Royce. They were where they ought to be. Camping out and cooking steaks on a fire. No Erlene, and no job to go to in the morning. No city lights to blur the stars coming out overhead. He had his campus queen and his new best friend, beer iced down at the house. Lord, what more could a man want? He couldn't think of a thing he didn't have.

"God I'm glad I ran into you, Royce," Doug said, this onrush of joy adding a tremble to his voice. "I didn't think I'd get to see you anymore."

"Things work out," Royce said. "It seems to me they do."

"I sure think they're working out for me. I don't know what I want to do. I'm still not sure about that. But it doesn't seem to worry me like it did."

"Maybe you already got it and don't know it."

Doug beamed at that. "Why that's what I was thinking, too. That very same thought. You think maybe I do?"

"Seems like it to me."

"My mother used to tell me, Doug, she used to say all the time, you can't get out of being what you are. She'd tell me that once or twice a day. I sure felt trapped. I believed that a real long time. She said a lot of other things, too. That woman could quote stuff right and left. She went to the library a lot. My dad, now he looked on the bright side of things. Right up to when they took him to the home. A girl'd come on the TV, she'd be standing in the shower. One of those shampoo ads or your Lifebuoy soap. He'd get up and stand close to that set, look right down the glass. He figured if he looked just right, he'd see her tits. He'd get up and do it every time."

"I had a uncle like that," Royce said. "Eighty-nine years old he wouldn't quit. Ordered him some seeds from California, started growin' bonsai sequoia in a dish. That man was a optimist first-class."

"Well I'll be," Doug said.

"A man knows what he wants, you can't hardly keep him down."

"That's the truth. I wish I'd learned that sooner than I did."

"There's no use hurrying things along," Royce said. He stuck a match between his teeth, studied Sue Jean up the road. "Some things got to come along when they do."

Doug thought about that. Maybe Royce was right. It made him feel better to think he hadn't just fucked around forever, changing jobs and getting married every hour and a half. Maybe he wasn't ready before now. Discontent wasn't enough. You had to figure timing in it, too. If he'd tried the high lonesome before, he might have screwed it up good. Royce, now, he'd just started out young and done it right. Drifting like a pro, not worried about a thing. Well there wasn't any use looking back. Where you are now is what counts.

The house was nearly dark; Doug thought how fine it would look with a kerosene lamp in the window, a cheery yellow glow in the night. That was the first thing they used to see, coming in for Christmas from Waxahachie or Oklahoma: a yellow light far off that said people were waiting up, that homemade fudge was sitting out on the table. The tree was up and lit, and you could find your own name on a tag.

"It's a mighty fine night," Royce said. "Sleeping out'd be better than sleeping in."

"You do you'll get a stinging scorpion right in your ear," Sue Jean warned. "They crawl in thinking it's a hole."

"I never heard of that," Royce said, lighting up a smoke.

"Well they do," Sue Jean said. "I had a cousin went crazy on a campout for Christ. That thing crawled around in her brain, they never did get it out."

"I heard of snakes coming up in a blanket," Doug said. "I know they do that."

"They won't if you lay a piece of rope around your bed," Royce said. "They won't cross the rope."

"Why not?" Sue Jean said.

"They just won't. It's a fact."

"I wouldn't want to trust that rope," Sue Jean said.

Doug stayed with Royce and watched the night close in. Sue Jean went in and lit a lamp. Royce cracked pecans beneath his boots. Even in the dark, Doug could see the fat man sitting in Royce's truck. He wouldn't go inside the house. Royce had brought his dinner outside. Brought back a plate untouched. The man made frequent trips to the brush. It seemed a wonder he could keep this up without taking something in. Sue Jean came back dragging Mousebreath on a leash. She pulled the cat across the porch. The cat dug in but Sue Jean didn't care. She pulled it back and forth like a toy that didn't work. Mousebreath and the man in the truck were in total opposition, thought Doug. One wouldn't start and the other couldn't stop.

"His name's Thack," Royce said, seemingly guessing Doug's thoughts. "Hasn't got anyone else to see to him so I do it."

"You ought to get some of that Kaopectate down him," Doug said.

"It hasn't got to do with his bowels. He don't feel comfortable with people he doesn't know. He doesn't know anyone but me."

"Thack what?"

"Just Thack." Royce flipped his smoke in the yard. "We all got problems. Thack's sorta mine. He'll be okay."

Doug waited, but that seemed all Royce wanted to say. He felt sorry for this Thack, but didn't mind if he slept in the truck. A man like that could be a problem indoors.

It was much too hot to get inside the sleeping bags, so they laid them side by side and stretched out on the top. Royce was outside with his friend. They had the big empty house to themselves, but Sue Jean wasn't in the mood. She thrashed about and complained she couldn't sleep. All those bony angles found the floor. She complained for maybe three or four minutes and she was gone. Doug listened to the owls outside, mice scrambling about upstairs. When he was a kid, most of the rooms up there were unused. He and his cousins thought the place was likely haunted. They'd creep halfway up the stairs and run back, pleasantly thrilled with fear. His mother's family had a history of ghosts. A great-aunt's husband appeared to her a week before he died. To Doug, this didn't seem peculiar at the time. His mother's folks were Whaleys, mostly from Alabama or Tennessee. They didn't do things in order like other people did.

He lay there and the memories flooded in. Green beans and okra, creamed corn scraped right off the ear. Cornbread and beans, ham and redeye gravy. His grandmother added a little coffee to the grease. Fried chicken which he loved. Chicken and dumplings which he didn't. This was a dish the old folks seemed to cherish. He remembered those people, his grandfather's family, coming out for supper, some special get-together. These people scared him. They didn't fit the world he knew. He saw them clear as day in his head, lined up at the table on the screened-in porch. They didn't look at all like your *Saturday Evening Post* Norman Rockwell cover. More like the sad sepia prints of old settlers just arriving in Montana, wondering why the fuck they'd made the trip. Hollow and worn out before their time.

He felt detached. Somehow free of all restraint. He knew why he'd kept this part of his life to himself. Why he'd never brought Erlene to this place, or for that matter anyone else. This was his. Something he couldn't share. A piece of the precious past more enduring than Waxahachie or Oklahoma City. It was sanctuary from the problems of growing up, from his parents, even if they were there. The rules applied to other places but not here.

He wanted Sue Jean. Looked at her curled up naked and was certain he had to have her. She wouldn't wake up, but didn't seem to mind. She was totally unconcerned. In the morning she might remember. Might ask him if she came. He loved her dearly for that.

Doug dreams he and Jesus are in old man Wetzel's model airplane store. The store is across the street from the dark and somber fortress of Lincoln Elementary. The school is two stories high but looks higher. There are towers crowned with concrete breastworks and sentry walks behind. Small mice and pigeons stand guard. Even on a Saturday afternoon, a cold December day free of imports and exports of Brazil, this grim wet structure holds the threat of Monday morning. Doug and Jesus stay clear. They keep to the other side of the street. They avoid looking up at the crenelated roof, the windows with pointed arches, the Norman arrow loops that the swallows have stuffed with straw. Doug imagines Mr. Britton donning battered helmet and mail. He mans the tower walls with a crossbow he's cleverly made in shop. Miss Crewley brings tubs of boiling soup from the cafeteria line. The Vikings howl in pain, drop their weapons and flee. They wish they'd never heard of Oklahoma.

The thick-boled elms that line the street are wet and bare. Doug feels ice on the bark. The clouds are steel and full of winter. The wind, out of the north, cuts corduroy knickers like a knife. The paint on Wetzel's store is flecked and dry as powder. The inside is the same; clapboard siding weathered ancient silver-gray. Wetzel's gas stove, big as a grand piano, fills one wall with its mass. Blue flame licks at the shaggy asbestos, blisters the wooden floor. The air is thick with heat. There is no way to breathe. Old man Wetzel stands stern and unforgiving behind the counter. This stupefying warmth is not enough. He longs for lazy Mesozoic days. His nose runs all year round. His chickenbone frame is wrapped in sweaters, one woolen layer after another, each the color of attic dust. A black stocking cap is pulled down across his ears. He watches Doug and Jesus through gold-rimmed glasses. He is waiting for them to steal. He knows all boys are thieves. Boys practice thievery and self-abuse. These are the things they do.

"What are you going to get," asks Jesus. "You still thinking about the Hawker?"

"Maybe," Doug says, "I dunno. What are you going to do?"

Jesus doesn't answer. His eyes are as blue as raw milk, blue as baby eyes. He looks at the model, hanging from a string overhead. A Spitfire shrieks through English skies. It dives on a doomed Focke-Wulf. Red yarn lances from the Spitfire's wings. White cotton smoke and orange tissue flames billow from the hapless Jerry's engine.

"Lo, the wicked shall perish," Jesus says. Doug sees sadness and understanding in his eyes. "They shall be consumed in flame, smitten over the channel and in the fields."

"Yeah, right," Doug says. "Listen, you get the Spitfire I'm still getting the Hawker. I'm not going to be no German."

Jesus keeps his silence. When he gets that look in his eyes, Doug knows there isn't any use trying to talk. Still, if he wants to be weird it's okay. He's the only kid Doug likes in 5A. When he first came to school, his folks made him wear these sandals and a robe. The other guys beat him up at recess for a week. After that he dressed like everyone else. Corduroy knickers with leather patches on the knees. The elastic is long gone out of the knickers, and they sag to his dirty tennis shoes. He has a checkered mackinaw and a checkered cap to match, earflaps down over his hair. And that's the only thing. His hair is as long as a girl's. Doug thinks Jesus is pushing with the hair. Your best friend turns up on the Sunday school lesson every week, it's asking a lot.

Doug already knows what he wants. He'll get the flying model Hawker and some glue. That'll leave twenty cents left over. Enough for the picture show and popcorn and Jujubes and a Coke. He knows what he wants, but he looks at every item in the store. He pretends he might get something different. He walks along slow, hands stuck down in his pockets. He looks at the long strips of balsa in the bin. Some strips are thin as spaghetti, some as thick as baseball bats. He covets every piece. He savors the rich smell. Sun comes in the window of your room. You sand down balsa and the air is rich with dust. He's looked up balsa in a book. Balsa trees grow in the tropics. He imagines how they look. You could pick up a whole tree and throw it.

He looks at the neat lines of airplane dope behind the counter, squat bottles of Chinese-red and sky-blue, black and green and silver and battleship-gray. He looks at the fine blades for carving, bright as new nickels and scalpel sharp, keen enough to lace a hand with scars in a single afternoon. He studies all the blue and orange kits on the homemade shelves at Wetzel's back. Every Comet model ever made is right there, everything from small nickel solids to the fliers for a quarter or fifty cents.

And there, on the very top shelf, where it's been for as long as he can remember, is a plane nearly three feet long. It is covered in black and red tissue applied with surgeon's skill. The wings are swept up like a gull's. A silver-chrome gasoline engine is mounted just behind the prop. Doug wants this plane with its bold pirate colors more than anything else in the world. He knows he'll never have it, but he'd like to touch it once and feel its magic. It has never crossed his mind to ask Wetzel for such a favor. There isn't a kid alive with the guts for that. Wetzel is watching him even now, guessing his thoughts. His eyes are cold as Spandaus, searching for hapless Bristols limping home. Wetzel knows. He knows Doug will buy a gasoline model about the same time he buys a new LaSalle. Wetzel can see right through Doug's mackinaw and knickers. He can see through flesh and bone and into pockets, see the quarter and two dimes clutched hot in Doug's fist. He knows to the penny what Doug has to spend. He even knows about the popcorn, the Jujubes and the Coke. He knows what's his and what isn't.

Doug and Jesus duck their heads into the biting north wind, close their eyes against the cold. Doug's ears are numb. He has to stretch his mouth to talk.

"You want to build 'em over at my house this afternoon? I got the table set up."

"Can't," says Jesus, "I have to be about my father's business."

"Is tomorrow okay?"

"Tomorrow's *Sunday,* Doug."

"Oh, yeah. I forgot. Anyway I got to clean up my room 'fore Mom throws a fit."

"That's good. Honor thy father and mother, Doug."

"Hey—we'll do it Monday after school. I got a new *Captain Marvel* you can borrow if you want."

"Monday's fine, Doug."

Doug wipes his nose on his sleeve. They hurry north, bent into the wind. The cold begins to chew at their bones. Doug feels the first rattle of sleet on his cap. The gray stone capitol of Oklahoma squats at the far end of the street. High steel derricks line the parkway, right to the building's front door. Ice slicks the derricks at their peaks, hammerheads groan and suck oil. The building and the derricks are the same dull color as the sky.

"What are you going to be when you grow up?" asks Doug. "I'm going to be a pilot, and shoot down Germans and Japs."

"Those who live by the sword—"

"Hey, I can be a pilot if I want."

"I know that, Doug."

"Yeah, well what are you going to be?"

"I guess I'm going to be what I am," Jesus sighs.

"What? A ten year old kid?"

"No. Something else."

"Like what?"

"I guess I'll be about my father's business."

"Sure, this *afternoon,"* Doug says, "you already told me." He's beginning to lose patience with his friend. Sometimes it's better just to walk with Jesus and not try to talk to him at all. "I mean later. When you grow up. What are you going to do then?"

Jesus doesn't answer. He stops and turns and looks back the way they came, past the bare trees and the school and the slate-colored sky. He seems to listen like a cat that hears sounds it doesn't share. Doug follows Jesus's eyes. He sees a small spot growing larger, the hard point of a pencil, punching through dark and brittle paper. The point grows, sprouts black horns and then a tail. Jesus doesn't move. He watches this dark and spinning star hurling toward him from a chill inverted sea.

"It is time," says Jesus, and Doug can scarcely hear his words. He stares in awe, in terrible disbelief. He knows the star and what it is.

"Jesus," Doug shouts, "it's a Fokker D VII and it's coming right at us!" He tugs at his friend, tries to throw him to the ground. Jesus is made of stone. The plane grows larger, fills the winter sky. Twin threads of yarn reach out and find their mark. Jesus cries out and falls. Doug looks up and sees the tattered double wings, the stubby shape. He sees no pilot, no one at all. Tissue paper shivers in the wind. The acid taste of glue is on his tongue. The plane snarls like a dog and disappears. Doug bends and takes Jesus in his arms. He is hit in the side and in his feet. There is blood in the palms of his hands. His face is set in pain and resignation. He looks at Doug and smiles.

"It's all right," he tells Doug, "it's okay."

"It's not okay, it's not!" Tears fill his eyes. He holds Jesus close against his chest. "I don't want you to die. You just can't!"

"I think I have to, Doug. I'm almost sure I do."

"You don't either. I'll never see you again and I don't even like anyone else."

"I'll be back. I promise."

"Oh sure. When?"

Jesus thinks a minute. “How about Easter? I’ll get up Easter morning early, and we’ll do the Hawker and the Spitfire together.”

Doug starts to tell him they go to church on Easter and eat out. He looks down and sees the fine blue eyes are white as marble. He’s seen war movies and how they close a guy’s eyes when he’d dead. It doesn’t work. The eyes don’t want to stay shut. He doesn’t know what to do next. Easter seems a long time away….

THE HEREAFTER GANG

The dream seemed to linger, to drift up with him out of sleep. Doug knew about dreams. They happened somewhere like the Twilight Zone where there was fog and funny music. What a dream wanted to do was be real. It didn't want to stay being a dream. When you started waking up it would hang on and try to get by, try to slide right through unnoticed. A real strong dream could nearly do it. It could hang on maybe half a day. He wondered how many ever made it. There might be dreams who'd gotten through. People you made up or didn't know oozing right into this world from another. Maybe they went out and got a job. Met a girl in a bar and ate ribs. And what did these people dream when they went to sleep? Where did they think they were? Once Doug dreamed he had french kissed the cat. Woke with the taste of Tender Vittles in his mouth. For a year after Lindy took off with the oil and gas man from Lubbock, Texas, he dreamed in serial form. The dream would leave him in a Fokker, shot up and spinning out of control. Going over South American falls, angry headhunters in pursuit. A new episode every night. The dreams had credits but he couldn't read the names. They stopped when he met a beautician from Biloxi, Mississippi. There was clearly some connection.

Royce was up making coffee and frying bacon. The radio was going in the truck. Bacon grease had fallen in the fire and smelled good. Doug made toast holding bread on a stick, turning it over the fireplace until it was brown. Sue Jean was still asleep and he sat and talked to Royce, then walked out back and looked at the farm. The day was already summer hot, the gravel yard so bright he had to squint. The orchard past the smokehouse was dead. There were peach pits hard as river rocks underfoot. He remembered his grandfather, stalking through the garden, a saltshaker clutched in his hand, pulling up green onions and eating them on the spot, going up one row and down another. That was the summer bees took over the smokehouse. There was no way the women could go in and get a ham. Doug's dad and his uncles flipped a coin to see who would go in and clear them out. His uncle Nat lost. The others dressed him up in thick potato sacks, and put a cheesecloth veil on his hat. Nat went in with a burlap kerosene torch. The bees fled the smoke, many finding safety down the back of Nat's neck, a flaw in his armor the others hadn't thought to sew up. Nat spent the rest of his vacation in bed.

It was a bad summer for bites. One girl cousin stepped on a centipede in the yard. A cottonmouth crawled up from the creek, found R.C. on his niggershack porch and bit his toe. R.C. screamed for help and Ellie came running with an axe, missed the snake but got R.C.'s foot, stopping the spread of venom right there. The most humiliating bite fell to Doug. Chiggers were an everyday event, a part of the summer plague. Calamine lotion was supposed to stop the itch but never did. Doug got a foreskin bite, and scratched it till infection set in. The skin turned a bright cherry red, started to swell and wouldn't stop. Doug was frightened out of his wits. At seven he was gaining some interest in this fascinating part and didn't much want to lose it. So far it wouldn't do much but pee but he suspected it was destined for greater things. In desperation he showed his mother what he'd done. Mother turned pale and called his dad. "Holy shit," said his father, with no expression at all. The swelling had reached staggering proportions. It looked as if a pink Crayola had speared a plum. The doctor said hot packs and rest. If the swelling didn't cease they'd have to *lance,* a word that filled Doug with nameless dread. Lance with what? A needle, a Bowie knife, a Hottentot spear? The doctor didn't say.

The worst was yet to come. Uncles and aunts were paraded in to see. Relatives drove in from as far as Corsicana. Perfect strangers would appear at the farm and ask to view this strange affliction. His parents' initial concern turned to pride. "It's a wonder, all right," his father would tell some couple from Minnesota, "you never seen anything like it I'll tell you that." People wanted to take pictures. Doug's father was all for it, but his mother said no. And Doug, who was too scared to protest, hid his head under the covers and prayed the swelling would go away. When it did, his father seemed vaguely disappointed. He looked at Doug as if he'd somehow betrayed the Hoover name. Doug kept to himself the rest of the summer, walking along the creek and looking at squirrels. He couldn't face his cousins, especially the girls. They knew. They hadn't gotten to see it but they knew. Everybody did. He considered running away, but didn't know where to go. He decided it wouldn't matter if he did. There wasn't a place in the whole country that didn't know who he was.

In the old brick kitchen where the stove used to be he found the hole where the black tin chimney had funneled smoke outside the house. Newspapers were stuffed inside against the wind. Mice had nested there for years and made confetti. A single panel from the funnies was still intact, the colors now soft pastels the shade of Swiss mountain blooms. Smilin' Jack was there with his neat two-stroke mustache. The fat guy whose name he couldn't remember was there too, a button popping off his shirt. A scrawny chicken waited to catch the button in his mouth.

"What I wanted was to get a good look at Waxahachie," he told Royce. "I don't guess I ought to do it. Erlene's likely called in the Guard. They've probably cordoned off the town."

"She might not bother you anymore," Royce said. He sipped on an after-breakfast beer, pulled another out of the cooler and gave it to Doug.

"You don't know her," Doug said. "That woman's determined to mess me up. I think I'll try for Oklahoma City."

"If you do, I'd stay off your major routes," Royce said. He spread a Texaco map on the hood, marked a path around Dallas with a number 2 stub. His pencil moved with a steady drifter's touch. He seemed to know roads the engineers had never planned. Balch Springs and Forney, sliding past Garland then Plano, up beyond Lake Dallas and Denton, a strange erratic course that finally picked up 35 again.

Royce seemed pleased with his work. "That ought to throw her if she's still hanging 'round. I'll lead off and you trail along behind. That Nazi car gives you any trouble just honk."

Doug was surprised and pleased at once. "You're going too? Lord, Royce, you don't have to do that."

"Isn't any trouble," Royce said. "I'd as soon go that way as not."

"Are you sure? You don't have to do it."

"If I didn't want to do it why I wouldn't, okay?"

Sue Jean appeared, pouty with sleep. She gave the map a dubious eye. "I don't guess there's any place to eat on this pioneer trail."

"Lot's of good stops," Royce said. "You won't likely starve."

"I heard that before." This time a telling look at Doug, then back to the house for coffee and a wake-up ciggie. He tried to read her mood. See if she remembered the night before. He wondered if she'd dreamed of violation. It didn't seem to show. He held the thrill of midnight plunder in his mouth, savored it like a hot cinnamon square.

He felt no regret at leaving the farm. He didn't feel he was leaving it at all, that in fact he was taking the true heart of the place with him, the creek and the bridge and the niggershack held by sedimentary magic to the bluff. He felt he had a hold on the past, that it was no longer slipping through his hands, that he could safely gather in the sweet tastes and dusty smells he'd left behind. Nothing was lost he couldn't retrieve. He suddenly knew that this was so. And with this understanding came a strange sense of calm and a rich intoxication, these two in seeming opposition yet the same. He wanted to shout it out, tell everything he knew. Share this with Royce and Sue Jean. Only he didn't know what to say. There weren't any words for what he felt.

He had thought the night before, when they were talking on the porch, that he could tell Royce anything he liked. He was certain of that now. They could sit there on the steps making smokes and drinking beer. Tossing green pecans at a tree. He could tell Royce the way he grew up, what he'd done and what he liked to think about. Erlene and the women in his life, all the do-nothing jobs he'd left behind. Royce could sure relate to that. He could even tell Royce about Cole Younger and Jesus and the pickup with Wyoming plates. Grat Dalton and German flying aces, all the other crazy stuff in his head that didn't even bother him anymore. Royce wouldn't tell him he was looney. He'd nod and understand, say, "that's the way it is sometimes."

Thinking about this made him warm all over. He wanted to stop right there, honk and get Royce to pull over and get out and just talk. He knew that was a dumb idea, but he couldn't help feeling like he did. The farm worked its magic. He wanted to shout out everything he knew, share the way he felt right now. He laughed out loud and scared the cat. Sue Jean gave him a look.

"You got a good joke you ought to tell it," she told Doug. "Isn't good manners someone sitting right here in the car."

"I haven't got any joke," Doug said.

"Well someone laughs you're going to figure they got a joke. If it's dirty I don't want to hear it."

"I haven't got a dirty joke, Sue Jean. I haven't got a clean joke either."

"I don't like those jokes about folks less fortunate than us. They sure can't help it if they got some ethnic persuasion. Fate could have just as easy give you a different race or skin. You could be out in the heat right now mowing lawns."

"I don't know any jokes like that."

"Well don't tell 'em to me."

"If I knew one I sure wouldn't tell it."

"You better not. I don't want to hear it."

"Sue Jean, I am busting out with stuff," Doug said, the words pouring out in a rush. "I don't know where to start. I met James McArthur Hill Dean. I used to window peek in Waxahachie. For some time I've been practicing immersion in the soil. I'm older than I look. Moles make love in the dark I've seen them do it. I saw Carl Sandburg once in a New York City elevator. Herb Tarchek I went to school with, he's got Cully Moon's daughter. He drives a Bentley car. I've been seeing Jesus a lot. He hangs out with Cole Younger in a truck. Doc Holliday's not as sick as he looks. Everything I see looks bright like someone drew a gold line around it. I wish I knew the names of marshland birds. I think I maybe do. All this stuff's coming out. I don't know how to keep it in. What's happening to me? I don't know. I feel good. I see a car go by I think, who's in that? What kind of coverage has he got? Did he ever use a Big Chief tablet? What did he eat for breakfast? Why do I have to know all that? I just do. Does any of this make sense? This is the prettiest day I ever saw. I'd like to get out and hug a dog."

"We going to get me something to eat or not?" Sue Jean said. "Royce said he knew a good place, I don't see anyone fixing to stop."

"What? I don't know." Doug's head seemed to shift into third. "I guess we will. We can if you want. Sue Jean, didn't you hear anything I said?"

"I heard you all right, I'm not deaf. You said you'd like to hug a dog."

"Well that isn't all. I said a lot more than that."

"That thing licks you on the face just don't come snugging up to me."

Royce stopped at a Texaco west of Renner, Texas. Thack tumbled out and made a dash for the restroom out back. Royce walked around and kicked the tires and Doug watched. Sue Jean put a leash on the cat and got all the quarters she could from Doug and Royce. The little mechanical clips started dumping snack prizes down the chute. Snickers and Tom's peanuts, oatmeal cookies and Hershey bars. Sue Jean asked the boy pumping gas for a sack. The boy admired the classic Nazi car, the way Sue Jean's cutoffs rode her crotch.

"We're making good time," Royce said. "Ought to hit Oklahoma 'bout a hour."

"Sue Jean wants to get something to eat," Doug said.

"I'm sure surprised to hear it."

"The stuff she's buying now won't do it. That girl doesn't get any mileage."

"It's hot out here I'll tell you that. This has been a summer and a half." Royce got a blue bandanna from his jeans and wiped his eyes. Off to the south, the skyline of Dallas seemed to rise in an insubstantial haze. Color was bleached out of the August sky. Doug remembered a service station Harry Truman's uncle used to run. The two men looked alike. People would stop by just to see. He thought that station was in Gainesville or Sherman. He looked at his sweetie and thought how bitch-cranky fine she was in the morning, eyes half-sullen and her hair still frazzled like packing in a box, the taste of sleep and ciggies on her breath. A hillbilly girl seemed to store up new tastes and smells overnight. Sometimes you'd lick one on the tummy and your tongue would come away with the taste of peanut butter. Just like that. She might have just dreamed peanut butter but there it was.

Doug had to pee, but wasn't about to use the restroom after Thack. He wandered out back and found ordinary gas station debris. Stacks of bald tires and a rusty trailer hitch. Unzipped behind a 55-gallon lube drum. A lady watched him from the Kwik-Wash Laundry next door. Shook her head to show she disapproved. Doug wanted to tell her about Thack. Make sure she understood. He felt a surge of good will. Ragged clouds rushed to Oklahoma, speeded up like the Weather Channel news. Doug felt dazed and unattached. Silly as a duck. In the mood for college songs. Whatever the high was he didn't ever want to lose it. And as he zipped up and watched the flaring sky he heard the sound coming in, the engine spitting through its teeth in the silver-colored air, saw the black knight's cross on the mustard-colored wings, heard the hum in the wires and saw the Fokker dip low, saw its shadow mark the Kwik-Wash Laundry, turn and bank in a curve so tight the canvas shuddered, went flat against the ribs like a runner sucking air. And Doug felt the throbbing engine's power in his legs, felt it coursing through his belly like a near-orgasmic thrill, smelled the gas and the overheated oil, saw Max Immelmann gently turn the Fokker on its side, wave and roll and flash away and out of sight....

THE HEREAFTER GANG

Past Lewisville and Denton, and names like Slidell and Krum, Ponder and Era and Celina now peppered about the map. Sue Jean appeared sated for the moment, appeased by the gas station goodies yet alert for Dairy Queens, feet on the dash, toes working out a new hit song. Squinting at a pamphlet the Texaco pumper had passed along, a clear understanding of Jesus's lost and secret years as a saucer navigator. And Doug, wrapped in fine hallucination of the clear cold skies of Verdun, of Spandaus blazing, and white scarves snapping in the wind, this scene now playing on a double mental bill with the James brothers' raid on Northfield, Minnesota, keeps a non-ethereal eye on the road and notes the magic of the sun-dazzled day is still about. That the highway here holds the ghosts of boxy Fords and Packard Clippers and LaSalles, a road that linked his Christmas holidays and summers, sandy bluffs and August creeks, country girls and turkey dinners. The long trips were never empty in his backseat fort with a stack of *Captain Marvels, Green Lantern* and *The Shadow.* And at night there were towns and lonely windows in the dark, the radio with Joe E. Penner, *Lights Out* and Fibber McGee, Jack Benny and Eddie Cantor and Baby Snooks.

Doug's Waxahachie grandfather lived and died in the house where he was born. He didn't care for Doug's father, and liked his other two sons even less. He pretended to have trouble with their names. His wife was long dead and people said he'd used her up. He had affairs with local widows when he could. He didn't care for grandchildren but tolerated Doug. He'd walk Doug down to the tracks and watch the trains. After thirty-five years in the yards he couldn't keep himself away. He had to smell the smoke and hear the hard clear concussion of the freights. At a one-room grocery that doubled as a railman's bar, Doug would get Nehi orange while his grandfather drank cold beer with his friends. The floor was made of asphalt scraps, narrow black strips from a thousand county roofs. Beer and soda pop caps fell directly to the floor.

Workboots and years ground the caps firmly in and left a bottlecap-asphalt mosaic, a spot where Doug could spend a good half day reading prehistoric brands.

And all that was gone, thought Doug, the past stolen clean away, summer days vanished and decoder rings lost. Even the long freights and the whistles in the night, and no one ever guessed they'd disappear. And Doug Hoover thrust into a present he didn't want, a world where freeways and do-nothing jobs consumed the day, where barbecue and hillbilly girls seemed the sole redeeming grace. Now some magic had made him whole and he felt as if the grown-up desiccated years had never been, as if he might find Oklahoma City just the same, Cully Moon sixteen, the big stove in Wetzel's store gassing kids into nickel spending sprees. And if he needed any proof the world was his, he could watch the August miles sweeping by, see the same deserted farms with their hollow window eyes, the haze of olive-colored trees he'd passed a thousand times before. Nothing changed; he'd simply fallen in the trap, swallowed the deception that it did, bought the lie that what he dreamed was the illusion and not the other way around.

"Well if you didn't have yourself a time," Sue Jean said. "The midnight prowler on the make." This out of nowhere, with no particular reason why the thought had come to mind.

"I didn't know you were awake," Doug said.

"Didn't say I was."

"Well were you?"

"Listen, you can't hardly do a girl she isn't going to know it. You wake up and find you been crazy-glued shut, you got a clue."

"Do you mind?"

"I don't recall."

"I couldn't tell."

"You don't have to know everything there is."

"Good because I don't."

Sue Jean licked her fingers clean, found a last bit of Twinkie and finished it off. "I'm surprised that pump's still holding. You can figure it'll go."

"I told you Royce said it wasn't the pump."

"That boy back there could've checked. You could've asked him and he would."

"That boy was more interested in working on your motor than mine."

"You think so?"

"I certainly do."

"You ought to read this thing. Says Jesus had a UFO and the devil shot him down. You believe that or what? I knew this girl thought God lived in Corpus Christi, Texas, on a boat. Said she read it in a book. It was Francine's sister is who it was, the girl who's a whiz at selling cookies. Mellisa Rae's got tits even bigger than Francine, you want to try and picture that. She had a day job in automotive parts and worked conventions on the side. Got a lot of that Kawasaki trade. She'd pop stark naked out of a ten-foot sushi every year. Lord, those little Japs'd go wild. This mountain climbin' bunch had a cake decorator do the major Everest routes on her tit. Francine's got full color shots. In case you don't know that's about the biggest mountain you can find."

"What'd they do on the other one?" Doug asked.

"What'd they do on the other what?"

"What did they do on the other tit? I guess she's got two."

"Well of course she's got two, what you think?"

"I just wondered what they did. Seem's like they'd want to use 'em both."

"What for?"

"I don't know, Sue Jean, because it's there. You ought to do something to it."

"Well I don't know a thing about that. If they did something else Mellisa Rae'd have a picture. I'd of seen it if she did."

Sue Jean looked annoyed. Went silent and lit a ciggie. She liked conversations intact. Didn't care for talk with a question on the end. And Doug saw Gainesville was ten miles ahead, and the first road signs for Oklahoma. Ardmore and Davis, Pauls Valley and Marietta, and he remembered getting drunk on Oklahoma beer the night of high school graduation, driving south with a carload of friends to Purcell. Picking up girls in the picture show there, finding out too late they belonged to local jocks. Getting bloodied up good and flat lost, out of gas in Anadarko without a dime.

Billboards showed him where to get whole life, fresh bait and truck springs in Gainesville, Texas. Junkyards and roadside cafes said the town was just ahead. Church spires and water towers thrust above the trees. The sun gave a hint of a white county courthouse on the square. And Doug in spite of joy and elation at the scene felt vaguely ill at ease, an itch at the center of his back, a tug at his line like a fish about to bite. A glance in the mirror quickly shattered his illusion of accord and inner peace. The mirror warned him objects seen are closer than you think, and he was certain this was true. Erlene and Pastor Jack were right behind, the white doctor Buick after that, and if this was not enough, a black limousine which he knew had a phone link to top mob centers in the West.

"Oh Jesus," Doug cried, "that woman's got illegal solutions in her head. That's a major crime czar on my tail!"

Sudden alarm shook his cookie out of sleep. Doug leaned desperately on the horn. Royce leaned out of the pickup up ahead. He seemed to understand at once, pointed and waved Doug to go on. Slowed and let him pass and took up the post behind. Doug saw him in the mirror, weaving and jerking about, maneuvers meant to threaten and harass. Doug raced ahead at Warp Two, or as fast as the near half-century-old engine would allow. He had never learned to translate kilometers into miles and had no clear conception of his speed. Gainesville disappeared in a blur. He prayed the local law had a waitress in the sack. That Thack didn't need to make a stop. He felt betrayed. Sunny D'Angelo had sided with Erlene. How had she managed that? You couldn't trust a criminal or a doctor either one. They'd turn right on you every time.

"Listen, I don't like your careless manner at the wheel," Sue Jean complained.

"We've been through this before," Doug said. "I'm not slowing down. That gangster's likely armed. I should've let that dog get squashed."

"Don't you say that about a little dog. He can't help it if his daddy's into sin."

"I bet there's not a penny in that overseas account. I bet Sunny lied about that."

"About what?"

"I am not going into that now. I got plenty else to do."

Royce was out of sight. Maybe holding the others off or maybe not. A sign said OKLAHOMA 2. Doug felt a slight surge of hope. Which didn't make sense but he felt it all the same. Now he could see the long bridge and knew the green stunted oaks, the high steel clouds to the north, everything ahead was Oklahoma. Maybe Erlene had a writ. It might not work out of state. He didn't know. Maybe that was the whole idea. Get him to cross the line. Take his under-age sweetie out of state and get the Feds on his back. Sunny had connections. He could help her out with that. The Nazi car quit. Rolled a few yards and stopped dead.

"Shit!" Doug said. Closed his eyes and pounded on the wheel.

"Well what now Mr. Race Car Driver?"

"I don't know. I got to think. Sue Jean don't you say it's that pump."

"Well I'll be. I didn't open my mouth."

Doug rolled down the window and looked back. No sign of Royce. It was ninety or a hundred outside. With the air off the car began to function as a stove. He didn't know what to do next. Sitting in the car wouldn't help.

"Hold onto the cat I'm getting out," Doug said.

"And do what?"

"I don't know. I haven't got any idea."

"Well just leave me sitting here burnin' to a crisp."

"Open the door, Sue Jean. Get out and walk around. Do something. Sit there. I don't know."

The bridge was less than twenty yards away. Hiking up to it double time he looked down, saw the red sandy bank, sluggish water the color of clay. Imagined catfish the size of submarines. A horn began to blare through the heat. He looked up and saw Royce coming at him flat out, waving out the window and sitting on the horn, the pickup weaving like a DWI on the run. He jogged back to the car. Royce skidded to a stop and jumped out.

"I got 'em jammed up and sacked," Royce grinned, "rattled and confused. But it ain't going to hold them too long."

"Listen, this foreign car has up and quit."

"Leave it. Get your gear and hop in the back of mine."

"What for? What good's it going to do?" Doug felt dazed. He seemed to lack purpose and direction. "It's the Red River, Royce. They can follow if they want. It's not like getting into Mexico or Poland."

"They try it, I'd say it's a clear invasion of your rights. I'd slap 'em with a suit that quick." He nodded down the road. "You going to sit here or what? I'd decide if I was you."

Doug looked back with alarm. Saw the blue Camaro coming straight up 35. Saw a vision of Erlene, bearing down with Lamprey resolution and affront. He didn't have to think twice. He opened the back door and tossed Sue Jean's pack and his box of belongings in the truck. Royce already had the truck in motion, driving in jerky stops and starts, Doug and Sue Jean trotting along beside him to the middle of the bridge.

"For Pete's sake, Royce, will you stop this thing?" Doug said.

Royce came to a halt.

"Well I can't hardly wait for this," Sue Jean said. "I don't like riding in the heat."

"Just do it," Doug said. He climbed in quickly and helped her up. Looked back and saw the blue Camaro and the white doctor Buick, the black gangster limo not a hundred yards behind. Royce got in and then Thack got out.

"Hoss, you going to have to hold it," Royce said. "We can't be stopping right now." He ground the gears into first and took off, left the Erlene caravan behind. Doug felt elated. She could follow him to North Platte, Nebraska, if she liked. Minot, North Dakota, or Saskatoon. He didn't have to go back and he didn't want to talk. She better get that straight in her head. Royce stopped abruptly near the far end of the bridge, left the motor going and walked back, leaned on the side and looked at Doug.

Doug felt alarm. "My God, why'd you stop? Let's *go!"*

"You sure you want to do this, now. You real set on it, that's fine with me. I don't want to get in no trouble later on."

"What! Get in trouble with who?" Doug wondered if he'd missed some key word or phrase. "For Christ's sake, Royce, I didn't rob a 7-Eleven, I'm running off from that woman. Her and that Daffy Duck job and Houston, Texas. I can't see why we're sitting here talking about this."

"Right," Royce said. "Let's do it." He gave Doug a wink, turned and got in the truck.

Doug looked at Sue Jean. "Now what was all that? I hope that boy isn't smoking something funny at the wheel."

Sue Jean doesn't answer. Royce starts up again and Doug looks down the road, sees Erlene's car and the white doctor Buick and the black gangster limo after that, sees they've pulled up just short of the bridge, that they aren't coming after him at all. It seems a curious thing to do, but maybe not. The girders overhead make shadows on the road. He watches them flicker by. Thinks about turtles in the river down below. Erlene gets out and seems to look across at Doug. She's wearing that short purple dress he likes a lot. Ham and Stew Geeter are at her side. Pastor Jack opens his heavy duty Bible on the hood. Doug thinks he sees some other cars too, a Datsun and a yellow Subaru, a Ford and a fuchsia Cadillac. And there is Sarah Dee and her true love Jane. Amos Fevre and three guys from the office he doesn't know. Janet and Shirley and Aimilee. Betticia and Parker Symmes. A woman he's met before and can't recall. They seem to get smaller as he watches, retreat in fine perspective, in geometric order to a single point of light, like the TV going on the blink. The pickup with Wyoming plates passes going the other way, stops at the far end of the bridge. Jesus and Cole Younger get out, put their hard hats on and get to work. Haul highway roadblocks out of the truck and set them up. Stick the yellow lights on top. Get back in and turn around. Pass Doug and wave and head back to Oklahoma.

"Oh Lord," Doug says, "I left the cat. She's back there in the car!"

"That kitty's just fine," says Sue Jean.

"You think she is?"

"Don't you worry 'bout a thing."

"Okay," says Doug, "I guess I won't." The bridge is gone now and the sky seems dazzling overhead. The Fokker comes straight out of the sun, does a quick and fancy roll. Doug recalls the tingly taste of Grapette.

Sue Jean falls asleep, her head rolling in his lap, rocking to the jerk-lazy cadence of the road. Her lips are sweet and open, pale and slack, leaving unconscious kisses on his thigh. The truck produces concrete taffy and extrudes it in a blur, and as Doug leans back against the cab he can see the ribbon harden as it slows, flatten and recede, vanish in obscure triangulation far behind. The drone and the clatter and the heat that warms his skin, the rush of the wind on every side leaves him out of synch but in, intact and unaware, cheerfully marooned. He feels absurdly sly, crafty and content, familiar states of mind from immersion in the soil yet distinctly more intense. And as his senses probed the earth and tasted stone, caught the scent of fetal mice, heard the sighs of farmers' wives, now he seems to venture further, touching wonders undefined. He is keenly aware that the ginkgo tree survived from ancient times. He knows Will & Finck made a first-class California dirk. He tastes the heat of old Monongahela rye. Sees a girl in Vera Cruz with a James Mason birthmark on her thigh. Knows a Paris hotel has hemstitched linen sheets. That mosquitoes have 47 teeth. Learns at once Genghis Khan had a deathly fear of air. That Kaiser Bill never pissed upon an ant. He fully understands that the odds are 20-1 against a rookie playing ball on major teams. That Omar Bradley's father liked to carve his own bats. That Judge Parker hung Rufus Black high in Fort Smith. That lifeguard Ronald Reagan pulled 77 people from the sea. That Sears offered the Marceau tenor trombone for sixteen dollars and ten cents in its 1900 catalog. That Caesar thought the Gauls were full of shit. That Jung dreamed of a penis nearly fifteen feet high. That Brontosaurus tastes better with a little pinch of thyme. He knows a man in Alabama married a small coniferous tree. That mice enjoy tiny cartoons of Marty Man. And in a burst of understanding, he sees that Oral Roberts and Madonna are clearly linked through a strange genetic trait.

Doug is plainly awed, significantly aslant. There are things he never knew or even dreamed. His mind is cable ready. He can feel the press of knowledge, the encyclopedic mass, the crush of answers to questions he doesn't know. Who would ever guess blue whales are the cause of mental illness in the world? That cockroaches enable us to speak? That stars are really giant galactic farts made by beings long ago? Who would know? Who would even imagine such a thing? Doug is dizzied by facts that dash drunkenly through his head like hornets in a jar. He flies like a bird. Learns that lice have an organized church. Breathes the dank Jurassic dawn. Eats a dragonfly seven feet long. He learns that photosynthesis feels great. Like coming in a tub and smoking pot.

And when his head unwinds, when the film slaps loosely on the reel, he falls deeply into sleep, smells the dusty blanket in the truck, smells forty-weight oil and a melted Hershey bar, hears the tires on the road and the engine in his ear, dreams of pale blue sparrows and Moroccan mint tea. Dreams Cully Jean Moon is solid gold and he has her on a leash. Dreams the pike top minnow swims in interstellar seas.

And when he wakes he sees the orange peel sky of afternoon, smells brick-colored Oklahoma dust. Finds Sue Jean dusky and appealing, sipping on a cold 7-Up.

"I sure had real peculiar dreams," Doug tells her. "I feel I got a quiz show in my head."

"Sleeping in the sun's what did it," says Sue Jean. "That heat'll bake your brains."

"Sue Jean, I know everything there is about your top historical kings. Stuff you can't read in a book. That and the germination of seeds. There's a lot going on in a plant. You ought to see those flagella whip about. A girl in Topeka's found the secret of skin care. You got any idea where we are? This isn't one of your major roads."

"Royce turned off a while back."

"I guess he did."

"You want a Coke? I got Coke or an orange."

"I'll take that orange if it's Nehi in a bottle. It doesn't taste right in a can."

Sue Jean digs around in the cooler. The bottle has ice on its sides. Doug recalls creek afternoons. The dirt road is narrow, scarcely room for two cars. Scrub oak scrapes against the truck. The pale afternoon seems to stretch out and linger, the day on hold and the sun a red strobe through the trees. And Doug thinks about a highschool field trip, the Arbuckle Mountains and Turner Falls, geology taken seriously in Oklahoma schools, the feeling then that oil would last two thousand years. Finding sandstone roses and a million fossil shells, learning more about faults than he ever cared to know. And on the long way back there are heartstopping feelies on the bus, romance in the dark with a girl in his class who'd never even said hello and never noticed him again. This picture from the past rushing in, the tape with better color, more intense than the happening itself, and with it Doug's new and heightened sense of events both great and small, a sweet narcotic mix of the familiar and obscure, revelation and reflection unconfined. The girl on the bus with the taste of cherry pie, the taste on her lips from a quick stop at Davis, Oklahoma, the touch of a new and secret breast in the summer sullen day, and a fresh understanding of the mountains bursting forth from the Archeozoic crust, the chalky taste of Ordovician seas. And for no apparent reason Doug can see, weather highs for 1932. Gossip from the court of Charlemagne. New data on foreplay in kangaroo mice.

And Sue Jean, in a surprising burst of carhop affection, snuggles in close and sits beside him as he watches the road unravel and slide away as he bounces to the rhythm of the truck. Sees the brief levitation of the dust and the bottle caps and bolts, sees the sun do its tangerine theatrics through a dark web of leaves overhead. And now he sees a slice of wooden roof, a quarter of a window or a door, caught for an instant then blurred among the trees. A house and then the corner of a barn, a fence and an Appaloosa horse, a hawk on a post and a Burma Shave sign. The pickup rattles over a loose wooden bridge and the smell of lazy water down below. Cottonwoods replace the stunted oaks, the red sandy road gives way to brick. The town is suddenly there on every side, the courthouse and the square, the falsefront stores and the evening slanting down across the street, the shadows stretching up the high curbs to dusty glass and the hint of goods behind. Vintage pickups line the curb. A Packard and a Dodge. Royce pulls in between a '39 Ford and a LaSalle, gets out and does a stretch, walks back and makes a smoke.

"Hop out and look around," he tells Doug. "Kinda nice little town. Meet me back here we'll go down and get a drink."

"Royce, I know a whole bunch of stuff," says Doug. "I don't know why, but I do."

"Well say that's fine."

"There's things we don't know about fish."

"Now I believe that. Sue Jean, go buy this boy a double dip."

"What flavor?" says Doug.

With that, Royce walks off toward the square, Thack trailing along behind.

Doug feels slightly off center, pleasantly deranged. Unhinged and light of foot. He wants to tell Royce what's happened in his head. What the Western ground gecko likes to eat. What Magellan did to cats. It doesn't seem to matter. Ice cream sounds fine. He follows Sue Jean up the walk, peeks into stores, looks at flies and crickets on display, looks at bamboo rods and minnow lures, patterned shirts and Stetson hats, pristine hammers that have never struck a nail. Out of the summery afternoon in the cool of covered walks, in the marbleized shade that a small town knows how to do, Doug discovers a canary bird whistle and a charter oak trunk. Montana hats and Texas ties. *Bluebook* and *Collier's* and *Liberty* magazine. *Action Comics* Number One. Vanilla extract double strength. A John C. Dueber pocket watch, a St. Louis washer and a fireproof safe. Cookies in a bin. Comet models and Tinkertoy cars. Gold-filled Masonic pins. *Sunbathers' Quarterly* magazine. Shepard's Blizzard Ice Cream Freezer and a Henry Disston saw. A Mickey Mouse watch. A Red Ryder air rifle and a Dick Tracy badge. Doug wants everything he sees. The ice cream is great. The store has marble-top counters and marble floors. A silverchrome fountain and a fan overhead. Marble-top tables and fancy wireback chairs. He gets a double dip cone, banana nut and Rocky Road. The dips are side by side like poached eggs in a cup.

"This is the best ice cream I ever had," he tells Sue Jean. "No kidding this is great. When I was nine we'd call up Veazey's Drug and order a carton of half orange sherbet and half vanilla. I tell you this or not? It came with a wooden spoon. I used to save those spoons and make a fort. The drugstore'd send a guy out on a motorcycle right up to the door. Five cents. You believe that? They'd send this five cent order right out. That was 1939. We lived on East 15th. What's that you got, vanilla?"

"Lemon custard," says Sue Jean.

"Now that's my favorite. I didn't know they had it."

"I used to wouldn't eat a thing it wasn't chocolate. I'd eat a Hershey bar for breakfast and another one for lunch. Get a hot fudge sundae about six. Grew a hundred pound zit and had to quit."

"What did you put on it?"

"On what?"

"On the zit. We had this stuff smelled worse than Camphophenique. Didn't do any good at all."

"I think I picked it is what I did."

"That'll just make it worse," says Doug. "What you got to do is dry it out.

You see people stay out in the sun they don't get a lot of zits. I never saw a farmer with a zit."

"That farmer eats enough Hershey bars, why he's going to get a zit," says Sue Jean.

They take their cones and start walking to the truck. The sunset is still holding strong, the clouds on fire spreading apricot and wine. Doug smells the creek and fresh dirt, sweet and woody smoke that says a barbecue stand is close by. Now how did he miss that? Royce comes striding up the walk, spots their cones and does his lopsided grin.

"Figured I'd find you all here, what'd you do try and clean the place out?"

"Royce, I flat love this town," says Doug. He grabs Royce by the arm. "They got stuff here you wouldn't believe. Delaware Punch in the bottle. Big Little books brand new. *Buck Rogers on the Moons of Saturn. Alley Oop.* They've got Tim *Tyler's Luck.* And every one of them's still five cents. I saw an Edgemere banjo and an upright grand. Lord, would you look at that sun."

"Can't beat a small town," says Royce. He tells Doug they'll walk some and leave the pickup where it is. Thack seems to be absent, and Doug forgets to ask. A warm breeze sweeps the square. There are big live oaks on the lawn, hiding the stone courthouse from view. People are walking about. Everyone nods. Once past the square, stores and shops disappear. Brick streets give way again a country block beyond town. They walk past houses warm with light. The sidewalks are buckled, the way sidewalks ought to be. Locusts rattle in the trees. Doug holds Sue Jean's hand, smells the honeysuckle from a yard, smells her hair, smells lemon custard ice cream.

"I love this town," he says again. "What's the name of it, Royce?"

"Don't know as it's got a proper name."

"Well it's got to have a name."

"No it don't."

"If I wrote someone a letter, where would I say it was to go?"

"You got me there."

Up ahead in the fading summer light, in the red-gold dusty August night, Doug sees the building set back among the cedars on a rise, sees the butterwax light from the kerosene lamps, hears the Tex Ritter whine, hears the laughter inside, sees the falsefront peak and the clapboard sides, sees the flat wooden steps and the batwing doors, sees the red dusty street, sees the sign that reads Pronghorn Saloon. And Doug feels happy as a dog, feels like there's forty-five music in his head.

"Royce, I got to see it," says Doug. "I got to see that place right now."

"Figured maybe you would," says Royce.

"I've got some kind of frolic in my feet. I don't know what. Sue Jean, I think I want to dance. You dance any at all? I don't guess I ever asked."

"I just might," says Sue Jean.

Doug sees six roan horses at the rail. A '23 Dodge. The pickup with Wyoming plates. A 1914 Silver Ghost. A '37 Cord. A staff car from World War I. A Harley painted Shawnee red. And as he walks through the batwing doors he feels silly as a duck, slick as bay rum on a Saturday afternoon. Every table's full and they're lined up at the bar. Johnny Cash is all a'quiver and there's sawdust on the floor. Everyone waves and shouts hello. Doug begins to grin like a fool. Royce finds a table and orders *Tres Equis* beer.

"Well what do you think?" he asks Doug.

Doug can't find the proper words. He feels tomfoolery on the rise. People are dropping by to shake his hand. Bitter Creek Newcomb and Charlie Pierce. King Fisher and Tom Horn. Cole Younger pulls up a chair, winks at Sue Jean and slaps Doug on the back.

"Sure glad you made it," says Cole. "Right nice to have you back."

"I'm obliged for the help," says Doug.

"Wasn't nothing at all. Glad to do it."

"Cole here's tricky as they come," says Royce.

"Shoot. Reckon you'd be one to know. Let's get this feller another beer. Looks to me like he's had a thirsty day."

Doug spots Max Immelmann at the bar, explaining some maneuver to Werner Voss. Both are wearing cutoffs and boots. Max sees him and waves and starts across the floor. Goes back and gets something from the bar. Brings a silver bucket of champagne, a plate of ribs and sauce.

"From me and von Richthofen and all the gang," says Max. "Good to see you, Doug."

"Hey, now that's fine," says Doug. "And nice flying, Max."

"Listen, let's you and me go up soon."

"Well we'll sure do it."

Doc Holliday stops and says hello. Grat Dalton shakes his hand, tries the champagne and decides to stick to beer.

"A great bunch of guys," says Doug, "they're really swell."

"Can't beat 'em with a stick," says Cole. "You need a beer, son?"

"I guess I'm doing fine."

"Well you holler if you're dry."

Doug chews on a rib and decides it's the best he ever had. Sue Jean licks her fingers clean. Royce says she looks like a raccoon at the creek.

Then the room goes silent, the conversation stops. All Doug can hear is

Kris and Willie, real low now like a radio in someone else's room. He follows Royce's eyes. Sees the man standing at the batwing doors, sees him tall in his white jogging suit, in his Nikes white as snow, in the white sweat band around his brow. And Doug knows him right then, knows the blue Aegean eyes, knows the pale silk hair and the beard as light as grain. The man walks straight for him, and Doug can scarcely breathe. He feels a fever in his head. Feels he's burning up fast and doesn't care. Synonyms for happy come to mind. Nothing seems to work. He wants to stand up and cheer but decides he'd better not. The man stops at his table, reaches down and shakes his hand.

"Doug, it's real good to have you back," the man says. "These boys taking care of you okay?"

"I'm doing fine," says Doug.

"Get settled in. We'll get together soon." He cocks his finger at Cole Younger, pretends to take a shot. "Cole, you behave now, hear?"

"You got it, Chief," says Cole.

"Drinks are on me," says the man. It seems to be a standard joke and gets a laugh. He turns and walks out. His image seems to linger in the air.

"Just walking in and coming straight to me," says Doug. "Making a special trip." He can't take his eyes off the door. "Royce, that's the nicest thing anyone ever did."

"He's got a way with people, all right," says Royce. "Isn't any doubt of that."

And Doug remembers being eight, his Uncle Lew telling his daddy he wouldn't amount to a thing, and he wishes Uncle Lew could see him now, see who it was just bought him another beer.

THE HEREAFTER GANG

Sue Jean pried him out of the Pronghorn Saloon at some early morning hour, sated on *Tres Equis* beer, chili and tacos and ribs, Doug vaguely aware now that none of the above seemed to affect him with excess. Having sung Hank Williams to a tee, explained to Werner Voss why the Albatros had problems with the wings, whipped Doc Holliday with three royal flushes in a row, the evening seemed complete. And walking back along the narrow dusty street, pleasantly weary and content, he saw the sunset had finally given way to blackest night, an intensity of stars common to Caribbean seas, stars so abundant, so vivid and undiffused, they had the slick and polished look of a costly special effect.

When they reached the house he turned in at once, walked through the gate without a word from Sue Jean. Walked beneath the grapevine arbor past the thick-boled pecans, up the porch and past the swing, through the wooden screen door that smelled of dusty afternoon. No one had to tell him this was his. Everything here was Doug Hoover, familiar to the eye. Worn and fashioned by his presence in the house. Every chair, every book, every slant of line and shadow on the floor. He walked through every room, down below then up the stairs, every room a confirmation he was home.

"Good to be back," Doug said. "Isn't anything like your own place." On the dresser was his skate key, an Indian-head penny. A gray gym sock with a hole in the toe.

"A person likes to have their own stuff," Sue Jean said. "Makes you feel settled in." She sat on the bed, a slight indentation on the quilt, the grandmother patchwork wonder where he'd waited for a dozen Christmas mornings to arrive, a hundred summer days. She looked slick and brown, cute as a bug. He felt aroused and wondered if he should.

"You got a place, too?" he wanted to know.

"Right down the street. Couple of houses down."

"Like mine?"

"Like me."

"Well sure, I guess so. You stay there a lot? Dumb question. 'Course you do it's your house. That's where you'd want to be."

"Hey. I can stay here with you. It'd be real simple just to ask."

"It's okay?"

"Doug. Everything's okay. All right? Don't try to figure it all out the first day."

He thought about that. Watched Sue Jean undress in yellow light, slip under the covers like a kid. Joined her then and snuggled up close, smelled her skin, ran his hands along familiar sweet terrain, fell asleep at once. Dreamed of Tombstone, Arizona. Dreamed of Minoan days and nights. Dreamed of Cheyenne smoky fires. Dreamed of stony Celtic walls and Druid bees. Dreamed of buffalo herds that took a week to pass him by. Dreamed of chalky British hills, dreamed of fishnets in the sun. Dreamed of hot Houston traffic with the AC on the blink, quickly put that dream behind.

When he woke he thought of macaroni and cheese. Leftover cold with the cheese on top hard as a rock. A Hires root beer. Thompson seedless grapes. Downstairs he found it all in the fridge along with Delaware Punch and Grapette. A chocolate eclair. Assorted German beers. Lemon custard ice cream. Got a dish of ice cream and a crusty cheese top. The root beer filled a glass with frothy brown. He took all this to the dark front room and sat in his favorite chair. The windows were open and summer smells came in the room. Moonlight striped the floor. A breeze rattled honeysuckle vines against the screen. He turned on the TV and flipped around. Watched Gary Grant cavort through *Gunga Din.* Watched *Jack* Benny and *Arthur Godfrey's Talent Scouts.* Watched *Dragnet* and *Gunsmoke,* and *Wanted: Dead or Alive.* Watched *Lost Horizon* and *Patton.* Watched *Casablanca* twice. *Ben Casey* and *Bewitched. Batman* and *Ironside. Rowan and Martin's Laugh-In, The F.B.I.* Watched *The Maltese Falcon. Citizen Kane. The African Queen.*

When he finally got tired he put the dishes in the sink and went to bed. Sue Jean seemed firm and electric. Warm as a puppy. Familiar and undefined. Doug was taken by desire. He felt tender and cheerfully debased. Felt his sweetie might dissolve in his hands.

"You awake?"

"I am now."

"Sue Jean, they even got cable."

"I know they do, Doug."

He touched her, slid his hands between her thighs. "Listen, you said it was okay."

"That's what I said." She turned and put her hands on his shoulders, pulled him close.

"You smell great," Doug said.

"You always say it, so I guess maybe I do."

"I was thinking. You know? Everything I like's right here. I can see any movie that I want. That fridge is something else. I guess when we're loving I could—what? Go all night if I want. Or shoot, maybe a week. Why I don't guess I'd ever have to—"

"Doug." She held him there with Tennessee eyes. "Just enjoy, okay? Don't push your luck."

Sue Jean was gone in the morning, leaving a neat sweetie fossil in the sheet. Fossils reminded him at once of Charlie Duckman, former agent of the F.B.I. and a whiz on past molluscular life. Duckman led him on to James McArthur Hill Dean. Dean to the Texas Tech honey who'd knocked him silly on the road. The honey on back to Sue Jean, his train of thought circled on the track. Boy, that frolic last night was a wonder. He was surprised they'd let you get away with that. Sue Jean said you could, but he figured he might check it out with Royce. Royce seemed to know all the rules.

Worn jeans were in the closet. His green college Keds. A Woody Woodpecker shirt from third grade that seemed to fit. Two Wings cigarette cards on the dresser. A Jap Zero and a Hawker Hurricane. The hard-to-get Yak 3. He opened the dresser drawer. Found socks and Clove gum. Stuck the gum in his pocket.

Royce was in the kitchen making pancakes and sausage. Scrambled eggs with cheddar cheese. Singing something with El Paso on the end.

"Didn't figure you was going to get up," Royce said. He showed Doug an off-center grin that might mean anything at all. "Have at it, there's coffee on the stove."

"Well now, this is real nice," Doug said. He poured a cup and sat.

"This here's your welcome home breakfast," Royce said. "I can do a fair supper if it's hash browns and steak, but breakfast is my pride."

"It smells good," Doug said. "What time's it getting to be?"

Royce got a laugh out of that. "Where you going, hoss?"

"I don't know."

"Well there you are. Slip some of those pancakes on a plate. There's orange juice in the icebox if you want. Man, where'd you get that shirt? Cole'll try to buy it. I kinda like those shoes. Don't start Sue Jean on a waffle. She won't quit. The boys are real proud of you, Doug. You come over standin' up." He slid a plate of sausage on the table. Added more Tabasco to the eggs. "That's a fine thing to do. Don't happen all the time. There's a fella in the park, wants to know if this train stops at Trenton. Asks me every day. Hasn't got the slightest idea what's going on."

"Like Thack?" Doug said.

Royce considered that. "Well now, it ain't quite the same with Thack."

"The man seems muddled up to me.

"He is some. Muddled's a good word. But Thack isn't looking for no train."

Doug waited, finally saw that's all there was. "Royce, I don't guess I ought to fault Thack. I got dreams of every sort. I got funny stuff turning in my head."

"It bother you that you do?"

"Not a lot."

"You worried sick?"

"I'm not worried about a thing."

"You feeling fine?"

"I'm feeling great."

"So enjoy."

''Sue Jean keeps saying that too."

"That girl's a cookie. She won't steer you wrong."

Royce got up and took the dishes to the sink, washed them with a quick and practiced hand, dried them at a pace revealing interstate empty pocket blues, overnight career moves in diners and cafes. He hummed as he worked, let his jaw chew on a tune. Doug decided Royce's face might have suffered in a quake, jerked and settled back a quarter inch out of line. He moved with a quick and awkward grace, as if a bone might have broken here and there, left to heal and poke through his skin like a shirt on a hanger hung wrong. Still Royce seemed a man complete, the way he ought to be, the old jeans and worn boots, the pinstripe shirt that made him look like a down and out dandy. Doug wondered why he didn't feel the same. Royce was right, he felt great. Yet his head contained an odd emotional mix. Puzzled and content. Whole and partially abridged. A sound ship with a compass on the blink. He wondered what he'd like to do next. Thought about looking at the creek. Maybe walk around town. Poke into the stores. All stuff he liked to do, but it wouldn't stop the itch. The itch was right there and he didn't know where to scratch.

Outside the yard was filtered yellow-green. All the shades he liked. The pecan trees were the biggest he'd ever seen, full of squirrels and jays.

"The place suits you, all right," Royce said, guessing his thoughts and stopping to build a smoke. “I couldn’t see you in that intercoastal dump.”

“I couldn’t either,” Doug said.

“Funny where a man’ll think he ought to be. Done it more than once myself. Want to walk? You and me got to stop by the courthouse, won’t take a minute.”

“What for?”

“You got a hat? Boy, we need to get you a hat. I’m thinking maybe a Montana bent. Black with a rattlesnake band. Never liked those silver do-hickeys on my head. Knew a man once he was constantly harassed by sparrows. Near picked his hat apart. Finally tossed all his conches in the creek.”

The town felt more like spring than mid-summer. The day was clear as glass. People shopped and wandered about the square. Doc Holliday waved from across the street. Doug thought he saw Bitter Creek Newcomb on a Honda. The courthouse was cool, clean marble floors and polished wood, full of open doors and stairs and scarcely anyone about. Royce led Doug down the hall to a frosted glass door. Inside was a yellow oak counter, a high-ceilinged room full of one row of shelves after another. The shelves were stacked with gray-backed official looking books, the kind every courthouse seems to buy. One book was open on the counter. Royce called out, and a pleasant looking girl came out of the stacks.

“Marcy Ann, got you a customer,” Royce said. “Come in last night.”

“Hi,” said Marcy Ann. “You have a nice trip?”

“Real good,” Doug said.

“He come over standing up,” Royce said.

“Oh my.” Marcy Ann seemed impressed. “Put your name right there. Do it so I can read it.” She turned the book to Doug. The page was half full of names. He didn’t see anyone he knew. He wrote his name and gave her back the pen.

“You get to keep the pen,” said Marcy Ann.

“You’re signed in, hoss.” Royce clapped him on the back. “You take care now, Marcy Ann.”

“That’s it?” Doug said in the hall.

“Well sure, what you think? That’s a right nice pen.”

A quick rain had passed by, leaving the brick streets smelling clean, pearls of water on the grass. Doug spotted Thack on a bench beneath the trees.

“He’s looking some better,” he told Royce. “I hate to see a man running for the brush all the time.”

“He don’t do it ’less I take him out of town. Likely should have left him here, but it shakes him up bad when I'm gone. He'll do okay. Old Thack's going to make it. Listen, him and me's got a class. You wander around and make yourself at home."

Doug seemed confused. "You going to school or what?"

"Something like it. You take care now. We'll find Sue Jean later on, run up to the Pronghorn and get ourselves a steak." He gave Doug a wink and walked away. Thack jumped up at once and fell in step, walking in his jerk-stop manner like there might be dance steps painted on the street.

Doug watched them go. Wondered what kind of fish were in the creek. Remembered he didn't have a rod and reel. Decided he'd better hit some stores first. Kresses had Hi-Flyer kites. Wind-up boats and trucks. Brand new lead soldiers, silver helmets glued on the top, uniforms baby-shit brown. Flash Gordon rockets and Buck Rogers guns. Every Big Little book ever made. Penny candy under glass. Doug went into dimestore shock grabbing everything he could. Wished he had a basket or a cart. Dropped goodies in the aisle. Got everything up to the clerk, felt in his pockets and found he didn't have a cent.

"Listen, can you hold this stuff?" he said, "I got away without my wallet."

"You new in town, huh?" The girl was a sweetie. She reminded Doug of Cully Jean Moon.

"Last night," Doug said.

"You have a nice trip?"

"Real nice."

"Up front," said the girl, jerking a thumb at the door. "I'll put all this in a sack."

Doug walked up the aisle, not sure just what he was trying to find. He walked past canaries and parakeets, tropical fish and pumps, decided right then he had to get himself a tank. A big 50-gallon job. Maybe a hundred. Neons and angels, swordtails and guppies. A little Volkswagen cat to suck crap off the bottom.

There was nothing in the store. He peeked outside. There was a fifty-five gallon drum on the walk. He wondered how he'd missed it. The drum was full of buffalo nickels. He filled up his pockets, walked back to the clerk.

"A dollar ten," said the girl, and handed Doug his sacks. "You come back soon."

Doug said he would. At the drugstore on the corner he found a *Bluebook* for November '42. *G-8 Battle Aces* for August '39. *Weird Tales* for September '41. At the hardware store he bought a flying model kit of the Gee Bee racer, the body in green tissue paper, wings and tail in white. A bamboo fly rod, waxed line and reel. Wet and dry flies. A fishing hat and net. At the candy store cinnamon squares and sour balls, Black Jack gum. The drum full of nickels seemed a sound idea, since everything in town was apparently five cents, bicycles and Hershey bars, typewriters and nails.

Halfway across the square he turned back and bought a kid's red wagon to haul his stuff. A man was selling hot dogs from a stand. He bought two with chili and onions, drank a root beer and a grape. Four German airmen rode by in a Lamborghini. Doug waved and the flyers waved back. Instead of going straight home he took the long way around. He wanted to see the neighborhood. Maybe find Cole Younger or Sue Jean. Houses seemed to vary, reflecting individual taste. Clapboard Colonial. California Greek. Doug was taken by a high Tudor keep with new aluminum siding on the walls.

He found the park by chance, came on it abruptly past a neighborhood street. There were low hills and paths, a fountain among the trees. The well-kept lawns stretched off to a line of cottonwoods beyond. Doug stood and watched. There were people in the park, sitting on benches or walking along the paths. The walkers seemed to move in some pattern he couldn't define. A mix of order and disarray. Jogger paralytics or maybe something in between. In a moment, he saw that this was so. Walkers followed two styles of motion, erratic or restrained. Speed varied between somber resignation and alarm. Doug imagined close order drill on the grounds of some asylum, decided not to stick around. Pulling his wagon behind, he hurried quickly by.

A man called out. Doug stopped.

"Listen, fella, you know if this train stops at Trenton?"

Doug wasn't sure what to say. Yes or no seemed incomplete.

"I don't know," he said, "I'm not sure."

"I've got important stuff to do."

"Sorry to hear it."

"Beth Alice has the car."

"All right."

"What the fuck am I supposed to do?"

"I don't know."

"Look, I don't have time to talk to you."

"That's fine."

"Get that wagon out of the way. I can have you arrested like that."

"Have a nice day," Doug said.

Doug was concerned about the people in the park. Royce was right. They were downright confused. Not having any fun. That man in the suit was plain rude. Not that Doug blamed him. Walking around wondering where you were was enough to cause severe irritation. Where did everyone sleep? There weren't enough benches to go around. If it were him he'd get his act together quick. Go out and find a burger and a beer.

The neighborhood was quiet, softened by the day, the houses lazing back in summer heat. Tall elms joined hands dropping gold coins of light in the street. Doug half expected Tom Sawyer with a brush. An icewagon dripping cold water in the dust. Other backlot movieland kicks. As he turned in the gate a white blur rounded the corner of the house, slowed to a fox terrier dog and leaped up into his arms.

"Well I'll be," Doug said with delight, "look at you. How you been, boy!"

Luke, the dog he'd had when he was six, squirmed in adoration and licked his face. From the porch came Brick the Boston bull from junior high. A cocker from Oklahoma City named Choc. Maxine Pepper, a blueback Waxahachie hound. Doug gave up and went to ground, let the dogs have their way. Let them drool on his pants, poke their noses in his pockets and his crotch. Finally shooed them all away, got his wagon up the steps and inside where he found blue drifts of Latakia, Cavendish and burley, followed this trail to the kitchen where he saw the man sitting there drinking iced tea, eating ginger snaps from the box, dressed in sky-blue tennis shorts and Reeboks, a Boris Becker shirt, a sweat band around his golden hair, two cats from Phara, Texas, named Floss and Mr. Pee curled asleep in his lap.

Doug was struck with wonder. He didn't know what to say. Ended up not saying a thing at all.

"See you been doing a little shopping," the man said. "You sure got a lot of cats and dogs. Might talk you out of that blueback hound. So how's it going, Doug?"

"It's going fine," Doug said. "Say, I'm real glad you dropped by. This is great."

"You like the town?"

"The town's fine."

"Well I'm glad. That pleases me to hear it."

"I got some lemon custard ice cream in the fridge."

"Thanks, the tea's fine. I thought you might feel like some tennis. We've got some real good courts."

Doug was embarrassed. "I never played in my life. I don't even know how."

"Sure you do, Doug."

"Well I haven't got a racket or any clothes."

"Hey, I bet you do." The man winked and tapped a briar in his palm. "Run up and change. I'll get these cats something to eat. Boy, where'd you get that shirt? Cole try to buy it from you yet?"

The man beat him 6-4, 6-3, 6-4. "You got a good swing," he told Doug. "Work on that backhand some you'll do fine. We got a tournament next week. You might want to sign up."

"I don't think I'm quite ready for that," Doug said.

"Get Sue Jean to help you out. That girl's a whiz at the net."

Doug squirmed at the mention of Sue Jean. He was sure the man noticed, but was nice enough not to let on. They were walking back from the courts. Rain moved in from the east, but looked as if it might miss the town.

"Those folks in the park got to you," the man said.

"I guess they did."

"They get to me too." His eyes looked Columbine blue, sad as the end of every day.

"I wanted to tell them it was all okay, they'd be fine."

"I talk to 'em some. It helps. Mostly, you got to figure it out yourself." He grinned at Doug. "I'm real proud of you, coming over standing up."

"I'd feel real goofy in that park," Doug said, and before he could change his mind, "Listen, I dreamed about you and me. Were we at old man Wetzel's shop or not?"

"If you dreamed it, I guess maybe we were."

"I get confused. I feel like me and then I don't."

"It takes a while. You're doing fine."

Doug saw they were back on his street. The man walked him to the gate. The dogs jumped up and had a fit. There seemed to be additions to the pack.

"Nice game," the man said. "Let's do it again soon."

"I haven't thanked you for the house. I sure like it a lot."

The man gave Doug half a smile. “Everybody’s surprised they got a place. I never can figure why. I mean, I said there’d be a whole lot of houses. Something for everyone. If it wasn’t that way, why I’d ’ve told ’em. Folks don’t seem to listen.”

“I guess not.”

The man stuffed his pipe. “Doug, you ought to go see your mother. I told her you were here.”

Doug felt slightly uncontained. It hadn’t occurred to him at all and he saw that maybe it should.

“It’s okay,” the man said. “You can’t do everything at once. Nobody expects you to.”

Doug felt relieved. “I sure appreciate this. You taking a personal interest and all.”

“Hey, I love people,” the man said. “Always have. You take care now, Doug.”

Doug finds some good ground chuck in the fridge, fixes himself a cheeseburger with lettuce and tomatoes, mayonnaise and bacon, onions and sweet pickles, finishes that off and finds cold cherry pie, spicy hot leftover Szechuan beef, Jello and bananas, feeds three more cats that appear on the scene and a yellow-eyed Shepherd named Duke. He hasn’t been out back and he finds he has a screened-in porch, a floor warped and sloped, a rocker that looks familiar with obligatory cat curled in the seat, a daybed that sags for summer nights. The backyard is a tangle, a natural intrusion, the trees veiled with lush Virginia creeper, grapevines that loop up in shadow out of sight, the light here diffused, green and hot and thick enough to cut, the whole giving a Tarzan bottomland effect. Doug feels hidden, sufficiently alone. There are neighbors somewhere but out of sight. He’ll go and say hello but not now.

Back inside he roams about, inspecting this and that. Finds things he hasn’t seen before. Books he can’t recall when he arrived. *Billy Whiskers in Mischief.* Minor English poets on paper thin as air. *Raggedy Ann. Heroic Deeds In Our War With Spain. Dave Dawson At Dunkirk. Cretan Kings. Lincoln the Tyrant. Egyptian Nights. Missouri Days.* Other things new or out of place. A tintype picture of a woman he doesn’t know. A stuffed owl and a bust of Daniel Boone. A postcard from Rheims in a spidery Spanish script he can’t read. He feels he lives in a Hoover museum. Exhibits are discreetly moved about. He wonders about this but not much. Enjoy, said Royce and Sue Jean and he does. Questions come to mind. Answers seem important or maybe not. Time release perception is the order of the day. He feels stable and detached in a pleasant sort of way. Increasingly aware of some internal fracture of the head, not alarming in the least, simply off in some multiple direction, a course both familiar and unrecalled, his compass gone dyslexic and out of whack. Not altogether different from the Doug he's known before, only now without confusion and alarm, now enhanced and unconcerned. His head no longer jerks with starts and stops. He's settled in an easy driving gear. He doesn't think he's on a train, he isn't walking in the park. He is who he is or maybe not. A town where everything is five cents seems the place to work it out, to let the Dougs unravel and have their way.

Starting at the bridge, he made his way upstream along the cool sandy banks, sometimes walking in the creek. The water's surface was lazy and undisturbed, the current below surprisingly cold and swift. The afternoon sun poked yellow laser holes through the trees. At the bend he found a big fallen oak, white and stripped of bark, wedged along the bank, over time catching branches and bits of stone, deflecting the stream's course and cutting a deep and scoured pool like the cover of *Field & Stream.* The sight nearly brought Doug to tears. He tied a dry Coachman to his line, his hands shaking with the act, flicked the fly upstream a few times and dropped it deftly on the deep blue pool. The fly was scarcely settled before the surface rose up with the violence of a full mortar attack, showering Doug with water and scaring him out of his wits. Something grand and silver thrashed the air, slapped the water and disappeared. The two-ounce rod bent double, the line burned along the pool. Doug played the fish well, gave it very little line, brought it nicely to the net. It was a sleek and heavy rainbow, fierce and mirror-bright. Doug admired its yellow eyes and dagger jaw.

When the pool settled down he tried again, hooked another like the first. Caught three more dandies after that. Each weighed a uniform thirteen pounds four ounces, and he wondered how he'd ever get them home. Leaving his catch wrapped in wet ferns, he made his way upstream, fished the current and caught six German browns, each weighing in at nine apiece.

Someone called out. Doug looked up and saw four men fishing some twenty yards ahead on the bank. Each wore red pantaloons and ruffled shirts. Beards and funny hats. Each was uniformly fat like his trout. Doug took them to be Spaniards, or maybe Portuguese kings. He waved and the men waved back. He wondered just how far he'd walked from the bridge. Fly fishing sure was fun. He'd always wanted to try it out. It wasn't near as hard as those guys on TV would have you think.

At the hardware on the square Doug buys a brand new five cent top-of-the-line hog, an Indian fat-wheeled machine circa 1939 painted black as Hitler's heart, painted silk-lacquer black and the rest all chrome, enough liquid silver trim, silver tubing spokes and valves to make a thousand forty-six good first-prize rodeo buckles, maybe seven more than that. And riding west out of town in the world-class twilight that seems to last forever, he sprays the road with ochre dust, leaves a red war bonnet in his wake. He feels fine, he feels free, or maybe not. All this racing and jazzing about, this noisy violation of snakes and birds, is in way of compensation and delay. This is Doug's way of saying that he'd rather be with Royce and Sue Jean. That he'd rather be eating prime steak and drinking beer, having aviator/outlaw shitkicker fun in the warmth of the Pronghorn Saloon.

The truth is he's flat scared to see his mother. He thinks riding out on a beetle-black hog that shakes him up like a malted milk machine will lend him strength. Tell him what to say and what to do. Fill his head with things mothers like to hear. Royce and Sue Jean said he'd do just fine. Doug's not entirely convinced. He can't forget the weekend that started on a Friday afternoon, dropped out of sight then surfaced once again Monday night. Waking up to find Houston, Texas, gone and Le Blanc, Louisiana, in its place, a disbarred deb turned part-time doper in his bed. Can't forget spending all day Tuesday in a search to find his car. Getting home Wednesday noon to find he'd missed his mother's funeral a day or maybe two. The family seemed to feel this was cutting it awful close.

So here's the true reason for sound and fury on the road. He remembers all this and knows his mother will too. Knows she never forgets a thing. If she can't forget Easter '62 when he didn't send a card, she'll sure as hell remember this.

The house was maybe four miles out, set back off the road nearly hidden by a thick grove of hackberry and cedar. Doug knew the spot at once. This place clearly belonged to her. There were hints of Waxahachie, a touch of Oklahoma City, lines and angles he didn't know which reflected those years before his time. The whole seemed to fall into place, seemed to work itself out, seemed at once to have a 1932 brick and shrub effect, a slat-sided classic cottage look, a bayou tanglevine Colonial collapse, a laid-back, semi-formal garden gone to seed. He parked on the road and walked up the gravel drive past snapdragons, sunflowers and weeds. Unfamiliar dogs came to bark. The screendoor opened and his mother stepped out shading her eyes against the sun. A smile touched her face and Doug's fears fell away. She wasn't mad about a thing. Not pissed off at all. She came quickly out to meet him, wiping flour off her hands, a dark-haired farm-pretty girl maybe twenty or twenty-five, a face both familiar and out of synch, a childhood blur and a black and white snapshot third from the end, between overweight uncles and skinny aunts.

"Well I'll declare," Mother said, "Dougie if you're not a sight."

Doug gave her a hug. She turned a cheek toward him for a kiss. She smelled of violets and salt, powder and cherry pie.

"Mother, it's good to see you," Doug said. "You look great."

"Well now I do, that's a fact." She held him off, picked lint off his shirt, showed distraction and concern. "Come on inside. I got iced tea and cake. I see you got old. You don't look bad but I'd stay about thirty I was you. You looked real nice in that suit you got from Sears. The light blue. You ought to dress up and wear a tie. The Hoover men are fine till they hit thirty five then they flat fall apart. Your dad blew his candles and went to pieces on the spot. You got some good blood on my side Doug that's where you get your looks. That and diggin' holes in the ground overcome your Hoover genes."

Doug was startled and surprised. "You know about that?"

"A mother knows a lot of things, Doug, don't ever think they don't."

Inside, the house looked like it should, though Doug sensed a certain Latin air that seemed vaguely out of place. Walls in a faded floral pattern covered three sides of the parlor. The fourth was bare stucco, hung with red chilies and a calendar from a bar in Veracruz. The iced tea was just fine. He was certain there was cumin in the cake. What all this meant he couldn't say.

"Well," Mother said, pulling up a kitchen chair, "you getting settled in good?"

"I've got a real nice house. Everything I need."

"The Chief come by here Thursday afternoon, said you was on the way. Called up last night and said you made it. Hear you come over standing up. Not me I'll tell you that. I walked in that park till I was blue in the face. Thought it was maybe St. Louis. They got a lot of parks. You been there or not? He finally sent in my brother Bob to set me straight."

"He's been a lot of help to me," Doug said. "We played tennis this afternoon. I got beat."

"He's real good at sports. Talked me into taking up golf."

"What do you shoot?"

"A pretty mean 64."

"Well I'll be."

Mother showed him a slightly foxy grin. "He's a real fine person. Nice as he can be. I sure don't care for those clothes. First time he come out I shooed him right off the porch with a broom. Didn't know who he was. Had silly looking hippie jock shoes. Next time he showed up in a real nice robe. I said, 'now that's a lot better. You come on in and have some pie'."

"You hear anything about Dad?" Doug said.

Mother shook her head and poured them both more tea. "That man'll hang on to the end, bless his heart. He don't know when to quit. Saved Coca-Cola bottle caps, one from every state. Had 'em framed out in the garage. I said, 'Hoover, they're every one the same.' Keep your eyes on that park. You see a fella selling lots for twenty-three dollars down that's him. You want some more of that cake?"

Doug's mother said she'd never felt better. She showed him around the house. Took him out back and showed him carrots and lettuce, cucumbers and cabbage coming up. All Doug could see was weeds. She was into Chinese cooking and ceramics. Automobile repair and industrial design. Pastel art and shodo-kan.

"I got some real nice neighbors," she told Doug. "Emma Tugg's down the way and Mrs. Terrence B. Hays. We're into contract bridge. There's several colored ladies in the group. Land, was that some surprise to me. I thought they'd have their own place. Why they're just like us. As nice as you could want. I can't wait to see your father's face. Doug, you shouldn't have taken up with that Lamprey girl at all."

"I guess you're right."

"A man's a weak vessel where a woman is concerned. You're about the worst I ever saw 'less you count your uncle Pete. That and not finding proper work. That's two things you did."

"Mother, I couldn't find a thing I wanted to do." Doug didn't care to get into this at all. "There's certain people not suited for a job. I think I'm one of those. I tried all kinds of stuff. Didn't like one any better than the next."

Mother made a face. "Liking's got nothing to do with work."

"Well it should. You ought to do things you like."

"You can't have everything you want."

"I can now."

"You want some more of that cake?"

"I'm just fine." Doug decided the little green things were bits of jalapeño pepper.

"The girls at bridge are into state politics. I swear I don't care much for it. I guess I will though if everyone else is going to do it. Mrs. Terrence B. Hayes says governor of Pennsylvania'd be nice. I don't know, I never been up north, what do you think?"

Doug tried to back up and find his place. "What do I think about what?"

"Son watch my lips. Try to sit up straight."

"Mother, I don't know what you're talking about at all."

"Oh, *I* see. You don't think I can do it."

"Do what?"

"Be governor of Pennsylvania."

Doug sat down his glass. "We're *here,* Mother. You don't have to be governor of Pennsylvania."

"You ought to be thinking on it, Doug."

"I just did."

"I don't mean me, I mean you."

"What about me, Mother?"

"Well, what do you think you want to do next?"

"Next what?"

"Next time you go out."

"Out where?" Doug didn't feel well at all. It might be the cake or maybe not.

"For goodness sake, Doug."

"Mother, out *where*?"

Mother reached out with a reassuring pat. "Son, don't you worry about a thing. You'll find something nice next time I just know. A real fine job and a wife who don't wear tacky clothes."

"Jesus Christ."

"Good idea," Mother said. "Something good comes up, why he's going to hear about it first."

He rode the black hog through the slowly fading light, through the red wine and terra-cotta dusk rolling slack across the sky. He felt suspended like the day, caught in some peculiar balance, caught in some remote reflection of himself, this perspective both obscure and crystal clear. There were certain indications of a motorcycle act, a neat prismatic trick that featured goofy mirrored Dougs in symmetric disarray. He thought the spectacle was grand and even cheered himself along, offered multiple hurrahs, apparitional applause.

All this from the encounter with his mother, revelations in the kitchen that had left him oddly fractured and uncertain in his head. Just whose idea was this? He was happy where he was. He liked the people and the town. Nickel economics was the best idea he'd ever seen. It was something he could grasp and understand. If his mother wanted Pennsylvania politics, great. Fine for her but not for him.

So he rode past the stores, past the courthouse and the square, and if he felt discontent, apprehension or concern, it was blurred by the giddy invocation of the town. He seemed detached from any worry or alarm. Trouble was an abstract wonder and it missed him by a mile. It couldn't touch the magic motorcycle act, the happy foliated Dougs. House rules kept him cheerfully immersed, secure and undisturbed. He parked the hog out front. Fought the crazed affection of a growing pack of dogs. Found Sue Jean was fast asleep and woke her up.

"Listen here," Doug said, "there's stuff you haven't told me. I'm missing vital parts."

"I don't much care for being jerked out of sleep."

"I got to talk right now. I can't put up with this picture in my head."

"What kind of picture's that?"

"Flunking chemistry again. Winding up a dentist in a panhandle town."

"Oh that." Sue Jean sat up and lit a ciggie. One little nipple seemed asleep, creased like a page in a book. "So how's your mom?"

"You sure do look good naked."

"That's beside the point."

"I don't like this business of going back. Just what's it all about?"

"You don't like it don't go."

"What's the catch? What happens if I don't?"

"Nothing happens at all."

"Well that's fine. I'm happy where I am. It looks to me like you and Royce could have brought this up."

"Doug, you're supposed to do some of this stuff by yourself."

"Seems to me they could tell you. It wouldn't be a big deal to get something printed up."

This seemed a little easy. He wanted reassurance. Wanted firm persuasion. Wanted to hop in bed and act silly and forget the whole thing. He thought about going to the kitchen for a snack.

"I can stay right here. Do anything I want."

"It's your house."

"That's some kind of answer."

"What's the question?"

"Well I don't see why anyone'd want to do it. I'm fine right here. I sure don't crave any further aggravation."

"All right."

"You're sure a big help."

"I guess not."

"It wouldn't hurt if you said how it's heaven in my arms."

"I could plain knock you silly, how's that?"

"Affection's a state of mind," Doug said. "I'm willing to talk it out."

"I'm willing to do anything but," Sue Jean said.

Caught in a happy cookie vise, he forgot bifurcation of the head, Dougs scattered and amok, Dougs stable and aligned. Campaign pictures of his mother by the road. As his sweetie plugged him in and pulled the switch, made him crackle like a looney tune cat, he considered growing rice, doing Pakistani chores, fucking valence up again. Knew for sure he didn't care for that at all. Daffy variations didn't make a bit of sense. You could end up in Panama as easy as not. Washing socks in Poland in an unheated room. Now who'd want to go and do that?

"I'm not going," Doug said, "and that's that."

"Then don't," Sue Jean said.

"I bet I never did before."

"Do you think?"

"Well did I?"

"For God's sake Doug, go to sleep."

He was talking to her back. She was curled in a post-carnal knot, scooping out a sweetie nest.

"If I did I bet I screwed up good. I bet I was a serf. I bet I had lice and some common irritation of the skin."

"You got a real shitty outlook, Doug."

"Well I wasn't any duke."

"You don't know if you were or not."

Doug turned out the light and snuggled close to Sue Jean. The quilt contained isolated spots of gravitation, cat mines scattered here and there.

"Him and me played tennis this afternoon," Doug said. "We had a nice talk."

"Bet he beat the socks off you, too."

"How'd you know?"

"He's real good I know that."

"He thinks I ought to go for tournament play."

"Then I would."

"You want to get something to eat?"

"I want to sleep, Doug. I don't guess I made that clear."

"Well that's easy for you to say. I got all this stuff in my head. I expect I'll be tossing all night. I can't get used to my mother into auto repairs. That and Asian martial arts. That bridge club of hers has put funny ideas in her head. You can bet this politics thing is just a lark. That woman won't stay in a hotel, that's the truth. Those wrappers on the toilet don't mean a thing to her. Doug, what good's that paper going to do, she used to say, they got foreign born help cleaning up? They could squat right down wouldn't anybody know. If that woman hits the campaign trail it better be around the block."

Dogs barked in the yard. A Maserati cleared its throat and whizzed by, outlaws and airmen on a spree. Doug thought about maybe getting dressed, going up to the Pronghorn Saloon. Maybe Doc or Cole Younger could tell him if he used to be a serf.

Doug dreamed of Lawrence, Kansas, Santa Fe and Powder River, dreamed of bitter tin coffee in a Cochise County jail. Dreamed he sailed with Danish Vikings on a raid to Saxon shores, dreamed of frightened Wessex maids who smelled of mice. Dreamed he sold a Persian orange to Alexander, thought he looked fat and short, not especially great at all. Dreamed he caught a glimpse of Royce at Babylon. Dreamed he ate a Cheyenne dog and threw it up.

And when he woke he found the dawn was nearly there, fuzzy underwater light about the room. He couldn't tell if what he'd dreamed was truly real or if he'd seen it on the tube, maybe read it in a book. Several Vikings had a Tony Curtis look. He didn't feel your average Roman smoked cigars, but who could say?

Sue Jean was in the kitchen making breakfast. That or simply messing with the food to see what would happen next. Bowls were on the counter, clearly batter in the works. Sue Jean tapped drops from a bottle into each. Stood back and studied the situation with intent. Added a drop of this and that. Poured the batter on a grid. Doug saw his sweetie had invented pastel waffles on the spot. He added syrup and took a bite.

"The green ones taste a lot like lime chiffon pie," Doug said.

"There isn't any taste to it," Sue Jean said. "That's harmless food color is what it is."

"I'd swear there's some real lime in it."

"Well there's not."

Doug watched a cat jump on the counter, sniff at a waffle and walk away. "Listen, there's something I got to ask."

"About what?"

"Where was I when I went? I'd like to know."

Sue Jean studied a peachy bite. "At the office. That dumb place you worked."

"I stopped to say goodbye to Sarah Dee. I guess I did."

"I'll say."

Doug set his coffee down. "Lord, I bet I shook her up good. I wish I hadn't done that. That woman's got enough on her mind. Did I linger real long or just go?"

Sue Jean looked right at him. "You got to do all this, right? You lingered. Hung on like a trooper. Tubes and machines and blinkin' lights. The whole *St. Elsewhere* bit, okay?"

"Boy, I bet everyone was sad. Erlene crying and carrying on, Ham and Stew wishing they'd been a whole lot nicer than they were."

Sue Jean threatened him with a fork. "I am not puttin' up with this, Doug."

"All right, okay. I just asked."

"I got two of these left. You want a purple or a pink?"

"Pink's fine," Doug said.

Pastel waffles didn't seem to be enough. When Sue Jean left he found cold roast beef in the fridge. Horseradish sauce and cheddar cheese. Half a banana pie. The day looked fine, so he fixed himself a plate and settled down in a rocker on the porch. The dogs were having a lark chasing squirrels. It was clear to both teams this would end up in a draw. Assorted cats looked away, embarrassed and aloof, switched about and found good spots to sleep in the sun. Doug watched the yard and read a *Collier's* for 1945. Put it down and started *John Carter of Mars*. He thought about cold cream soda and considered a morning nap. The thought seemed enough and he felt refreshed at once. A calico cat, one he couldn't quite recall, climbed the screen and gave Doug a silly look.

A good night's sleep had cleared his head, left him more or less alert, left him suitably detached. The idea of going back still left him cold but didn't bother him at all. No thanks, he'd had enough. One disaster would do him fine. You walk off from an airline crash you don't hurry and buy a ticket somewhere else.

Sue Jean said she'd done it lots of times and wouldn't go into details at all. No big surprise there. That girl could leave a question just hanging out to dry. He thought about Royce and kind of hoped he'd say it didn't make a lick of sense to him. Royce was a drifter, but he knew the high lonesome when he saw it. His mother was something else. Doug knew the cause of that. His father was to blame; he wouldn't take her anywhere at all. If he had, she wouldn't be running off now to get elected in the east.

The dogs let off chasing squirrels and took out barking to the front. Someone knocked, and Doug made his way to the door. A man stood smiling behind the screen.

"Doug Hoover?" he wanted to know.

"That s me."

"Philo Akers," said the man, "I'd like to take a moment of your time. No problem if I don't. I can leave if you like. I can come back Thursday afternoon. How about Tuesday after next? Sorry to intrude. I won't trouble you again." The man turned away and walked off.

"Come on in," Doug said.

"Well that's fine. This is working out good. Say, what a nice place you got here. Understand you came over standing up."

"I guess I did."

"Not me. I thought I'd got lost at the zoo down in Jackson, Mississippi. You been there at all?"

"I've got some iced tea in the fridge."

"I'll take a cookie if you got it."

"You fidget an awful lot," Doug said. "I sort of wish you'd sit down."

The man did. He wore a three-piece polyester suit on a beanpole frame, no socks and no shoes. Your classic Dole pineapple shirt and a bow tie to match. He sat on the couch and laid a clipboard across his bony knees, then opened up a 1937 Parker fountain pen fat as a fifty-cent cigar, a wicked writing tool and a weapon in itself.

Doug felt under imminent attack. "I don't much care for these polls," he told Akers. "If you're getting into that, let's not."

"I'll be out of your hair in a jiff," Akers said. "Say, you play a musical instrument or not? I got you figured for a mean tenor sax. You don't have to read notes."

"That's good 'cuse I don't. What's that you're writing down?"

"You got a borderline first tenor voice. I'm thinking maybe lead in a mixed quartet."

"Well don't."

Akers scratched it out. Doug served iced tea and Oreo cookies on a plate. Akers split the cookies in half and ate the icing part first.

"How you feel about the ballroom dance?" Akers said. "I'd say that's an art in itself."

"I don't like to waste your time."

"Your mother's taking band trombone and modern tap."

"I'm not a bit surprised."

"The whole course is five cents. You can't beat it with a stick."

"I got a lot of things to do."

"You going to throw those cookies out or what?"

"They're all yours."

"Well I'll be." Akers stuffed cookies in every pocket he could find. "All the sounds of the earth are like music, who said it?"

"Oscar Hammerstein, *Oklahoma!*"

"Shoot. You got a knack for this."

"No I don't. You have a nice day."

To his wonder and delight, the house continues to absorb the convolutions in his head, to sort and sift and rearrange in shy collusion with his dreams, to disentangle fractured Dougs and set them more or less aright. The house seems adept at this geologic act, clearly practiced in the art of shifting artifact and mood, fossil smells and relic tastes where they belong. As revelations flicker on his multi-feature screens, a shelf or a wall or the corrugation of a room provides a lap he feels he's run or maybe not. Slipped among his books he finds *Arizona Trails. Seven Celtic Bards. Eburones Wars* and *A Cowboy's Delight. Poems of Hunt and Clare. Samantha at Saratoga. Bill Cody's Campfire Chats* and *A Look at the Macedonian Wars.* On his dresser upstairs he finds a new pack of Steamboat cards. A scatter of Minoan beads, an ivory Thor. On the wall above his bed, a dun-colored daguerreotype of Liberty, Missouri. In the kitchen there's a bone-handled corkscrew from a Coffeyville, Kansas, saloon. And scribbled on the bathroom wall in faded hand he reads,

My Peggy is a young thing,
Just entered in her teens,
Fair as the day, and sweet as May,
Fair as the day, and always gay.

My Peggy is a young thing,
And I'm not very auld,
Yet well I like to meet her at
The wawking of the fauld.

Doug reads these lines again and thinks they rhyme real good, that it's better than what you see on your average Houston Texaco wall.

After lunch he found a kit for the *Eindekker* Fokker E II, got his airplane glue and a single-edge blade by Gillette, laid everything out on a card table on the screened-in porch. Made himself a pimiento and peanut butter sandwich, opened up a Delaware Punch and got to work. He seemed more adept than the kid in Waxahachie, he could see his fingers fly, see the clean sharp lines go where he liked and hardly ever out of whack. He was drunk on the smell of balsa dust and the tangy taste of glue, the touch of fine tissue paper stretched taut as a soldier's bed. In a dizzy rush of wonder at his skill he saw a whole panorama spreading out, a spectacle that would fill the whole house with every Fokker and Halberstadt, every Rumpler, every Albatros and Pfalz, every Dornier and Hanse-Brandenberg. He felt a mission in the works, a fine obsession on the brink. He'd do them all, every one, every great Kraut machine that ever flew. Or maybe not.

He had the fuselage complete and the wings looking good when Immelmann and Boelcke roared up in a brand new Derham Duesenberg painted red, a Mack truck chrome-plated bulldog head with ruby eyes mounted high upon the hood, mudflaps with silver dome buttons spelling *Jagdstaffel 11*, Janis Joplin belting *Lili Marlene* on the tape. They braked to a stop by the white picket fence, bringing Doug a case of cold Dortmunder Kronen beer, tins of Romanoff beluga caviar, chocolate-covered truffles, and five pounds of Fort Worth east-side barbecued ribs.

"Well I'll be," Doug said. "What a nice thing to do."

"Nothing *at* all," Boelcke said, peering over Doug's shoulder at the plane. "You got the cowling real good, but them Spandaus is maybe just a tad close together."

"How's that?"

"That'll do her."

Boelcke grabbed two beers, flipped off the caps and handed one to Doug. Max wandered in the kitchen and came back with a diet 7-Up and a plate of cherry pie.

"You doing all right," Max said, "settling in okay?"

"Doing fine," Doug said. "I got a lot of stuff going in my head, but Sue Jean and Royce say it doesn't mean a thing."

"Right on," Max said, "you're flat hittin' on eight." He propped his boots on the table, picked up the *Eindekker* and studied it a while, closed one eye and moved the angle of the wings just a hair. "You got to let things work kinda slow," he told Doug. "Get your feet on the ground."

"Go with the flow," Boelcke said.

"Play it nice and cool," Max said. "How's your ma?"

"Happy as a clam," Doug said. "Seems to play a lot of bridge. Got a garden out back full of weeds. Carrots 'bout as long as a baby's little dick. I don't much care for this politics scheme I'll tell you that. She'll run into scalawags and tramps."

"Sure enough," Max said.

Doug looked at the fliers straight on. "You guys ever do that or not? I mean go back out and try again."

Boelcke looked surprised. "Well sure we have, Doug. Lots of times."

This wasn't what Doug wanted to hear. Max seemed to read him plain enough. "Look, you don't want to worry about that," he told Doug. "Whatever you want to do, why that's going to work itself out."

"I feel like I might've been a serf," Doug said.

"You might have been some kinda earl, you think of that?" Boelcke said.

"I sure don't feel like an earl."

"Well not now you don't."

"Listen, I'd flat remember if I was. If I had me a title and a flag why I figure it'd show. I don't feel like I got a noble mien. You wouldn't go from a castle to a PR job in Houston, Texas. That doesn't make a bit of sense. I think I might've worked a farm in southern Gaul. Walked out in the woods to eat a root and got clobbered by a Hun, no offense."

"None taken," Max said. He finished off his beer and stood. "Doug, I want you to get this shit out of your head. You got to let her ride, all right?"

"I guess so," Doug said.

"What we come by to tell you there's a knockdown howler at the Pronghorn tonight. Got friends coming in and going out. You want to be there sure.

Doug brightened at that. A party seemed like just the thing. "I sure won't miss it," he told Max. "Listen, you know a skinny little fella with a big Parker pen?"

"Shoot," Boelcke said, "I'm a tarantella whiz. Got the shimmy down pat."

"Them Oberursel engines was the pits," Max said. "An inline six won't let you down."

The Pronghorn was jumping when he stepped in the door. Chandeliers yawed with dizzy light. The floor seemed about to call it quits. Sonic damage seemed a cinch. The jukebox retarded forward motion; it took some time to find Royce and Sue Jean. He made his way through outlaws and airmen doing Cotton-Eyed Joe, doing jitterbug waltz, doing punk Virginia reel, slinging pretty girls about. Every girl he saw was a long-legged dream, a Dentyne apple-tit honey with hillbilly Popsicle eyes. Doug considered sly deeds, misdemeanors of the heart. Thought of Sue Jean and knew she put all the others in the shade, but he might want to think about that.

Royce saw him coming. He handed Doug a lop-sided grin and stood and clapped him on the back. "Hey, how's it hanging, hoss? Sit it on down while I clear these empties and find us something wet. You want some ribs?"

"Sounds great."

"Well you got 'em." He filled his hands with dead Becks and made his way through the crowd. Doc Holliday waved from across the room. King Fisher came by and said hello. Doug watched Richthofen do the Spanish jig, watched him stomp on his hat and eat a hard-boiled egg on the run. *Jagdstaffel 11* cheered him on. Doug figured the Pronghorn was in for tremors and quakes.

"Well hi there, hon," said a voice behind his back, and Sue Jean leaned down to plant a chili kiss on his cheek.

Doug turned and his heart slipped a gear. "Say now, look at you. Lord, Sue Jean, I'm flat dazzled by your charms."

"Shoot," Sue Jean said, "I saw you eyein' those Tennessee debs."

"You're a long-haired scamp. You put those ladies in the shade."

"I guess I heard that once or twice." She slid in a chair, decked out in white leather, leather buckskin vest with little pearls and a fringe, white shorts and white carhop boots. The white against her tan stirred serious perversions in his head.

"I haven't seen you all day." Doug said, "Where you been?"

"Had a class."

"You doing that, too?"

"I guess I am."

"I'd like to hear about that."

"Not now."

"Boy, you and Royce are just alike. I had two major Huns drop by and do the same. Never said a thing except you're doing fine, Doug, way to go."

"You feeling bad?"

"I'm feeling great."

"Got a worry in your head?"

"Not a one."

"Then hush up and drink your beer."

Royce arrived with fresh supplies, *Tres Equis* and Shiner beer with frosty sides, white bread and ribs. The ribs looked thick and dark, pepper welded solid to the fat.

"Boys are havin' a jalapeño fest," Royce said. "Sam Bass has got thirty-two down and the Reno brothers is close behind. I got a nickel on Sam." He opened beers all around. "So what kinda day'd you have, son?" He shot a wink at Sue Jean. "I hear you're a plain shopping fool."

"What'd you do to your hair?" Doug said.

"Well I didn't do a thing."

"You look different than you did. I think your jaw's out of whack."

"What's this boy had to drink?" Royce said.

"You don't look the same and that's a fact."

"Babe, you got that head of yours working overtime," Sue Jean said.

"I got a squirrel cage going is what I got," Doug said. "You want to know what I did? You want to hear? I made a Fokker E II. I watched a cat eat a leaf. I talked to some fella wants to put me in a band. What I did was just walk around the house and try to figure who I was and who I am. I feel like a party snack plate. Some of this and some of that. Boelcke says I might have been a earl. Feeding an earl's pigs is what it was, I'll tell you that. I bet I was married to Otta Gee."

"Hon, you got serfs on the brain," Sue Jean said.

"Isn't any use getting in a rush," Royce said, "you got the time."

Doug gave them both a look. "Well you and miss rodeo queen here could help. I don't see how that'd hurt. I can't get an answer out of anyone at all."

"Answers got a way of showing up," Royce said.

"Now what's that?" Doug said. "Is that a riddle? I sure don't need to hear a riddle."

"You want some more of these ribs?"

"I think you cut your hair. You look like you but you don't. Royce, have you been back out or not? I want to know."

"I sure have, hoss."

"What for?"

"Something I had to do."

"And you think I ought to do it, too."

"I think you ought to do what you want."

"What's the catch?"

"Isn't any catch at all."

"How's it feel?"

Royce grinned. "Well now, how did it feel to you?"

It was an answer he half expected and didn't much want to hear. Too simple and direct. Too easy and complete. He was hoping for something else. A super high with a benefit package on the side. Some reason to leave a place that had everything he liked. Familiar dogs and cats. A fridge full of import beer and cherry pie. Five cent Maseratis and Sue Jean. It didn't make sense to leave that and maybe shovel camel shit in Bangladesh. Maybe sell cheap term in Tupelo. Doug felt oddly disengaged. Collectively aware of some derailment on the tracks, yet conscious of the on-time arrival of accord. Revelation and disarray, insight and clutter in a goofy Doug mix that seemed to work.

Applause broke his thoughts; he looked up and saw couples pause on the floor, saw everyone stand, heard the music fade away. Ernst Udet and Tom Horn hoisted the Sundance Kid atop the bar. A dozen champagne corks popped at once. Someone gave Sundance a bottle and he held it up high and drank it down, foam streaming over his shoulders and his chest. This feat brought a cheer and then the crowd went quiet. Doug looked up and saw the Chief walk in through the batwing doors and make his way to the bar. He wore Converse shoes, Adidas jogging wear in an Easter-lilac shade, a matching band across his brow. The Kid scrambled down and the Chief shook his hand, said a few words that made Sundance grin.

"Ol' Sundance is going back out," Royce said. "Real fine thing to see. I expect he'll sure do it up right."

"What's he going to be?" Doug said.

"Getting into ballet, as I recall. The boy's a whiz on them *grand plies.*"

"Lord, that dancin' is a art in itself," Sue Jean said.

Doug perked up at once. "You mean you get to pick? You can be what you want? Sue Jean, you never said a thing about that. Well I'll be. I'm not saying I'd ever do it. I might consider the South of France. I'm keen on your idle beach life."

"Hon, you just settle down," Sue Jean said. "Don't bounce in your chair."

"I'm just fine."

"I'm going to take you home and give you an alcohol rub."

"I don't want to go home, I'm having fun."

"We'll have a whole lot of fun at the house."

Doug watched a girl with an Alabama gait. "What I want to do is dance. I got a feeling I could glide with little effort on the floor."

"You need to get this boy a hot chocolate," Royce said.

"I'd say your eyes are different too. I don't recall that nose."

"You sure got me coming all apart."

"I'm not too sure of that chin," Doug said. He wiped the cold off his beer and ate a rib. Three men came in the door. He recognized Ben Thompson and Cold Chuck Johnny right off. The other looked happy and confused. Unattached and silly as a duck. Symptoms he could see in himself.

The Chief left the bar and walked up to greet the new arrivals. The violet Adidas shirt and pants looked great with the gold in his hair.

"Another fella come over standing up," Royce grinned, "or close to it."

Doug felt touched by the moment. "I never thanked you two for bringing me in. That was a nice thing to do and I appreciate it a lot. If you go out again, why I'll do the same for you."

"Ol' hoss, you already did," Royce laughed.

"I guess I don't recall."

"You want to dance with that honey, have at it," Sue Jean said. "I'm going home and anoint my whole self with a quart of Shalimar."

"Shoot, let's go and do it," Doug said.

THE HEREAFTER GANG

Walking home through a spring and summer night, through a honeysuckle smell and cricket dark, under stars bright enough to read a lease, bright enough to make a cat consider shades, Sue Jean and Doug happily toss their shoes aside, share the feel of dusty streets warm as waffles from the day. In the yard they make their way through a cheery flock of dogs, spirit goodies from the fridge and up the stairs, shoo the furball team from off the bed and hit the hay. Once again Doug's entangled in his cookie's sweet delights, in the magic of her touch, in the wonder of her hillbilly Dr Pepper thighs, in the heady taste of adolescent wine. And as she takes him past the giddy speed of otter lust, sends him off on Indy thrills, he remembers in an instant all at once every motel encounter, every bedroom event, every backseat adventure, every trailer court romance, every Friday at the movies grope and feel. This encyclopedic blast of former fun knocks him silly, out of synch, leaves him more or less intact, leaves him rattled and complete.

And as he holds his cutie close he drifts away, beyond sweet hallucinations of the past, drifts from there into dreams without the scent of dusty skin, where the smell is harsh and raw, the taste of leather and despair. He tries to hold the hazy ghost of candy lips and salty hair but they quickly slip away. He falls without a net into cold Missouri days, into Albuquerque nights, into backtrails and hot caliche draws. He knows the taste of sandy bread, the smell of woodsmoke in his clothes. His throat is dry and tastes of clay. He feels the rain pour off his hat. He shoots a boy from West Virginia in the jaw. Sees a scorpion bite a dead Mescalero in the eye. He pees against the wall in a cold Nebraska jail. Sees a man he thinks he knows. Sees a girl who never cries. Royce is somewhere about and then he's not; he wanders in and wanders out. He's shooting another picture on a set across the lot, they'll get together for a lunch. The pictures are rated S and R for semi-real. Violence and tears, language and regret. Constipation due to fear may be unsuitable for adults. Doug takes it in his stride, he lives the dream without concern. B-movies are a drag and he's done it all before.

Doug woke with the feeling there was something he'd forgotten or remembered to forget. He knew he'd seen a little of himself, familiar pictures here and there. Snapshots from the attic of his mind. Nothing too intense or really clear. And there was Royce—Royce and a man he ought to know and couldn't place. A friend or, closer still, someone plainly in his past. Doug felt vaguely discontent. He couldn't doubt it anymore. He had a past for sure which meant in spite of how he felt he'd gone out somewhere before. There were Dougs back there before the Houston-Waxahachie Doug he knew. Now why would he want to do that? He felt betrayed. That fellow was a sneak and likely funny in the head. Well he sure as hell wasn't anymore.

Sue Jean was still asleep. Shoving cats aside he went down and put the coffee on the stove. Fried thick-sliced bacon, made scrambled eggs and toast. Found oranges in the fridge and squeezed a quart of fresh juice. Royce was very much on his mind. He kept hanging on from the dream. Peeking out of the wings with a lop-sided grin and a wisecrack Doug could nearly hear. He looked different and the same. Like he had the night before. Now why was that? He didn't know.

Sue Jean came down looking slick as a pup in her sky-blue jumpsuit and heels. Earrings the shape of baby seals and a ribbon in her hair.

"Say, I got a great idea," Doug said, feeling a tug here and there, recalling keen acrobatics in the night.

"I know you do, hon," Sue Jean said, "I can't do it, gotta run." She grabbed a 7-Up from the fridge.

"Well what for? I got eggs and fresh juice."

"I got a class, I'm running late."

Doug put down his fork. "You just hold on. I want to talk about that."

"'Bout what?"

"About this thirst for education, that's what. You and Royce. And I bet there's some others in it, too."

"For goodness sake, Doug."

"Sue Jean, I won't be put off. You got a corkscrew mind, you got my ire up good. You talk like a secret Nazi spy."

"Isn't anyone doin' that, hon."

"Well yes they are. Nobody tells me a thing, I'm in the dark."

"You're a sweetie, that's what," Sue Jean said. She bent to plant a kiss, fussed her hair, studied him with serious intent.

"What's the matter?" Doug said.

"Not a thing. You're lookin' younger, babe, for sure. Hard as a fender, on the mend. Ready for the prom. Well, bye!"

Doug sat and watched the screen door. Heard the dogs say hello, heard the gate squeak shut. He was vaguely aware that she'd snookered him again. Aware of the taste of scrambled eggs, of the 7-Up kiss, of the drift of Shalimar. In a minute he got up and found a mirror in the den. Looked at a face that he recalled. She was right. He wasn't fifty-seven. He was maybe thirty-three. Take away six carry your one. Which meant he looked some short of twenty-two with the soil immersion factor thrown in.

Well I'll be.

He needed to talk to Royce. He didn't know why, but it seemed like Royce could give him answers if he would. If you could get past the riddles and the grins. Royce was real good at that. Him and Sue Jean both. Doug felt like a quiz show host at a home for the deaf and dumb.

Royce wasn't at the square. Doug looked in the stores and asked around. He bought a sack of cinnamon squares and talked to the sweetie in the shop. She understood he came over standing up and hoped he had a nice day. Bitter Creek Newcomb drove by in a Pantera painted Nile green, cowhide doors and a Mickey Mouse clock on the hood.

Doug walked back toward the house. He didn't know where Royce lived but his place shouldn't be hard to find. He'd run into someone he knew. Everybody knew everyone else. At the corner where the town sloped down, where the paved brick street became a dusty rural road, he stopped and looked into the park. Nothing much had changed. People wandered idly about. Slow, fast-forward and reverse. Sometimes a touch of all three. Doug shook his head and walked on. Stopped a moment later as something odd caught his eye. Someone had put up a tent. Not just your everyday campout tent, but a tent big enough for a 4-H event, a travelling carnival show. Crossing to the park, he saw a crowd had begun to gather or at least give it a try. The walkers made every effort to chart a semi-daffy course. Some missed the tent altogether, getting it right maybe the second time around; others veered haplessly into the trees.

Doug stood at the back behind the last row of chairs. Up front someone raved and bobbed about. Doug followed a pompadoured head and saw it went with a squat little frame. The frame prowled restlessly back and forth, shouting at the crowd. Doug was taken aback. He felt seriously impaired. Distinctly uncontained. Didn't like the looks of this at all.

"Sit down, Doug, take a load off your feet."

Doug turned and saw the Chief. He sat alone in the very last row He wore a basketball suit the color of Delaware Punch, the number 2 on his shirt. Doug sat.

"You want an apple?" asked the Chief.

"I guess I do."

"Real nice day. We're going to get a little rain this afternoon. Be good for the grass."

"I guess it will."

"You feeling good?"

"I'm feeling fine."

"You like the town?"

"I think it's great."

"Well I'm sure pleased to hear it."

The tent wasn't filling up fast. The walkers found arriving at a single destination hard enough. Actually sitting down required major docking skills.

"I don't know why you put up with this at all," Doug said. "It's sure a big mistake you ask me."

"Hey, what can I say?" The Chief gave Doug a weary smile. "I put out the word. Nobody's got to listen."

"You look tired."

"I guess I am, Doug."

"You ought to get up there and set 'em straight is what I think."

"I'm not into that anymore. How's your backhand coming? Haven't seen you on the courts."

"I been meaning to come out."

"Let's take a walk."

Outside the tent they made their way through the shade of tall pecans across the lawn. Doug didn't see the man waiting for a train, and wondered if he'd found his way out. A lady with a Lord & Taylor sack searched for bargains in the trees. Two Hare Krishnas hopped by in semi-harmonious reverse. The Chief found a handful of nickels and dropped them in a cup.

"I don't care for that park," Doug said, "makes me feel out of sorts."

"They'll come around. A lot of folks don't take to change."

"Listen, I hope you don't mind. I got a lot of things churning in my head. I could use some friendly aid and dialogue."

"That's what I'm here for, Doug."

"It's that going back out again stuff. I can't seem to get relief, it's got me whipped."

"Don't let it."

"Well I figured out I did it, and it looks like maybe more than once. I still don't know if I was a serf. I haven't got to that yet."

"Get off of that serf kick, Doug."

"Well I will. I mean that's what I'm endeavoring to do."

"You're giving it a go, I know that," the Chief said. The sky seemed caught in his eyes. His beard and fine hair caught the brilliance of the sun, the color of his bright athletic wear. He looked at Doug and grinned. "You know what? You're dropping those years like ticks off a dog. Getting younger every day."

"I guess I am."

"You got a good head start. I'm crazy about that soil immersion prank. Hardly anyone ever thinks of that. You're a rascal and a half. You into any classes yet or not?"

"Now that's another thing," Doug said.

"I'd do it."

"You think it'll help?"

"Trust me, okay?"

"When you think I ought to start?"

"When it feels good, Doug."

"And when you think that'll be?"

"That's kind of up to you."

"I guess it is.

They were out of the park, halfway to town. The stores were having a half-price sale and there were people all about.

"I got to run by the courthouse," the Chief said. "Sign a bunch of stuff. You going to town or what?"

"I guess I'll head back to the house," Doug said. He didn't really want to go, and the Chief seemed to know it. He looked warmly at Doug.

"Listen, you're doing real fine," he said. "Don't think you're not. You let me know what you need. Anytime. Just ask for it and you'll get it. Look for it and you'll find what you want. All right?"

"I sure do appreciate the help," Doug said.

"You play any basketball at all? I'd guess you're a rimshot whiz."

"I played a little in school."

"Well there you are," the Chief said. He gave Doug a wink and started off, weaved quickly down the street, darted this way and that, fooled pursuers with a fake and dropped a dandy in the net.

Sure enough, the afternoon brought a pleasing summer rain that cooled the day and released the thirsty smells of dry grass and dusty streets, the thorny scents trapped within the folds of bark, the veins of leaves. The rain freed the brittle tang of books, the musty wine of old wallpaper, dinner chairs and rugs. Doug puttered about the house doing this and doing that, but when the rain began to stroke the shingle roof he retreated to the porch in the company of cats. He sat back in his rocker and watched the rain drip off the eaves, watched the birds take a bath, recalled the rains in every house where he'd lived and decided this one had to beat the others hands down.

For a while he tried to read. His attention seemed to wander off the page. Doug knew exactly who was there. Royce was still upon his mind; he had lingered since the dream the night before, tagged along throughout the day. The revival in the park had left him slightly unhinged and on the loose. Back home he recalled what he'd set out to do, which was track down Royce or find his house. He clearly hadn't reached either goal, and now the fine rain was here and he didn't want to venture out at all.

He thought about potato chips and beer. Peanuts and cheese. A person ought to have a snack to watch the rain. The idea was sound but the effort seemed immense. The rain was humming in his head. A cat slept like a stone in his lap. Cats carry feline narcosis in their eyes and they'll infect you with a look. Doug could feel nap fever in the air, knew it struck one person out of six, knew he didn't have his shots, knew the smell of bitter sage, the smell of lizards on a rock.

Long shot of desert flats, pallid strands of olive green, land bleached with summer heat. Quick cut to Mexican girl with feather eyes. Cut to hawk against the sky. Cut to Charlie Bowdrie flat and nearly dead. Surprised to find he's gutted on the ground and it doesn't hurt at all. Cut to Rudabaugh scared and heading south. All this is cable clear and Doug knows who's in the cast. Pan to the house, sable night and ochre moon. There's Royce, and all the changes in his face are complete. Doug can see him plain, see him walk in the room in the half-shadow dark, see him walk real soft with his boots in one hand with his Colt in the other. He knows what happens next, that there's little more to see, just a second of surprise and bright regret.

Well I'll be, says Doug. He puts a name to Royce, knows who he was at once, sees it all clear as day. He's got Royce flat but he isn't even close to himself. Doesn't know any more than he did. He feels sure he's done it wrong. He's fairly certain this is not the way it works.

THE HEREAFTER GANG

When he woke from his nap he felt refreshed, full of pep and revelation, full of vim and enterprise, full of harmony and zip. He had an itch to mow the lawn. Some desire to climb a pole. He couldn't wait to tell Royce he'd stumbled on a former spree.

The rain had left the day with glitter in the air, clouds painted on a set. Doug waded through the dogs with a greeting here and there. There were maybe twenty-six, but the lawn was immaculate and green, not a one had made a pyramid surprise. Walking seemed the thing on such a day. The black hog gleamed outside the gate like Montego Bay at night. He liked to ride it fine but a car seemed in the works. A classic MG in racing green. A Ferrari Berlinetti or a Porsche. Hey, a Rambler station wagon would be a kick.

As Doug turned the corner he heard the click of pruning shears and the tail of a country song. Pausing by the fence he parted thick trumpet vines and peered in. The yard was full of roses, every color in the book. White and yellow and gold and every possible shade of red. Cole Younger was on his knees in faded cutoff jeans, a shirt with the sleeves cut out and a Panama hat. He looked up and saw Doug and waved his shears.

"Why come on in if you can find the damn gate," Cole said. "It's somewhere off to your left."

Doug felt around and finally located a latch. The vines had taken over, covering the fence and running wild up the trees and over the house, a heavy green tangle everywhere except the well-kept beds of bright blooms. The house seemed Italian neofascist with a touch of river shack, but it was kind of hard to tell. Doug liked the effect, and made a mental note to start some vines of his own.

"You doing good?" Cole said.

"I'm doing fine."

"You got a worry in your head?"

"Not a one."

"Well sit and have a beer."

Cole kept working but pointed Doug toward a cooler on the porch. Doug opened a bottle and made a place for himself on the steps. The porch was full of blue tick hounds in apathetic disarray.

"There's always somethin' to do with these buggers," Cole said. "Feeding and cutting and this and that. Weeds is a lot less trouble, but you sure don't get the same effect."

"They're real nice," Doug said.

"The dark ones over there is your Margaret Thatcher reds," Cole pointed out. "Them whites is your Betty Friedan double bloom. Grew that one myself and nearly took best of show. Ol' Clay Allison faked me out with his Pat Nixon pink. That son of a bitch is a rose growin' fool. Say Doug, you're looking spry as you can be. I'd put you down at maybe twenty-two."

"Must be something in the water," Doug said.

"Well yeah I guess there is."

Doug sipped his beer and watched the dog collection breathe. There didn't seem to be a pattern. He liked the trumpet vines a lot. Humming-birds buzzed around the blooms. Doug thought about Billy Dale Hoover, who'd dreamed of training hummers to do Spad and Fokker antics at the fair. His mother likely had a point. The Hoover men had trouble getting projects off the ground.

"Cole," he said finally, "you ever go back out? You think that's something I ought to do?"

Cole answered without looking up. "I been out, sure. What I think you ought to do is what you want."

"That's what everybody says."

"Well that's the house rules. I guess you figured that one for yourself."

"I guess I did," Doug said. "Only it doesn't seem to help."

"Just give her time, Doug. Don't let it hurt your head. You feelin' good?"

"I'm feeling fine."

"Well there you go. The Chief says he seen you in the park. Said I ought to talk you up for basketball."

"I'm not much into sports."

"I can see you just streakin' down the court."

"He thinks I ought to take a class," Doug said.

"Then I would. The man won't steer you wrong."

"I don't know, maybe I better do it." Doug stood and set his empty on the porch. "I got to get unraveled if I can. I feel there's a major motion picture in my head. I don't think I know my lines. Look, I need to talk to Royce. Can you tell me where he is?"

"A block over," Cole said. "Third house on the right. You want to get into roses let me know. You might do fine with a Betty Boop red. You ever think about the dance? I bet you got ragtime in your feet."

"I bet I don't," Doug said.

"Shoot. I can see you doing a nifty buck and wing. Hummin' your favorite show tune."

"Those are real fine dogs," Doug said. "I sure thank you for the beer."

Doug said goodbye and started off to find Royce. There seemed to be great interest in the arts. Song and dance was all the rage. It didn't appeal to him at all. He remembered Mrs. Becker's School of La Dance, which was Mrs. Becker's empty front room, and you had to use the john before you came. Mothers made their kids go. The idea was to get a jump start on social grace. You had to wear a coat and tie and the girls wore pink frilly dresses and patent leather shoes. There were two maybe three pretty girls and they danced with boys they knew. The rest of the girls were fat. Every fat girl in Harding Junior High. Once a week they could breathe on a boy and they never missed a chance. Their mothers said if you can dance you'll be popular with the boys. Like a fat girl stomping across the floor is a lot more attractive than standing still. The class was full of fat boys too, hoping to meet a skinny girl, hoping Dad's Aqua Velva would do the trick. And after maybe six months of Listerine and sweaty hands, of the fox trot and the Oklahoma slide, of *La Paloma* which was Mrs. Becker's all time hit, everything was back the way it was. The kids who were going out before still went. The fat boys and girls stayed home. The boys jerked off and dreamed of Cully Jean Moon. The girls had slumber parties and danced across the floor, closed their eyes and dreamed of quarterback lust and chocolate pie, dreamed of backseat fun and Hershey bars, heard Vaughn Monroe tell them love was on the way.

Erlene liked to go out and dance but she mostly liked to sit. She didn't like to get up on the floor. What she liked was to wear tight jeans and drink beer, wink at cowboy doctors on the make, hum the music in her head, dream she was maybe Debra Winger on a spree. What Doug liked to do was stay home. Get in bed with Erlene and do the horizontal waltz. Dream she was maybe Debra Winger on a spree.

Doug wasn't sure if he'd done all this or if he'd read it in a book. It seemed to be him but maybe not.

He could hear the piano going half a block away. Chords seemed to lift on the wind and come at him through the trees, seemed to tinkle in his head and then thunder in his chest. Pausing a minute to listen, he decided he liked it fine. One of your heavy classic tunes, but it sounded real good all the same.

Walking further down the street he got another new surprise. If Cole had it right, that music was coming straight from Royce's door. Doug didn't know what to do. He stopped and studied the house. Adobe Renaissance with a touch of Norman keep. He wondered if he ought to interrupt. Maybe Royce had a high-class date. There was a girl in Tulsa got off on the theme from *Meet the Press.* He walked up and knocked. The music was so loud it hurt his head. Doug knocked again and it stopped. Royce came and peered through the screen, blinked as if he'd set some other thought aside.

"Well hey there, hoss, come on in," Royce said. "Wasn't expectin' to see you."

"I come at a bad time?"

"Not a-tall." Royce stood aside to let him by. "Understand you might go out for basketball."

"I might not," Doug said. "I don't look right in a skimpy suit." Royce looked exactly like he should. Doug could see it plain as day. He wanted to tell him right then what he knew, see how surprised he'd be.

Royce caught his look. "Now what's the matter with you?"

"Not a thing."

"I got spinach on my teeth?"

"Not a bit."

"Well come in and rest your feet."

"Boy, that's sure some stereo you got," Doug said. "You can hear it all the way down the street. I like that tune a lot." Out of the corner of his eye he caught the tail of a frock coat scrambling up the stairs, a little scent of Ovaltine, a little soot left in the air.

"Old Thack's sorta shy," Royce said, "don't take no offense."

"I sure didn't mean to run him off."

"Won't hurt a thing, it's just his way. You want some lemonade or beer, I got both."

"Beer's fine," Doug said.

Royce left for the kitchen. The shades were half drawn. Doug's eyes got used to the light. The room had limestone walls thick and cool, books scattered about the shelves, Kashan carpets on the floor, busts of Mercian kings, a stuffed Chuckwalla and a chipmunk lamp, a picture of Jane Austen in the nude. And filling one end of the room, a Steinway grand black as silk, legs carved with legends of the Utes, a case of canned peaches on the top.

Doug was taken aback, struck with sudden thought. "Hey Royce," he called out, "you play this thing? Was that a record I heard or you?"

Royce appeared with a sheepish grin. "I guess it was me. I kinda pick around some."

"Well I'll be." Doug took his beer and found a chair. "You sure do play good. Some of that stuff sounds to me like they dropped a sack of notes off a truck. But I like yours fine."

Royce sat down and ran his fingers over the keys. "I been fiddlin' with that concerto in A. That Schumann is a tricky sum'bitch. Them semiquaver notes is flat giving me a fit." He played a little more and then stood and drank his beer. "You ought to get yourself a instrument to play. There's a lot of satisfaction in a song."

"I don't think I'm up to that," Doug said.

"Well you sure don't know you ain't tried." Royce scratched his nose and gave Doug a studied look. "You feeling fine or not?"

"I'm feeling great."

"You got a ache or any pain?"

"Not a one."

"You figure you're goin' to tell me what's working in your head?"

"What do you mean?" Doug tried to look surprised. Royce wasn't buying it at all. He looked at Doug and didn't say a thing.

Doug had to grin. "I guess I had this dream."

"All right."

"It was raining and I kind of took a nap."

"Okay."

"Well I dreamed about you is what I did. I mean that's how it turned out to be. Rudabaugh and Bowdre were there. A pretty Mexican girl and a lot of other folks. I just saw the whole thing. Saw you go into Maxwell's room that night, and saw Pat Garrett there too. I knew what was going to happen and it did. Two shots ring out in the dark and that's all. Royce, I didn't mean to intrude."

Royce put down his beer and studied the floor. "Shit, Doug, if you don't beat all." His frown broke into a grin. "You ain't supposed to do *me.* You're supposed to be figuring out you.

"Well that's nothing new with me," Doug said. "I got this problem putting things the way they go. I do stuff backwards sometimes. Listen, do I call you Royce or Billy? I don't figure you like The Kid. Whichever you want's fine with me."

"Royce'll do," Royce said. "Stick to that." He looked curiously at Doug. "Hoss, you think you're gettin' anywhere close? You got to work this out. Spottin' me ain't going to help you any at all."

"I'm doing what I can," Doug said.

"You off of that serf kick or not? You want to drop this baseborn shit I'll tell you that."

"I guess I am. I'm kind of narrowed down out West."

"Glad to hear you got a start."

Doug had a thought. "You remember me at all? We might've rode the high lonesome together."

"That ain't the point, Doug."

"I guess not."

"You want another beer?"

"Listen, were you really that fast? I know a lot gets twisted in your Western tale and lore."

Royce looked tired. "You got to get through your follies and misdeeds," he told Doug. "You don't want to hang onto what's been and that's the thing. Gettin' on is where it's at."

"I guess it is," Doug said.

Royce nodded at the stairs. "If I could get that over to ol' Thack I'd have a leg on helping him over the hump. He *knows* who he is, and that's what's hanging him up. He's flat stuck. Can't get off the fence. I figure writin' that *Vanity Fair* shit's what got him hooked. Got his head swole up and he don't want to do nothing else. Your English writer fellows got some kind of bug up their ass. I seen it slow down more'n one."

Doug thought about that. He looked at the wall, at the sun making brand new patterns on the rug. "He doesn't *have* to do it, does he? I mean you and Sue Jean said it's okay to stay right here if that's what you want to do."

Royce showed Doug an easy understanding smile. "Hoss, I know that's how you see it now, you ain't hardly got your feet on the ground. And that's fine. You'll get her worked out. But old Thack, now, he knows it's time to get off the pot. He just ain't going to budge and that's that. He's a pure aggravation, and sorta being on the cusp don't help. Most of the old boys in our bunch done their minor poet thing, caught consumption or the dreads and got out. Went into Kraut flyin' or the outlaw trade, then the PR and advertisin' stuff. That's where Thack got hisself fucked up. A half-ass poet wasn't good enough for him, he had to go and write some books. Now he's got that in his craw and wants to go on back and finish up. Maybe do some night soaps or get a good movie deal." Royce shook his head and built a smoke. "See, that's the thing. You don't never finish up. It ain't the point. But old Thack can't see it."

"So what's going to happen?" Doug said.

"Something'll work out. It always does. I got a couple of thoughts on the matter if I can get Thack to listen." He looked at Doug. "You do some cogitatin' on yourself now, Doug. Don't strain your head, just let her kinda drift. I'd take me some classes if I was you."

"The Chief said he thought I should."

"The Chief's right." Royce eased himself up and showed Doug his best lop-sided grin. "I got to put in some time on the keys, you don't mind. You're welcome to sit and listen if you like, ain't trying to chase you off."

"I guess I better run along," Doug said. "You gave me a lot of stuff to think about."

Royce walked him to the door. "Like I said, just go along with it. Run down and get yourself a cone. Buy a car. It'll work itself out when it's time." He laughed aloud at Doug. "You comin' up with me, if that ain't something else. Can't wait to tell Cole. You got yourself a cock-eyed filing system, boy."

"I guess I can't help it," Doug said. "Hey, you see Pat Garrett any at all? Is he here?"

"Was," Royce said, "but he's gone back out. Him and me used to pack a lunch and fish. Go down to the creek here with Olinger and McSween. Went on to be advance man for Margaret Mead. Plays second clarinet now in an Oslo band, if I recall."

"Well I'll be," Doug said.

Outside, he walked down the street in light filtered the shade of butter through the trees, saw gold dust suspended in the air, heard Royce or Billy finger Handel's *Water Music* on the keys and wondered just how he knew that.

Doug didn't feet like going home. Boy, Royce had sure filled his head. There was stuff in there doing acrobatic pranks. Thoughts going this way and that. Frisky little East bloc cuties doing flips on a pole. He felt goofy and aslant, oddly incomplete, dizzy as a fish.

And what about this minor poet deal? He sure didn't recall being that. Which didn't mean it wasn't so, shoot how would he know? The way Royce put it that was two whole going outs back. He couldn't even figure what he'd done right before, couldn't properly recall Tuesday night.

He thought about movies on the moors. Gazing real serious out to sea. Say, that might've been a kick. Horsing around with old Leigh Hunt and Keats. Hanging out with your footpads and knaves. Some saucy little tart in the hay. Maybe go right into a faint. Fainting was okay, guys did it all the time. He sure did like those poet shirts. They billowed out good on the heath. You could think up a rhyme and look at clouds. Just sort of fuck around, do a poem now and then about sheep.

If he'd done it he'd remember some time or maybe not. Royce kept saying take it easy, let it flow. Sue Jean and Cole said it too, and he guessed that was what he ought to do. Fine, but he hoped something solid would hit him soon. It was like being part of a trapeze act, the Flying Hoovers on the road. He couldn't tell if he was swinging or in the air. He was likely that jerk just missed without a net.

Maybe he was like old Thack. On the cusp and out of whack. Daffy as a goat. He could get a frock coat and trail around after Royce. He didn't see he was much better off. What good did it do coming over standing up, if you didn't know where to hop next?

While his mind wanders off, while his wits take a hike, while his head's on an expedition somewhere round the horn, his more or less higher self gets his compass on the mark, gets his heading on the beam, makes a proper course correction to the square. Guides him to the corner and the ice cream shop and a double-dip lemon custard cone. The sweetie at the counter says he's sure looking young, dropping birthdays all the time, getting more like a sock hop rascal every day. You feeling good, she wants to know, I'm feeling fine, you got a worry in your head, not a one. Doug flips the girl a nickel and strolls away, windowshops and watches people passing by, minds the balance on his cone, licks the melt on every side, knows the act of drip confinement to a tee.

Past the square he wanders down the brick street to the far edge of town, where the paving gives way to a dusty avenue into the woods. He hears the sound of water and follows that. The creek appears through a rich green window in the trees. Looking down he sees trout against the white gravel bottom. The trout are fat as sausage in a sack. From the top their bright flanks are out of sight. Their backs are the color of old moss. Doug remembers this spot; the deep pool by the log is just ahead. A well-worn path follows the creek and he walks along the bank, watches trout dart about, watches minnows on the run, watches turtles do their submarine act. Around the bend fat Portuguese kings are still fishing up a storm. Doug waves and gets a greeting in return. Velvet pantaloons seem hot for summer wear.

The woods get deeper as he goes, a color sample book of green, the air immersed in every shade. Doug feels as if he might see a bear, Shawnees on the prowl, Jim Bridger in a tree. He feels alert and unimpaired, unaccountably aware, sly and cleverly concealed.

Further on he sees folks across the creek, RVs among the trees and a picnic table on the bank. They might be Macedonian Greeks or maybe not. Bronze seems hot for summer wear.

Doug isn't sure where he's going, but then again he is. Inner gears are on the job, a navigator's in his head. He's on the trail to class, he knows that. The multi-fractured motorcycle act very clearly knows the way, locks his rudder on the goal. He feels collectively at ease, nicely dazzled and askew, slightly crafty and perverse. The path seems to twist and curve about, lead him this way and that. He finds a bridge across the creek, wanders that way and this, finds another bridge to cross or the one he found before. The sky through the mantle overhead shows an evening streaked with gold, spread with marmalade and cream. The woods are soft with muted light, the air befogged and indistinct, maybe forty-watt vision up ahead. It can't be very far, he decides. He ought to be there soon enough.

Doug feels a little fuzzy in the head. Cicadas drone and rattle in the trees, a turtle slips into the creek. The day is hot and still, full of drowsy saturation, full of sullen green accord. He feels inclined to take a nap. Every sight and sound conspires to this event. Still, he stays upon his feet, keeps an eye peeled for intramural pranks, happy students on a spree. Instead he finds a herd of plucky Goths by the creek, stops and waves and says hello. Fur seems hot for summer wear.

As dusk lingers on, which it often seems to do, he sees a rift in the trees, spots a clearing up ahead. Now he'll see what this academic fuss is all about. He wonders if you wear a beanie cap. He breaks into a run through the last stand of trees, he imagines ivy walls and campus fun. Wonders if they've got a winning team. He leaves the woods behind, finds a too familiar scene. There's the town up ahead, there's a lemon custard puddle in the road. There's the spot he went in, and where he came out again.

This flat isn't working out at all. Your road to education's full of oak trees and trout. Folks from foreign climes. Picnics and turtles on a log. He wonders where he took a wrong turn. He figures maybe Lincoln Elementary, April 1938. If he'd gotten Miss Flood instead of Mrs. Obberdott he'd have got it all straight in his head.

The day was still on hold, the sky in its John Deere free calendar pose, when Doug made his way up the road to the square. Diehard shoppers were on the loose. Bentleys and pickups lined the curbs. He thought about a steak. Maybe fat onion rings big as baby buggy wheels. He spotted Doc Holliday, lazing on a courthouse bench. Porsche shades and jeans, a Ralph Lauren shirt, grinning at a 1937 *Fort Worth Press.* Doc saw Doug and waved him in.

"Well hi there," he said, "stop and sit. Boy, them Katzenjammer Kids is somethin' else."

"I guess they are," Doug said.

"You're sure looking young and fit. I understand you got some nifty hoopster tricks."

"I won't say I'm going to play," Doug said. "I'm not sure I've got the moves. Doc, I don't know what to do. I can't seem to get it right, I got a puzzle in my head. I can't get her into gear."

"You feeling good?"

"I'm feeling fine."

"You got a nickel in your jeans?"

"I guess I do."

"Well there you are. Sit and give it to me straight."

Doc made room on the bench. Doug sat and studied pigeons on the lawn. "I tried to find me somewhere to take a class," he told Doc. "It didn't do a lick of good. I flat wandered all over those woods. I might've heard a bear. I saw some of your historical types on the creek. I sure didn't find any school."

Doc thought about that. "Might be, Doug, that you ain't quite ready for it yet, I dunno. I mean it's something you got to really want to do. You get the proper spell in your head, why you're going to find your way through the woods."

"I think I saw this in *Snow White,"* Doug said.

"Say, them dwarves is a caution."

"Well I sure looked, I know that," Doug said. "Everybody says I ought to get in a class, well fine. I can't do it if I can't find where they hid the school." Doug slumped on the bench. "Royce and Sue Jean say I ought to play it slow. Just let it kind of simmer till it's done. I been doing that too, only nothing seems to work. Doc, I tried to let her flow and get a line on me. What I did was dig Royce up instead."

Doc slapped his knee and laughed. "Blew the Kid's cover, did you? Well I'll be. Can't wait to tell Boelcke and Sam Bass."

"I can't even figure that," Doug said. "Shoot, everything's over my head. Why didn't I know Royce was Billy right off? I knew you and Cole and about everyone else."

"Don't work that way," Doc said.

"Well why not?"

"Your escort types has got to play it real cool on the job, that's the rules. You got your recollection post-lag factor after that. The Kid and Sue Jean was who you asked to pick you up."

"I don't recall doing that, I guess I did."

"You ain't supposed to get everything at once," Doc said in a kindly tone. "I figure that's what you're trying to do."

"I guess I am."

"You feelin' trim?"

"I'm in the pink."

"You got a beer in the fridge?"

"I got a case."

"Well there you go. You shouldn't ought to let this shit hurt your head. You come over standin' up, you're doing fine."

"I guess I am."

"Just let her slide, boy."

Doug thought about a beer and wished he had one now. That and a piece of cherry pie. The sunset had decided to call it quits. The sky was edging into mulberry dark.

"Doc," he said finally, "I suppose you've been back out, too. Most everybody has."

"I done my share," Doc said.

"You like it all right?"

"Some's a pain in the ass. Some's as fine as ice cream."

"See that's the thing," Doug said. "I like it fine right here. I got a house and lots of dogs. I got a bunch of model planes I want to do. I'm not hot to leave town."

"You don't have to do a thing."

"Sure, that's what I hear," Doug said, "only everyone else has got the bug. Shoot, my mother's into state politics. I don't think she'll take to hotels."

"Now you can't ever tell."

"That woman won't eat a bite on the road. Doc, I'll tell you this. Being Doug Hoover's flat all I can handle. I can't figure who I was, and I'm not real crazy about who I'm going to be. I've been hearing lots of stuff. There's dance and music in the air. I got strong misgivings on that."

"I see you doing clarinet riffs," Doc said. "I bet you got the knack."

"I bet I don't," Doug said. "I don't feel I got a muse. I don't have the itch to tap. I sure don't see me in your woodwinds and brass."

"Just take her as she comes," Doc said. "I'd like to see you suit up. Shoot the melon down the court. Get your Nikes on the move."

"I don't know, I guess I might."

"You stop by the Pronghorn tonight we'll sign you up. You into comic books at all? I got a entire collection at the house. I got *Action* and *Marvel* both, number one. That Human Torch is a whiz. I got the first *Donald Duck.* Bruce Wayne's folks was foully slain when he was ten. That's what got him on a Batman kick."

"I'd like to see 'em," Doug said.

"Well you drop on by when you can."

Doug got to his feet and Doc rose to shake his hand, sat back down with the *Fort Worth Press.* Laughed aloud and shook his head. "That Little Orphan Annie is a curly-head scamp. You ever get your own mug?"

"I think I did," Doug said.

It was almost night when he walked by the park. He saw the tent was gone, and decided that the walkers found the navigation problem too immense.

By the time he reached home the day had yielded to the night, bringing dark-time flavors into play. The earth released its summer spice in collusion with the tannic brew of cottonwood and oak, hickory and pecan. Doug could smell the honeysuckle fragrance in the air, moonvine and hyacinth and blooms he couldn't name. And overwhelming all the rest, a scent of stupefying girth, a diabetic overdose, a floral tide that choked the air. He knew Cole's Rose Bowl parade was blocks away, firmly seated in the ground; still he wondered if they might have gotten loose to take a stroll.

A car he didn't know was parked beside the gate, a brand new '48 Ford, a slick two-door with wire wheels, wicker trunk on the back, plaid seats and chamois dash, a chrome Andy Gump on the hood. Doug maneuvered through the dogs. He could smell fried chicken inside, hear it singing on the stove. The house was dark except for yellow country light, and he wandered through its tunnel to the end.

Sue Jean heard him and turned from the stove. "Well hi there, hon, what you say?"

She came to him for a hug, skinny in a man's dress shirt that hung halfway to her knees. Her hair was pulled up in a knot and he tasted sweet and sour on her neck. Salt and shampoo. Chicken and 7-Up.

Doug held her off and looked. "Say, I like that outfit fine. You got something on underneath?" He grabbed to find out and she hopped out of reach.

"I'm readin' some sexual innuendo into this," Sue Jean said.

"You're a scamp is what you are. You look like a deb who's got the weekend off."

"I guess I do. You want to try this chicken out or not? I got gravy and biscuits and iced tea."

Doug sat and watched her move, still taken with her high school charm. He felt inclined to some backseat offense, some drive-in Saturday night lark. Sue Jean took a chair and spooned sugar in her tea. She found a sprig of mint fully houseplant size and dunked it in, took a sip and grinned at Doug through the brush.

"I feel a Jap sniper on the loose," Doug said.

"I doubt that's a deb thing to do."

"I've known one or two. Coming out in Waxahachie's not the same as your back East romp. Hey, does that car out front belong to you? It's sure a beaut."

"Picked it up this afternoon," Sue Jean said. "I'm a fool for classic lines. I got tradition in my genes. You ought to get yourself some wheels."

"I might do a Rolls or a Nash," Doug said, "I don't know."

"I kind of see you in a Cord. Maybe Del Monte green. 'Bout thirty-two coats hand polished by a craftsman from the Saar."

"I like the sound of that," Doug said, reaching for a second piece of breast. He went at the chicken with a surgeon's art and zeal, getting all the crust first and then the skin, finally working on the white, dabbing extra honey and pepper on the meat.

"We ought to do Szechuan some time," he said. "I run a pretty mean wok."

"You think you're good, huh?"

"I can do a hot duck'll make you quack."

Sue Jean seemed impressed. "Lord, I'm a fiend for spicy Chink. I might trade my maiden goods for Kung Po."

"Shoot, let's get at it."

"Let's see the duck first," Sue Jean said. "I been taken on a Hunan ride once or twice."

He helped her clear the table and put the dishes in to soak. The cat squad crowded in for treats. The kitchen was the way Doug liked to see it best, oilcloth and kerosene light, an aftersmell island in the dark. Sue Jean lit a ciggie, and Doug heated coffee on the stove.

"Now that was a fried chicken feast," he said, filling both their cups. "If you want, why I'll do wok magic tomorrow night."

"Get your stuff down at Mao's by the creek," Sue Jean said. "He's got some fresh ginger won't quit."

"Then I'll do it first thing. Your virtue's good as gone. I'll have you on the mat by the egg drop soup."

"We'll see if you do or not."

Doug didn't care for any reference to the creek. It brought his disappointing trek back to mind. He wasn't sure what to say to Sue Jean. It might be good to put it off. He felt lazy and content. Absorbed by the after-dinner scene. There was no good reason to fuck it up, bring his boy scout antics to the light, so he spilled the whole thing then and there.

"Sue Jean, I got it in my mind to go to class," he said at once. "I didn't get anywhere at all. I had me a good nature walk is what I did."

"So I hear," Sue Jean said.

"You mean you know?" Doug wasn't pleased with this at all. "Well that's just fine. That annoys me good, you know that? I guess you got a extra sense perception in your head."

"I guess I got a call from Doc at the square," Sue Jean said. "Told me that you might be in a snit."

"He sure is right about that," Doug said. He burned his mouth on the coffee and set it down. "Doc said I maybe wasn't ready. That I might need a Walt Disney spell."

"Doug, he didn't say any such thing." Sue Jean tried to look patient. "He said you had to *feel* that's what you want to do."

"Well then I guess I don't. I sure didn't find any school. I found a lot of guys could use a good men's store. Sue Jean, that's the thing. If I did find the place, why I wouldn't even know what to take. My mother's into ceramics and martial arts. I don't care a thing about that."

"She isn't doing that stuff at the school," Sue Jean said. "We're not talking handicrafts."

"Well then what?"

"Things you need to know."

"Things I need to know."

"That's right."

"Well fine. That sure clears it up, Sue Jean. Thanks a lot."

Sue Jean got up and found a biscuit on the stove, took a bite and perched on the counter and crossed her arms. "What it is, Doug, is you. Up close and personal. That's what class is all about. Who you are, and what you want to do with yourself."

"Good," Doug said, "I can save a lot of time and stay home. I know about forty-three things I want to do. I want to catch some more fish. I want to do Kraut fighters on a thirty-second scale. I want to get some good ivy on the house. How many's that?"

Sue Jean let out a sigh. "Doug, you *think* that's what you want to do, and I guess maybe it is right now. Only that's not all there is to it."

"Not all there is to what?"

"To what I said."

"And what's that?"

Doug seemed perplexed and out of gear. She caught confusion in his eyes. Dropped off the counter and went to perch in his lap.

"Hon, just get it all out of your head now, you hear?" Sue Jean said. "You're doin' good. Isn't any need to push."

"I don't feel like I'm doing good at all."

She kissed him on the cheek. "Hey now, you sure pulled a fast one on Royce."

"You're changing the subject, Sue Jean."

"I'm not doing any such thing. That's what I mean, babe. You're flat comin' up on it. You're kinda tacking across the course, but that's fine. I figure sideways to east is your natural born bent."

"I was kind of embarrassed about Royce," Doug said.

"You don't need to be at all."

"You sure don't weigh a whole lot."

"I guess I don't."

"I sort of thought me coming up with him was some kind of intrusion at the time," Doug said. He watched a cat slick leftover chicken off the stove. "Royce is all worked up about Thack."

"I know," Sue Jean said.

"I wish there was something I could do."

"You're his friend. That's what he needs most now. The Kid'll work it out all right."

"I guess maybe I'm worried that he will," Doug said.

Sue Jean gave him a look. "Now what's that supposed to mean?"

Doug wasn't sure himself. "I don't know. It's just something working in my head."

"Well you got enough in there without addin' something else."

"I guess I do."

"You feeling good?"

"I'm feeling fine."

"You full of chicken up to here?"

"I couldn't eat another bite."

"Well there you are." Sue Jean got up and took his hand and led him out past the light to the porch. The trees seemed overwhelming in the dark. Insects were out on a dozen lively gigs. Dixieland jazz in the hickory by the fence. Bug progressive in the oak.

"You want to walk up to the Pronghorn or not?" Sue Jean said.

"I'd just as soon stay here," Doug said.

"Well then, that's what we'll do."

Doug settled in on the daybed, stuffing soft pillows to the wall. Sue Jean went back for a cherry 7-Up then scooted out a place by his side. All about the house, cats sensed a sleepfest in the works and hurried in to find a place.

"Everything except here doesn't seem like it ever was at all," Doug said. "I try to think about Erlene and Pastor Jack and Sarah Dee, and Sunny D'Angelo and Ham. Going to work at Clinton-Fevre. None of that seems to matter anymore."

"I don't guess it does," Sue Jean said.

"Meeting Royce and finding you at Mary Anne's, then picking you up on the road. That seems real to me." Doug leaned up on one arm and looked at Sue Jean in the dark. "Doc says it was me figured all that out. Everything that happened. You and Royce coming out to bring me in. I don't recall doing that at all. I don't remember being here before or who I was."

"That'll all come to you, hon."

"I guess it will." Doug put a finger on her nose. "I pinned down old Billy. Might be I'll come up with you too."

"You think so, huh?"

"I just might."

Sue Jean gave him a Tennessee stare. "You just *might* try and get your ownself straight, Doug Hoover. You ain't on a daytime quiz. The idea's to figure you, not everyone in town."

"You said take it easy, let her flow. That's just what I'm doing, Sue Jean, shoot I'm flowing all I can."

"You might ought to check those pipes," Sue Jean said. "I don't see nothing coming through."

"Well I can't help that."

"I guess you can't, babe."

"I haven't got some real big incentive, you want to know," Doug said. "The more I find out about me, the closer I'm going to get to the Budapest string quartet."

Sue Jean grinned and offered a 7-Up kiss. "You don't want to worry 'bout that."

"Well I do. I can't help it. I don't want to be that or a tap dance whiz. I haven't got any music in my head. Maybe everyone else has got the restless urge to waltz but I don't."

"Doug, you don't have to do a thing."

"That's what I hear, all right. What I see is the Kid going at those ivories like a fiend. Everybody hummin' on a tune. Boelcke says he loves the tarantella, and Sundance is into ballet. I suppose you're headed for a brass quintet."

"I think I got a bass cello in my soul."

"That figures," Doug said.

"You going out for basketball? I hear you're a slam dunk marvel on the court."

"I might suit up, I don't know," Doug said. "I'm not sure I got the reach."

Doug dreams of the horse General Shelby rode to war. He dreams of a girl with blue eyes. He dreams of a hollow, smells dew and gunpowder in the air, sees a bug that a bullet cut in two, sees a boy lying still without any eyes at all. The boy has the look of Pennsylvania in his hair, in the bones about his face. His soldier blue coat is hardly stained, his gun is propped neat across his knees as if he set it there to rest. Doug dreams of clay hills, riding fast through the night, making coffee in the rain, eating biscuits on the run. Dreams of gnats in his mouth, dreams of gravel in his teeth, thinks he maybe knows his name.

Then his engine slips a gear, knocks him squarely off his course, lets him flounder out to sea, takes a Krazy Kat encyclopedic fix. Now he sees that the sea bass can fertilize itself, that Hitler peed in the shower all the time. That John W. "Bet-a-Million" Gates made a killing in the barbed wire trade, and Plastic Man swings either way. Charlie Brown smokes pot. The bay scallop has several rows of pretty blue eyes. Napoleon's dick sold for nearly four grand. Oola gave Alley Oop the clap. The Western ground gecko has eighty-six orgasms every time it mates but doesn't have the sense to know it. Doug Hoover hasn't any idea who he is.

THE HEREAFTER GANG

They held the big game on an open-air court out back of the Pronghorn Saloon. Doug suited up under protest, mostly to please Cole Younger, who'd made a big thing out of bringing new athletic wear by the house. The uniform was two shades of blue, symbolic, Cole explained, of the skies over Ypres and Amarillo. Sue Jean said he looked real cute. Doug said he looked like a jerk. She could call it a basketball suit if she liked, it was still blue underwear that grabbed him in the crotch.

"Shoot, you're going to score real big," Sue Jean said, "you wait and see. I'm expecting major shots down the court. The crowd's on their feet, they're flat comin' unglued."

"I might stay home and watch the tube," Doug said.

"I might bean you with a Delaware Punch."

"They got a Nina Foch filmfest going, Sue Jean. I had the hots for her in Harding Junior High."

"You had the hots for Minnie Mouse," Sue Jean said. "Get those deviled eggs out of the fridge."

Doug helped her fill the picnic basket, a job that took his mind off looking like a jockey short ad. Sue Jean had made sure they wouldn't starve, since they'd likely be gone the afternoon. Potato salad and Danish ham. Peanut butter and champagne. Sweet pickles and 7-Up. Lime marmalade and ribs. Fritos and lemon chess pie. Doug fed the cats and dogs, loaded up the '48 Ford. The Pronghorn wasn't that far, but he told Sue Jean they had too much to carry on foot.

"You're afraid folks'll see you in your suit," Sue Jean said.

"You got it," Doug said.

"That's the dumbest thing I ever heard."

"I had a dream last night but I didn't get a thing. It started off good then my wheels went off the track."

"You'll get there, babe, wait and see."

"There's a lot we don't know about your lizards of the West."

"Is that a fact."

"They're missing out on bedtime delight. The gecko doesn't know if he's any good or not. I don't know about snakes. I've seen 'em do it on *Nova,* but you can't tell if they're having any fun. Boy I would if it was me. I'd be a diamondback stud, I'd be a cottonmouth rake."

"Just drive," Sue Jean said.

Doug didn't like the look of things at all. Long before they reached the site he could see there'd be a crowd. The road was full of Greeks, Portuguese kings and Polish nuns, Zulus and Mormon CPAs. Everyone on the creek was out in force and they'd all be looking right at him. Doug Hoover the underwear whiz. Well they couldn't make him do it, he didn't have to play. He'd sit and eat his picnic lunch and tell Cole he'd sprained his knee.

"Don't even think about it, hon," Sue Jean said, without looking from the road. "Just find a place to park. It was your idea to bring the car."

"The athletic program here is out of hand," Doug said.

"I'd talk to the Chief if I was you."

"Yeah, right."

"You're going to do just fine, you're going to dunk that melon in the tub."

"I'm going to look like Goofy in my shorts."

"You're going to look like lightnin' on a stick," Sue Jean said. "Now just hush." She leaned in and kissed his cheek. Doug parked and got out, retrieved the picnic basket from the trunk. He couldn't see the court for the crowd. Booths were set up all about, and two or three bands played at once. It looked more like a fair than a basketball game, but everyone seemed to like it fine.

"What it is," Doug said, catching up with Sue Jean, "I'm not into your contact sports. I don't care for that locker room stuff. I don't like to shower down with guys. I'm not too fond of smelly socks."

"You got a attitude problem's what you got," Sue Jean said. "You got a pre-game fidget in your head. You hear that crowd you're going to swing, you're going to snap into line."

Doug didn't try to answer that. Sue Jean made her way through a pack of Hittite youths, ghetto blasters going full. Doug noticed there were no chairs or bleachers at the court; the crowd spread their blankets on the grass, walked and talked, sang and danced, watched their dogs and cats cavort. People washed their cars on the road. Couples wandered off in the trees. A man wrestled with a pig.

No one appeared to watch the game, which was clearly underway. Doug stopped to look and saw the other team wore purple and olive green, peach-colored Nikes and avocado socks. He began to feel good about blue.

"Lord, look at that," Sue Jean cried, pointing at the court. "Go get 'em, Mannie, go!"

Von Richthofen raced down the court, faked to Udet, turned and shot the ball hard to Cole Younger who dropped it in with ease.

"We got the *team,"* yelled Sue Jean, "we got the *guys,* we're going to poke 'em in the *eyes!"*

"Yeah, great," Doug said.

Sue Jean spread her blanket near a mixed bag of Lombards and Franks. Doug felt a surge of team spirit or maybe not. He was annoyed and relieved. Pleased and out of sorts. They'd gone ahead without him, didn't need him there at all. Well, fine. He could sit and eat a rib, wouldn't work up a sweat, wouldn't have to run around like a fool.

Sue Jean had struck up a conversation with a Frank in yellow tights and a feather in his cap. He leaned in close and whispered something in her ear. Sue Jean laughed aloud. The Frank sneaked a look at her legs. He traded Sue Jean a jug of wine for two diet 7-Ups.

"Well who's that?" Doug said.

"He's a guy from down the creek," Sue Jean said, "I think I got an awful good wine."

"That's great."

"You want to try a little slug?"

"No I don't."

"Just what is eatin' you, hon?"

"Not a thing. I'm just as fine as I can be."

"Doug, will you behave? They are real nice fellas and as smart as they can be. There ain't a thing they don't know about tax law and fur."

"I'd like a peanut butter if you got it," Doug said. "If you haven't traded that off, too."

"They're right here and just hush. Isn't anyone likes an old grump."

Doug bit into a sandwich and tried to watch the game. The purple team started down the court. Charlie Pierce stole the ball, passed it off to Bitter Creek Newcomb who worked his way quickly past a guard, then tossed to Werner Voss beneath the net. The other team seemed confused and out to lunch. Voss caught the ball in midair and dunked it in. Doug felt depressed. Cheerfully deranged. He didn't like the game at all, wouldn't play it on a bet. If they begged he wouldn't budge.

Doug smelled barbecued shrimp and saw some whalers had a small hibachi going to his right. They seemed to be working things out with some pretty Mayan girls. There were sure a lot of people on the creek. It must be hard to keep them straight. There were probably a lot of other squares, a lot of other courthouses stacked full of heavy record books.

"Shoot, boy, you goin' to eat all day or get your tennies on the court? You need to get that uniform wet."

Doug came out of his thoughts to find Boelcke standing above, grinning and toweling off his face.

"Well, yeah," Doug said, "I guess I can. Hadn't anybody asked. I figured you were all full up."

Boelcke laughed and took a cold Dr Pepper from Sue Jean. "This ain't exactly your NBA playoff hit. You want to play you go in. You want to leave and take a piss you go out. Get on your feet, sport. I want to see them magic fingers dance."

Doug grinned like a fool. "Why I'll sure give her a try."

"Go get 'em, hon," Sue Jean said, and sent him off with a kiss.

Doug followed Boelcke on the court. "Hey, it looks like we're doing all the good. I'd say we're really on the run."

"We're doin' fine."

"Who's the other team, I don't guess I even know."

"Them Berbers and some Teutonic knights," Boelcke said. "They don't know shit but they're a good bunch of guys. Put it to 'em, son." He slapped Doug on the butt and disappeared.

Doc Holliday winked at Doug and tossed the ball right into his hands. Doug came in low beneath the net and scored at once. The purples got the ball and couldn't get it down the court. Max Immelmann dribbled fast to Tom Horn. Horn passed to Tulsa Jack Blake, Blake to von Richthofen who poked one in off the rim. Doug missed once and scored three more times. The game seemed casual at best. There weren't any coaches he could see, no benches or officials and no way to really tell the score. Players wandered in and out. At one time there were only three members on his team, twelve on the other side. Then the balance seemed to shift and there were seventeen blues on the court, as the Berbers made a rush on the snowcone stand leaving only two purples in to play.

Doug felt elated. Dizzy as a duck. Sue Jean met him with a hug. "Lord, hon, I'm so proud I could bust. You washed 'em out and flat hung them out to dry."

"I guess I did."

"You're a hoopster and a half, you're a killer on the court. Listen, Royce came by, he wants to see you if he can. He was going to be over by the road." Sue Jean seemed to hesitate some. "I think you ought to talk to him, babe."

"Is something wrong?"

"Not a thing."

"Are you sure?"

"Sure as rain."

"I'll go and see," Doug said, and picked a sticker off his shoe.

"Get me a couple of those corn dogs, hon, and a Nehi Orange if you can.

"I'll sure do it," Doug said, and started off through the crowd. It felt good to wear the blue, folks could tell he was a jock, they could see he'd made the team. He walked as casually as he could, he looked alert and self-assured, he looked thoughtful and intense. He looked as if he might just hook another long one off the boards.

He passed some airline stews and Persian guards, he passed some Amish fry cooks and Turkish cops. The lines were long at every food and drink stand. There were handy nickel barrels placed about. He decided to go and find Royce first and try again.

Doug saw a girl he thought he knew. T-shirt and shorts. A twitch-butt cutie on the run. He looked again and she was gone, swallowed up in the crowd. Moving on he saw her image in his head, saw a walk that made him shake, saw a hipbone razzle dazzle slide that made him weak, saw a motion that defied the rules of heat and sweet abrasion, broke the laws of thermal bliss. It couldn't be and yes it could. Turning back he ran through the crowd where he'd seen her disappear. Past the hot dog stand and a place that sold balloons, past the saltwater taffy and an apple on a stick. He finally saw her by the ice cream stand, doing battle with an Eskimo Pie. Doug's heart took a leap. Oh, Lord, it was Cully Jean Moon, the queen of Harding Junior High, there was no mistaking that! Those fuzzy green eyes, that saucy little mouth, that Oklahoma sweetie pelvic thrust that had driven Herb Tarchek from soothead to wealth and carnal cheer.

Doug rallied junior high courage and walked up to say hello, sauntered up and said, "Hi there, Cully Jean Moon, remember me?"

Cully Jean's tilty eyes took him in, searched her cookie data bank, put a smile upon her face. "Well I'll be, Dougie Hoover, is that you? Why it is for a fact." She gave him a hug and a chocolate cold kiss, poked Riviera pears in his chest. "I heard you were here, I didn't know just where."

"Right here in town," Doug said with a grin.

"They said you came over standing up."

"I guess I did."

"You want to walk around and talk?"

"I sure do."

"You want an Eskimo Pie?"

"I think I will."

Doug got himself an ice cream and a spare for Cully Jean. They walked along through the crowd taking in the sights and sounds. He bought Cully Jean a fat pink stuffed bear, had a thought about that, and got another one to take to Sue Jean.

Cully Jean was as nice as she could be, considering she spoke to maybe two or three guys in ninth grade, Doug Hoover not being one of these.

"You look nice in your uniform," she said. "I wish I could've got to see you play."

"Sports is where it's at," Doug said, "I kinda like to keep fit."

"Well isn't that the truth."

"It's a way of life with me."

"I ought to keep myself in trim. I think maybe volleyball's my game."

"Why shoot, Cully Jean, I'd say you stay in shape just fine," Doug said. "You look as slick as you can be."

"That's nice of you to say, it really is." She gave him a Cully Jean smile that broke his knees.

"You've grown up some but I'd know you in a wink. You're still a honey and a half."

"I sorta like twenty-six. I might do it for a while."

"I sure think you should," Doug said, "it suits you fine. Do you live nearby, are you anywhere close?"

"Just across the creek, down a ways," said Cully Jean. "I'm with a pearl-divin' bunch and some actuary folks."

"Well I'll say. And which one of those were you?"

"Dougie, I don't even know," Cully Jean gave a sigh. "I'm trying to get it straight but I'm having me a time."

"Is that the truth?" Doug stopped and put a hand on her arm. "Cully Jean, it's the same way with me. I think I'm on the track and then I'm not."

Cully Jean laughed. "Well I guess I'm not the only one around. You reckon everyone from Harding Junior High is kinda slack? You think we're pokey on the draw?"

"We might've got a overdose of Gru Hackley and his Silver Moon band."

"The Black Hotel!" said Cully Jean.

"The Skirvin Tower!" said Doug.

"String of Pearls!" said Cully Jean.

"Ghost Riders in the Sky!" said Doug.

They strolled along holding hands, happy days in their heads, good times that seemed Technicolor bright and not ever black and white. Doug hoped Sue Jean didn't pop right up behind a tree. She likely wouldn't care, but you couldn't carve hillbilly logic on a rock. She might pick it up and kind of toss it at your head.

He liked to hear Cully Jean walk, liked to hear her motor hum, liked to listen to the sweet lubrication in her stride. There weren't that many fine cookies in the bin, and Cully Jean was a prize macaroon. The fact that she'd never looked him squarely in the eye, never given him a glance, never given him the proper time of day made her something special, too.

"You ever get together with Clayton Ricks?" Doug asked. "I kind of figured you two would make a pair. High school sweethearts and on to wedded fun."

"Fun was all there was," said Cully Jean, "and that went sorta flat. Clayton Ricks and that Tonto sidekick of his Harley Fish got a motorcycle shop. I think they both might've done a little time. There was talk of stolen parts, maybe carburetor coke. My folks sent me off up to Smith. That place is something else I'll tell you that. It isn't Oklahoma a-tall. Those girls were either skinny or they was fat. I don't guess they ever saw a *Vogue* fashion magazine 'cause they all wore Keds and campin' gear. My roommate was taking Old Norse. Had a picture of Hitler by her bed. I was 'bout the only girl there had given any thought to tits. I gave those Harvard boys a fit. Took my junior year abroad where I met a German count and got married right off. That didn't work at all. He was into those Borzoi dogs and wanted me to have some pups. I flat took off with a sack of Nazi gold. Set myself up in Paris, France, and got to be a major high fashion queen. You might've seen me in an ad. I had money in the bank and a villa down in Cannes. Two or three of your white Rolls cars. I did a movie down in Nice, I went to parties on a yacht. Went through Arabs and Swiss banking dudes like minnows through a net. Shoot, those fellas wouldn't let me alone. They'd never seen an Oklahoma girl and I drove 'em up the wall. I met a British Labor leader and a Czech athlete. Neither one had a dime but they were both kinda cute. Begged me to marry, and I said I wouldn't have them either one. Said I didn't need that, said the single life was fine enough for me. So they took off together and left me flat. Stole everything I had. I 'bout starved for a while and had to take up hooking on the side. Made all my money back in maybe eight weeks time and got a plane back to Oklahoma fast. Married the first guy I met hadn't ever eaten a snail. Turned out he had oil and real estate. Turned out he knocked me up on the plane to Cozumel. Left me swellin' on an Amarillo ranch and took off to find some oil. I saw him about every fiscal quarter when he dropped in to drink and wreck the house. Like it was me personal done the windfall profit tax to screw up his life. When the baby came he flew into town to say hello, found I had a girl and flew out. I learned about then he was humping this girl geologist looked kinda like Nixon in drag. I think she might've gone to Smith. Well I didn't say a thing. I mean, what was I going to do? I had a kid to raise and no means of support besides him. There I was in Amarillo. I got a stack of magazines and a cable TV. I got cars in the garage which I'm not allowed to drive. I got whatever house money this jerk decides to send.

"One day this fella shows up says he wants to mow the lawn. He's your Tom Cruise type only grown up nice with little lines around his eyes. He mows the lawn and leaves and comes back the next week and mows again. He clips the hedges up good and we kid and joke around. He treats me real fine and says yes ma'am a lot and pretty soon he's coming in for iced tea. And pretty soon after that we're going at it on the laundry room floor. Well I don't see the harm in this at all and he doesn't even charge me for the grass. He says it's sure been good and he'll drop by Tuesday if I like. I say that'll be fine and I'm happy as a clam. I got me a man and I'm comin' back to life. I can hardly wait the week, I'm gettin' randy as a bear. When Tuesday rolls around I hear a knock and I'm running to the door. I'm wearin' something black comes up to here. Well that's when I see my luck hasn't turned at all. Instead of that good-looking boy I got a three-piece lawyer in a hat. He says get packed up and take the kid. You don't live here anymore, here's a ticket for the bus. Who says, I want to know, and the lawyer says your husband, that's who. Sign here unless you'd like a real messy-type divorce. I got a videotape and you're the star.

"Well I knew right off it's that girl oil seeker set me up but there's nothing I can do. Monday I'm a oil baron wife. Tuesday night I'm on a Greyhound bus. Thursday afternoon I'm slinging hash in Fort Worth and shacked up with a rodeo clown. That lasts about a week before he slips out of town and I'm stuck with the trailer park rent. It kinda goes downhill after that."

Cully Jean paused, and finished off her Eskimo Pie. "I'll tell you what, Doug. Being flat out lovely's got a price. It hadn't all been a cup of tea. There's times I kinda wished I had a zit, a little pimple on my ass, but that never was to be. Shoot, I was a stunner to the end. And I raised a daughter that was prettier than me.

"She's a sweetie, all right," Doug said before he thought, and tried not to look at Cully Jean.

But Cully Jean just smiled and said, "Doug, why I bet you saw my girl with old Herb. Now don't they make a fine pair?"

Doug was surprised to say the least. "You mean you know about that?"

"Well of course I do, Doug," said Cully Jean, "Lord, what kind of mother you think I am? What happened is I saw this picture in a *Forbes* magazine one day and said, that's Herb Tarchek himself, I do believe. I was working for a dog and cat vet and had a beauty shop job on the side. I was drinking quite a bit but it didn't cloud my head. I saw this picture and it came to me, Doug, like a vision on a TV show. I sat down right then and got a letter off to Herb. I knew that's what I had to do. It wasn't but a week before he showed up at the door, had a car outside 'bout half a block long. I said, Herb, I don't know how you did it but you did. It's clear you found your wits somewhere and made it big. I'm down on my luck and I can't see it picking up fast. I got a girl thirteen now, Herb, and if she stays here with me she's got a future like a flat 7-Up. You mooned after me from first grade and misery's all you ever got. This child's going to look like me, and that's trouble and a half. I want you to take her, and see she gets raised up right. I don't want a thing for myself. I just want your promise that you won't ever touch her till she's grown. Just promise me that and you got a Cully Jean. 'I promise,' Herb said, and that's all he ever spoke. He took my girl right then and that was that. Doug, I knew I'd done the right thing. I knew he'd worship that girl and she wouldn't come to harm. I watched them drive off and got a drink. And then I guess another after that. When the bottle got done, I walked down the street to stock up and got struck unawares by a yellow Reo truck."

"Well I'll be," Doug said. "Was it one of those high-cab diesels do you think?"

"It might've been," said Cully Jean.

"So what you think you want to do next?"

"My bunch is heavy into wild game and fish," said Cully Jean. "It looks like forest work for me."

"I might go into brass or modern dance," Doug said.

"Well that's just as fine as it can be. I expect you'll be a hit, why I'll bet you're goin' to swing."

"I guess I will," Doug said, "or maybe not."

"You hang in there, love," said Cully Jean, "and come and see me when you can." She kissed him real nice and walked away, and Doug watched her disappear, watched her heels and little toes, watched her sleek and racy lines, watched the happy oscillation of her shorts. He tried to remember where he was, tried to figure out his name.

Sue Jean was packing up, tossing picnic goodies on the run, missing seven out of ten, mostly shaking up a storm. The Lombards and Franks had broken into martial chant and Sue Jean had caught the beat, had the top forty ballads on the run.

"Well hi," Sue Jean said, giving Doug a bawdy wink, "come over here and jive, hum a tune, fling a ditty in the air."

"I don't think I got the knack," Doug said.

"I bet you got a cantata in your head."

"Did we win?" Doug said. "What's the score?" No one seemed to notice that the teams were off the court.

"Beats me," Sue Jean said. "I expect we whipped 'em good. A bunch of Brits from the Anti-Corn League and some Jap dental types flung a challenge in our face. We're going to play them next week."

"Why we'll pin them to the floor."

"We'll flat wipe 'em out."

"Say, I brought you a bear," Doug said.

"Why that's real sweet of you, hon. Where's my corn dogs and my orange?"

"Oh Lord, I flat forgot."

"Uh-huh I guess you did. From what I could see she's a cutie and a half."

Doug felt slightly out of synch. "I guess you mean Cully Jean. She's a real old friend from way back."

"You got any old friends without tits?"

"I guess I don't."

"Did you ever find the Kid?"

"I didn't see him anywhere."

"Did you look?"

"Not a lot."

"Shoot, Doug Hoover, you're a world-class mess," Sue Jean said, "you know that?"

"I guess I do," Doug said.

He thought about fat Nancy Lash who went out with Harley Fish. She likely didn't get to Europe like Cully Jean Moon or meet a count. She might've got to Baton Rouge or maybe not. A person was a lot better off not knowing where they wouldn't get to go or where they would. If Cully Jean had sought a higher education in the state instead of running off to Smith, she wouldn't have gotten caught in that lawnmowing deal. She might not have had a daughter looked just like her. And Herb would've spent his whole life shaking lint and getting smart, and still never got a Cully Jean. Boy, you sure couldn't ever tell. Life could pitch a curve any time, and you didn't even have to be at bat.

Doug called the Kid at home that night, when he and Sue Jean got back from the game. No one answered and he called until it got pretty late. Thack was likely there, but Doug knew he wouldn't pick up the phone. After breakfast next morning, after Sue Jean got off to class, after Doug fed the cats and all the dogs, he walked over to the house. Royce's pickup was gone, but he knocked on the door just the same. Thack was inside; Doug could hear him spooking about from room to room, see him peeking out the shades.

"Tell Royce I came by," Doug called out, and started off up the street. Royce would get the message or maybe not. Doug wasn't sure how the two communicated, since he'd never heard Thack say a word. Maybe Thack talked when no one else was around. Maybe they wrote a lot of notes.

The day was looking fine, cool and green, working up to lazy hot, the seasons stuck nicely on the dial between spring and summer fun. Doug walked toward the square in case Royce had gone to town. The square seemed empty, sleepy and serene. Everyone who'd come for the game had gone home. A few shoppers were about, and some couples on the courthouse lawn. Doug checked the cars by the curbs. The pickup wasn't there, so he walked along the street, did some shopping in the stores. He bought a Kashan rug like the one at Royce's place. He bought a *Collier's* magazine for August 1946. He bought a Behringer bicycle with big red reflectors on the back, twin foxtails on the bars. He bought some red hots and Three Musketeers. He bought a Prince tennis racket and some balls, a Patek Phillipe silver Donald Duck watch. He bought some sherry and some wine and a case of Grapette. He bought an Acme Queen Cathedral Gong Clock with a nifty bronze rider on the top. He was taken by a fine set of Baccarat Ovaltine mugs, and picked up a box or two. They had Annie and Sandy, Punjab and the Asp, and Daddy Warbucks etched upon the sides.

When he was done he had a load he couldn't budge. He figured this was as good a time as any for a car. Down the street he bought a brand new five cent '37 Cord. Turtle green with a zippy rag top, white sidewalls and a chrome hula girl on the hood. Folding down the top he put his stuff in the back then drove past the square and out of town. Driving seemed a good idea; he didn't want to go home until he tracked down Royce. Doug felt a little bad about missing him at the game. The Kid didn't go in for much talk. He wouldn't have left word with Sue Jean unless he really had something on his mind. That was how he was and Doug liked him that way just fine. When you sat down with Royce you didn't hear a bunch of crap like the money market's up, or some dumb current event you didn't even need to know. Guys at Clinton-Fevre used to do it all the time. They'd talk about a pitcher for the Astros and what he ought to make. Who was doing what overseas and did Bush have a honey on the side. Royce wouldn't do that at all. He always had something real interesting to say. He could list every bar in Fort Worth, tell you who'd likely be in each one on a Friday afternoon. He knew when bass liked to take a rubber frog. He could tell you every sunrise he'd seen, and what the beer tasted like at the time. The only thing he wouldn't talk about at all were his outlaw days on the run. Just mention Fort Sumner or the Lincoln County War and the Kid would clam up quick as rain. Doug figured he had a reason and didn't push it too far. Like Royce himself had told him more than once, you had to look ahead and not back. Maybe he'd do the same, Doug decided, if he could remember anything to forget.

. . .

He found himself circling on back, past the low line of trees that hid the creek. The Cord sounded fine, like there might be a big sleepy dog beneath the hood. He drove past his mother's place and thought he really ought to drop by. It seemed like the right thing to do, but the truth was he didn't want to stop. Maybe when he got a little straightened out himself he could deal with Pennsylvania politics. It wasn't something he could handle just now.

Back through town he checked the curbs again for Royce, then drove past the house to check there. Thack was out front doing something with a rake. When he saw Doug's car he scrambled quickly out of sight. Doug shook his head and drove on. Lord, that fella's got a problem and a half. He didn't envy Royce at all.

And when he parked before his own white fence there was Royce's battered truck. The Kid himself was in a rocker on the porch, his boots propped up on the rail.

"Well I'll be," Doug said, "I've been looking 'bout everywhere for you."

"Everywhere but here," Royce grinned. "You got some good cold beer in your fridge. Go get yourself one and maybe bring me a spare."

Doug returned with beer and some Fritos and dip. He pulled another rocker up close.

"It's a right nice day," Royce said. "I kinda like that car. I bet it's got a lot of zing."

"It's a honey," Doug said. "Drives like you're sleeping on the couch. Royce, I'm really sorry that I missed you at the game, I sort of got off the track."

"I hear you dunked a few good ones in the hole."

"I guess I did."

"I hear you ran across a friend." Royce shot Doug a lazy wink. "You're something else, son. There's a cookie in the store, why you're goin' to seek her out. I guess you got the knack."

"That was sure a funny deal," Doug said. "Running into Cully Jean like that. I was about as surprised as I could be."

"No reason why you should. Hang around long enough you'll see 'bout everyone you know."

"Yeah, but Cully Jean. I mean it's not so much just happening across her again, I can see how that'd maybe be. But Lord A'Mighty, Royce, the things that girl's been through. I would've never figured that. I thought sure Cully Jean had it made. A girl looks like that has got a good running start on a life of chocolate fudge ice cream. Instead of that, why her looks turned around and did her in. I guess you can't say what's going to be."

"You got it right there," Royce said. He sucked on his beer and looked out across the yard. "Folks do what they kind of need to do, and that's the thing. It ain't always the smoothest road to take but it's what they got to do. A man gets hisself a load of jalapeños on his plate; he knows if he eats all that he's going to pay. But he's just got to do it, got to go ahead and see. You got to try about nine-hundred girls and see how much whiskey you can drink. Sometimes you got to hurt yourself bad and pile misery on your head. All that is is checking shit off your list so you won't have to do it anymore."

"I guess it is," Doug said, and tossed a Frito to a dog. "Cully Jean sure checked off a lot. That girl had a intercontinental itch."

"Throwin' up is hard to take," Royce said, "but it sure feels better when it's done."

"You want a beer?" Doug said. "I got an empty here myself."

Royce shook his head. He picked himself up straight and set his bottle on the rail. "I guess what we ought to do is talk, old hoss. There's kinda something that I got to get done." He looked right at Doug. "It sort of has to do with what we've been going over right here. I wanted you and me to sit so I could tell it to you straight. Didn't want you to hear it at the Pronghorn or over at the square. Doug, I'm going back out for a while."

For a minute Doug felt a little empty, like he might not have eaten all day. "I guess I kind of figured on that," he said at last. "I told Sue Jean I was afraid you might work things out. I know that's the wrong thing to say, it's just I sure don't want to see you go. I haven't got this going back business real clear, you know that. I see what you mean about checking stuff off, but I still can't get it in my head."

"It'll come to you, son," Royce said. "You're going to do just fine."

"I guess I will," Doug said. "I guess it'll work itself out." He started to say something, then stopped. He knew he had to get up and go. Leaving Royce on the porch he went in and just walked around the kitchen for a while. Opened up the fridge and didn't see a thing he wanted inside. Grabbing up another beer he walked out to the back and stood and looked out the screened-in porch. There were fifteen or twenty cats and dogs stretched out to catch the sun. It looked as if a bomb had hit the yard and done them in, tossed them all in odd contortions, in unlikely attitudes. There might be a prize for looking warped and out of joint. Doug took his beer and an extra one for Royce and went back out to the front.

"Listen, I didn't mean to act like that," he told Royce. "I'm just going to miss you, that's all."

"I appreciate that," Royce said. "I kinda got used to seeing you again, too."

"And I'm glad it worked out with ol' Thack. I know that's been troubling you a lot. Royce, you play a real mean piano and I know you're going to make it just fine. I don't go for your classics too much but you play 'em awful good I know that. Shoot, you're going to be a hit and a half. I expect you'll do some records and a tour."

Royce held his beer up close and looked through it at the sun. "That ain't exactly it, for a fact. I don't guess I told it real good."

"What?" Doug said. "You're going to play something else? You think you might get a horn? I wouldn't blame you if you did. It might be hard to make it on the keys."

Royce kept looking at the sun. "What I mean is, I'm not going to do that at all. Least not right away. Doug, getting Thack squared away is what going back out is all about. See I'm taking him too, that's the thing. I got him all primed up to take the leap, but he isn't goin' to make it by hisself. That ain't ever going to be. I ought to have seen it sooner, it just took a little time. I got to go in and jump-start Thack or he isn't going to do a damn thing. He's going to sit right here and not ever get it going a-tall."

"My Lord, Royce." Doug couldn't think of anything to say. "Is that what you really want to do?"

"It's going to be just fine," Royce said, "I got it worked out good. We'll kinda grow up close in one of your back east ghetto neighborhoods. Thack don't much care for that but it'll do. We'll get fucked up right off and do your street kid action by the book. Cut school and get a jacket with a dragon on the back. Steal a lot of Eye-talian fruit. When we're maybe thirteen we'll rob the corner liquor store and get blown away quick on the spot. In and out, get her done."

Doug stared at Royce. "That's it, that's the plan?" He wasn't sure he was getting this right. "You and Thack. You do this cop show scene and that's it."

"That's it, what do you think?" Royce showed Doug a broad grin, certain now Doug could see the light. "I give it a lot of thought and talked it over with the Chief. He'll buy it just fine. Shoot, Doug, there ain't no way Thack's ever going to handle your major outlaw role. Least this way it'll count, and I can get the thing done. Might give him a little confidence in himself. He can rest up some and think about his PR and advertising stunt. That one's a pain in the ass, I don't have to tell you that. Lord, I spent thirty-six years in the forth worst agency in Chicago, Illinois. We never did get to be third. Lived right on the lake and froze my ass. Wanted to make damn sure I didn't ever have to do that again."

"Sounds to me like you had it a whole lot harder than me," Doug said.

"I guess it's all about the same. Some's bad and some's worse. You ought to talk to old Doc sometime. Your outlaw trade's good practice, that's for sure. Gets you toughened up for what's to come."

Royce sat up and rolled a smoke, stretched and stood and looked at Doug. "I'm going to miss you, hoss. You're a kick is what you are."

"The same goes for me," Doug said.

"Well there you are."

Royce started for his truck and Doug trailed along behind. "I don't like to see you leave your music though," he said. "I know you been looking forward to it some."

"Shoot, I can handle that," Royce said, "won't do me any harm. I'll get her going next time sure." He gave Doug a grin. "I figure I can use the practice time."

Doug stood by the fence. "You're doing a real fine thing," he told Royce. "I hope Thack appreciates that."

Royce waved his words away. "Isn't anything to it. Me and Thack we go a ways back. I reckon I'm obliged to see him through, and it's what I want to do." He squeezed Doug's shoulders and looked him in the eye. "There's going to be a big to do at the Pronghorn, late tomorrow night. I want to see you and Sue Jean there. But I wanted us to talk without a bunch of folks around."

"I'm sure glad we did," Doug said.

"You just take it easy, let it flow. You're going to make it just fine."

"I guess I might be kind of slow. I don't catch on fast."

Royce got in his truck and shut the door. "Fast ain't what it's all about. Don't you go forgettin' that, now."

Doug stood in the street and watched him go. He felt resigned and out of sorts. He felt distressed and in accord. He felt lonely and at ease. He felt as if he might need a bacon and tomato and a nap.

Doug dreams a sweet Phoenician girl gives him seven kinds of clap, dreams that Crete is awful hot, dreams that Minos is a wimp. He dreams that mice like to sing, that badgers love to lead the band, that the red abalone has a foot. He thinks he might have been a Pict, he thinks the Visigoths are grand, he thinks the Angles and the Jutes are hardly any fun at all. He finds the same girl again in the southern part of Gaul and itches all the way to Kent. He dreams that squids can play the flute, that the yucca moth is gay, that woolly mammoths couldn't handle oral sex. He dreams that Plato smoked some pot, that Euclid counted on his toes. He dreams that Stonehenge was a house of ill repute and the Druids shut it down. What he doesn't dream about is who he is and what he thinks he ought to do. He dreams a Hoover travelogue and never brings it close to home, never gets it off the fence, never brings it down the line.

And in the morning on the shelf he finds *The Sweetheart of the West, Silas Marner, Moby Dick, Fifty Ways to Cook a Snake, Millard Fillmore's Secret Life.* He finds a marshal's badge from Butte, a bust of Alexander's cat, a Fargo lock without a key. He finds a peanut butter jar full of Brasher gold doubloons, he finds a picture of Lillie Langtry on a moose. He finds a stuffed horned toad from the St. Louis Fair, and the lost credit cards of Kubla Kahn.

And on the bathroom wall above the tiling by the tub he finds some writing on a slant, a verse in lilac-colored ink that sets the day:

Busy, curious, thirsty fly,
Gently drink, and drink as I;
Freely welcome to my cup,
Could'st thou sip, and sip it up;
Make the most of life you may,
Life is short and wears away.

Now that's kind of nice, Doug decides. It rhymes real good and it's a poem about a bug. There's all kinds of poems about bowers and trysts and some fags hopping round in a glade. But there isn't that many of your poets will take the time to sit down and do a poem about a bug.

Max Immelmann had asked Doug the day before to drop by the field and see the guys and maybe take a little spin. Doug didn't even know there was such a place and was itching to go and see. Then he got caught up in the game and heard the news about the Kid and plain forgot. Now with Sue Jean off to class and the dishes in the sink it seemed a grand idea. Sitting around thinking about Royce or if he might like to play the clarinet wasn't any fun at all. Everyone said let it flow, take it easy in your head and so he did.

Hopping in the Cord he took off past the square down the road across the bridge. The directions Max had given seemed simple at the time. Straight for a mile and turn right and then turn right again. It wasn't too long before Doug was flat lost. The day was real fine and he didn't let it bother him at all. One thing he'd learned about the roads around the town was while they didn't always go where they should, you always seemed to get where you thought you ought to be. Sure enough, very soon he saw a sign that said: *Jagdstaffell 11,* and when he turned down a narrow dirt road there it was. Doug thrilled to the sight. It was just like he thought it ought to be, just like *Wings* and *Dawn Patrol.* The wooden hangars with their corrugated roofs, the flat meadow rutted down to dirt, the grass where it remained pressed flat and streaked with oil. Set about the field was a scattering of olive tents and huts, boxes and barrels, vans and parts, everything coated with a fine film of grease. And the planes, oh Lord, just look at that! Doug felt a chill and tried to take them all in. Halberstadt and Albatros and Pfalz. A Roland and a Rumpler and a few he couldn't name. And there was von Richthofen's bright red Fokker taking in the morning sun, and there was Boelcke's old Eindekker II. He had the itch to hear the wind in the wires, tack a picture of Mary Pickford to his bunk, hear Strauss on the gramophone machine. Smell the gas and castor oil, find a sweetie down at Douai.

Max Immelmann saw him coming and came grinning to the car. "Well hi there, Doug, I kinda figured it was you. Say I like those wheels, they really got a lot of class. I bet you're flat burnin' up the road. Step out of there and sit a spell and talk."

"I guess I will," Doug said, and followed Max across the grass. He couldn't take his eyes off the magic of the field, off the planes lined up just as fine as they could be. "Boy this is something else, I'll tell you that. I feel like I'm standing right in France. I feel like I ought to get a scarf. I feel like the Tommies might jump us right at dawn."

"I guess they won't," Max said, "but they might drop by and get a Coke. Those boys are suckers for a carbonated drink."

"Is that a fact?" Doug said.

"I seen Billy Bishop get an RC high."

"Well I'll be."

"You feeling good?" said Max.

"I'm feeling fine."

"You got all the dogs you need?"

"I got a covey and a half."

"Well there you go. Let's hoof it on out of this heat, I feel the need for something wet."

Half a dozen fliers were slouched about, hunkered down in lawn chairs and cane-back rockers where the hanger made some shade. They all stood and shook Doug's hand and said hello.

"Sure glad you dropped by," Boelcke said. "I got some cold champagne and a box of ginger snaps."

"You want a beer or 7-Up? We got a lot," said Werner Voss.

Mannie Richthofen found a clean glass, filled it up with champagne. "You're a slam-dunking fool," he said, passing a drink to Doug. "You really led us down the court, you got the magic in your shoes."

"I guess I do," Doug said, "I really like to wear the suit." He took a handful of cookies from the plate. He was happy as a clam, really glad to be around. He didn't much care for the way the group dressed, but he sure wasn't going to say that. Boelcke and Voss and Udet wore cutoffs and dozer caps and rubber shower shoes. Richthofen had on a shabby white robe and he'd spilled a lot of stuff down the front. Immelmann and Lowenhardt were clearly dressed for golf in baggy knickers and silly hats. It sure didn't look like dawn behind the lines, getting ready to go tangle with some Spads.

Max told the others so long, grabbed a bottle of Moët from the ice and walked Doug across the field. Doug stopped to thump the wings of a Fokker D VII. From a distance, the planes looked tough as scrappy dogs; up close he could see you might poke your hand right through the fabric with hardly any trouble at all.

"I hear Billy's going back," Max said. "I know you ain't too happy about that."

"That's what he's got to do," Doug said. He kicked an empty can across the grass. A breeze picked up and rattled across a hanger roof. "He's doing it for Thack, and I sure can't fault him for that."

"The baron's goin' out again soon," Max said. "Plans to go into Dixieland jazz. He's something on a horn. I sure do like the Kid, I'm going to miss him while he's gone. I think I might've liked the West, I was sorta on the cusp. 'Course flying was a kick, but I might've made a felon on a horse."

"I bet you'd 've done just fine," Doug said. "I can see you on the run, a bunch of marshals in pursuit."

"Well now, that's real nice of you to say," Max said. "It sure is." He seemed pleased with the image and pursued it in his head.

Doug stopped to look as an engine coughed and hacked, choked and had an asthmatic fit then rattled into life. Boelcke bumped across the field in his Eindekker II, turned into the wind and revved her up then roared down the meadow dragging dust, all nine cylinders firing more or less at once. Doug watched in awe as the Fokker banked hard and came back, streaking by not fifty feet above. Boelcke waved and Doug waved back.

"Lord, I believe that's the finest sight I ever did see," Doug said. "It's a wonder and a half."

"You ought to hop into one of these crates and take her up," Max said. "Get your ass off the ground, get your spirit on the wing."

"I would but I don't know how."

"Well shoot, I bet you do."

"You think I might?"

"I'm as sure as I can be."

Doug watched the plane circle high above the field; the sun pierced its mustard-colored wings turning spars into traceries of bone.

"I don't guess I ought to soar," Doug said. "I kinda got stuff pinning me to the ground."

"Don't let it," Max said.

"I don't know how to do that, Max. I haven't got a care, I'm as fine as I can be. But I can't get a line on myself. I can't straighten out my head, I can't find my way to class."

Max waved him off. "You aren't in a track meet, friend. You don't have to hurt your feet."

"That's what Billy said, too. He said fast wasn't it."

"The Kid's right as he can be."

"Maybe so," Doug said. Boelcke's shadow swept the field. Someone popped a cork down the way. "Right now I seem to have a little verse creeping in. I guess it's from the me before last, I can't say."

"You got you some spillover's all," Max said. "Don't worry about that. I used to catch myself saying *copse* and *whither* all the time. Crazy stuff like that. It can't do you any harm."

"I guess not," Doug said.

"You get a mind to take something for a spin you let me know. You're sure welcome any time. I bet you'd get her off the ground, I bet you'd set her on a dime. I bet you'd be a rascal in the sky."

Doug thought he would too, he thought he'd be a Fokker whiz. He thought he might want to get a leather coat. Only now didn't seem the right time. He didn't want to hear wind in the wires or see the clouds trail below. What he wanted was for Royce to stay put and not steal Italian fruit, or get a jacket with a dragon on the back. He wanted everything to be like it was and not ever have to be something else. Once you got things right it didn't make a bit of sense to go and mess them up again.

Every Kraut ace and outlaw in town is on hand to see the Kid and Thack off, and the party at the Pronghorn's the best that's ever been. There's champagne and ribs and caviar and a herd of sweeties too. Doug does the conga with a girl from Tennessee, does the tango with a girl from Mindelheim. Does a neat cakewalk with a girl from Brandenberg, does the reel with a girl from Arkansas. Hokey Pokeys with an Alabama doll who maybe used to be a Lapp. He's happy as a frog and forgets what the party's all about. He flirts with Sue Jean and does a flip. Barks like a dog and nearly gets a laugh from Thack. Drinks a bunch of Grapette and spills his chili on the floor.

And then the room gets quiet and the Chief gets up, makes a speech and asks the Kid to say a word. Billy says three or four and the crowd gives a holler and a cheer. He shakes a lot of hands and gets a lot of hugs and kisses from the girls, gets a lot of champagne along the way. He finds Thack in a corner and makes his way across the floor, says some more goodbyes and tells the Chief so long. And then he stops right there and looks around and finds Doug across the room. He meets Doug's eyes and leaves a wink and a grin, leaves the picture of a whomper-jawed look and a nose that's out of whack. Doug gives him back a smile and half a wave, stands there and watches till he can't see Billy anymore.

Sue Jean doesn't say a word, she just holds him real tight. And Doug feels mellow and alone, slightly fractured and complete, happy and compelled to eat a rib.

"You come on and dance with me, hon," Sue Jean says, very softly in his ear, and Doug says that's what he'd like to do.

Standing on the dark back porch he could hear the soft rattle of the leaves, hear a bird have a dream, hear a squirrel turn over in its sleep. Now and then he could hear them at the Pronghorn Saloon, hear a wave of fun and music rolling in and fading out, a tinny, hollow kind of sound like it reached him through a pipe, like the music in your car on the road to Abilene. He sort of wished he'd stayed around or maybe not. If he was there he'd have to talk about Royce, and he didn't much want to do that. He liked to think about the Kid, remember all the fun they'd had. But he wanted that to stay in his head, didn't want to let it out. It was fine in there and he could bring out a thought and look it over when he liked, take his time and put it back. When you talked about someone it didn't seem the same after that. As if you lost a little something when you said the words aloud, like change slipping down inside the couch.

He heard the house creak, heard a dog thump on the steps, heard Sue Jean hum a country tune.

"I'm whipping up some scrambled eggs, hon," she called out. "I got some bacon in the pan."

"Shoot, I couldn't eat a thing," Doug said. "I must've had about ten pounds of ribs."

"I'm putting in a whole bunch of cheddar cheese, going to be awful good."

"I guess not," Doug said. He heard an owl in a tree, heard a cat catch a leaf, heard a mouse take off its shoes and go to bed. In a while he wandered in and sat and watched. He always liked to watch her cook. Liked to see the way her hips went out of whack when she scrambled up some eggs. Liked to see her bite her lip, see her eyes go intent when she lined up the bacon on a plate.

"That was a real nice sendoff for Billy," Sue Jean said. "Just as nice as it could be."

"I guess it was," Doug said.

"I thought he gave a fine talk. I kinda like my speeches short and sweet."

Doug tried to remember the event. "I don't guess I heard what he said. My head was kinda on the blink."

"Well I know it was, babe," Sue Jean said, "you're entitled to a lapse." She brought a plate from the stove and bent to kiss him on the ear. "I'm going to miss him some too, you know that."

Doug got a 7-Up and watched her eat. She patted down the eggs until they made a little hill, then crumbled up her bacon on the top.

"You make good scrambled eggs, I'll say that. You know how to get 'em right."

"I guess I do."

"Not everyone does. They'll either get them too wet or too dry. A lot of people don't know eggs'll cook for a while when you take them out of the pan. They don't allow for lag time."

"You sure you don't want some, hon?"

"I'm fine," Doug said, "I couldn't eat another bite."

Sue Jean nibbled on a little piece of bacon, working all the edges off until she had about a gnat-size bite. She gave the speck a look then sucked it off her thumb. "About the best sendoff I ever saw besides the Kid's was when ol' Bill Doolin went back," she told Doug. "He was kinda like Thack only he didn't keep off to himself. Just didn't want to go. Liked to raise tomatoes and wouldn't hear about anything else. Had no use at all for the PR and advertisin' trade. Charlie Pierce and Bitter Creek, and the Daltons who'd worked with Bill before, why they'd all been out and come back. And Bill was still here just messin' with tomatoes. Wouldn't budge out of that yard."

Doug waited. He took a bite off Sue Jean's plate. "So what happened then?"

"Well, he just went, that's all. Got up one day and went to class. Got to be an academic whiz. Never even looked at those tomato plants again. Went back out and they say he got the Campbell's Soup account."

Doug took Sue Jean's fork and scooped another bite of eggs. "Royce had a real awful advertising job. Said it like to drove him nuts."

"That's what I heard."

"Said he wouldn't want to do that again."

"I thought you wasn't hungry, Doug."

"I'm not I just want a little bite. Looks to me it'd take a lot of nerve to go back out again after that. The Kid got burned pretty bad."

"Well he isn't going to do the same *thing,*" Sue Jean said. "He's doing something different this time."

"I know what he's doing. And it doesn't sound a whole lot better, you ask me. Even if it does get Thack straightened out. I kind of feel like Doolin, Sue Jean. Growing tomatoes here is better than doing most anything else back there."

"If that's the way you see it, babe."

"Well that's the way I see it," Doug said. "It just doesn't seem right the Kid's going back out after what he went through. Anybody had a advertising job in Chicago ought to get a little break."

"Doug, doesn't anybody much like their advertising stint," Sue Jean said. "It's just something you got to do."

Doug gave her a curious look. "So you had a big time then or what? I bet you had a New York job and went to parties every night. I bet you saw plays all the time. I don't think you ever said."

"I don't think you ever asked," Sue Jean said.

"Well then what?"

"It wasn't any big thing."

"No, come on I want to hear."

Sue Jean pushed her plate across to Doug, handed him her fork and got up. Went to the counter and started cracking eggs.

"It wasn't any New York and I didn't see a play," Sue Jean said. "Where it was was in Greenville, South Carolina, and I didn't go to parties every night. As a fact, I didn't go to parties at all. I grew up with your average mom and dad. Went to school and had a bike. I was pretty till I hit sixteen then I swelled up like a toad. Didn't matter what I ate. Must've been a faulty gene 'cause I shot up from one-seventeen to a hundred ninety five in 'bout a week. Went straight from what I am right now to your regulation blimp. I could've worn my old cheerleader suit on a foot. All my boyfriends hit the road. My sex life was hardly off the ground and it came to a halt on the spot. I went home and hid out and wouldn't even leave my room. I stayed there a year and two days. When I finally came out I weighed two-thirty-six. I wasn't about to go to school and hang out with girls that looked like me. So I went down the classified ads and looked for work. It wasn't any big surprise to find no one was lookin' for balloons.

"Well I finally got lucky, and nailed down the worst job in town. Didn't anybody want the thing but me. It was a big old furniture store that specialized in glit. In case you don't know, that stands for glue and shit. There wasn't an honest piece of wood in the place. It was bad taste city and they couldn't keep the showrooms full. They put me out back out of sight and said I'd be a junior copywriter. 'Course there wasn't any senior copywriters, just me. I had a desk and a Royal upright and half an hour off for lunch and not a soul around but me. I thought, shoot, that's fine, I got nothing else to do.

"Well I'd never wrote an ad in my life but I guess I got the knack. I churned those mothers out in style. All you really got to know is SALE and SAVE and ACT NOW, and that decorator colors is everything from black to white. I got a raise every year, I gained two pounds a week. They were flat out delighted with my work and even sprung for a heavy duty chair. They had a showroom stretched maybe six or seven football fields, and I'd go and pick my specials out at night. I was hitting maybe three-twenty-nine so they wouldn't let me out when there was customers in the store. Like maybe Lady Di would drop in to get a plastic dinette."

"I sort of forgot to count the years. I just sat in that room and puked it out and got bigger by the day. I did the Fall Recliner Frenzy, I did the James Polk Birthday Marathon. I did the Spring Whiz Bang Flamingo Lamp and Rocker Sale. I tipped the scales at four-oh-two.

"About that time I just quit going home. I was too damn big to even get on the bus, and there wasn't a thing to do in my room. I'd just get me some junk from the snack room machine, get a TV set off the floor and crap out on a stack of Ducky-Downs. If anybody knew I started living in the store they didn't say a thing.

"Well the seasons went by, and when they did I'd kinda try and celebrate. We'd wind up the Thanksgiving Fold-a-Bed Sale and I'd color-key my supper for the night. Get a Nehi Orange and some chocolate M&Ms and sorta decorate my plate with plastic leaves. On the Fourth I'd try to eat something red, white and blue and that's a challenge and a half.

"That Christmas, I thought up the big Senior Citizens' Lava-Lite Sale. Lord, it was an all-out hit. We had oldsters backed up, we had the traffic at a stall. Word was I was in for a plaque. The next day I found a quart of good domestic gin on my desk with a ribbon on the neck. I almost cried at the sight. Recognition don't come real easy in the advertising game, I don't guess I have to tell you that. Well I had me a real Christmas party that night. Red hots and green gum drops set the key. I watched the Christmas specials and I even sang some songs. I drank most of that gin. Which by the way was the first drink of booze I'd ever had, except stealing Sally Leek's daddy's bourbon at a slumber party once.

"I guess I kinda got out of hand. I recall waddlin' all about the store singing Elvis Christmas hits. That and drinking gin, and wondering if I'd hit four-twenty by the spring. The last I recall is sitting down to take a break and doing

Jingle Bell Rock. What I sat down in was a packing crate for Lazee-Dad recliners which I'd figured for a neat tie-in with the Super Bowl Sale. What happened is I got hauled out the next day. Fork-lifted to a dumpster out back and straight to a land-fill site. I don't guess the store ever figured where I went. It wasn't the very best Yule season I ever had, but wasn't any of them hits."

Doug didn't say a thing for a while. Sue Jean brought her new scrambled eggs to the table and poured herself some juice.

"My Lord," Doug said at last, "that's a real awful story, Sue Jean. You didn't have any fun at all. I didn't do near as bad as that."

"This plate you see here is flat mine," Sue Jean said, jabbing a finger at her eggs. "You got that real clear, hon?"

"See it's stories like this put me off," Doug said. "I hear shit like that and I don't get a lot of incentive in my head."

"I don't guess."

"Well I don't. It doesn't make any sense at all."

Sue Jean put down her fork. "Hon, we've about worn this out, don't you think? You've told me three hundred times what you're not going to do, all right? So don't."

"I might and I might not. I can't say for sure."

"I'm real surprised to hear that."

"I just don't get the point," Doug said. "I'm just fine right here. I can't see rushing back out to get fucked up again. Royce says you got to check shit off your list so you won't have to do it anymore. Well fine. I'll check it off right here. I know all about me I want to know."

"You do, huh?"

"I sure do."

Sue Jean licked egg off her lips. "If you do, Doug, you wouldn't have gone back out before, now would you? You ever think about that?"

"That's different," Doug said.

"Oh, sure."

"Okay, so why did I?"

"Well why do you think?"

"I don't know. I'm asking you. What's the point of getting here and going back out again? I can learn all about me in the comfort of my very own home. This is flat the finest place there is."

"That's just not so now, Doug." It was a very nice reproach, gentle and restrained. "I mean it's real fine here, but this is *not* as good as it can be."

"Well then, what?" Doug was basically confused. "You know a better place to live? They got a nicer town down the creek? Fine, let's run out and see it."

Sue Jean got up and put her dishes in the sink. She seemed to be thinking something out, going through it in her head. Finally, she lit up a ciggie and leaned against the sink. "Hon, we're not talking about down the creek," she told Doug. "Don't you realize that? That isn't it at all." She paused and seemed to get the right gear. "Listen to me, Doug. You know how things start to change when you're driving on into Fort Worth? First you got your mobile homes, and your junkyards and dance halls and such. Then you get past the used parts stores and the rusty tool and pipe. You keep on driving through your new builder homes and you come to the residential stuff. Well, drive a little more and you're right down town. You got skyscraper banks and your offices and such and—well, see? There you are." Sue Jean spread her hands and grinned.

Doug looked blank. "There I am where, Sue Jean?"

"Maybe I'm not doing this right," Sue Jean sighed.

"Maybe not. You're sure flat missing me."

"What I'm saying to you, babe—I mean, I kinda thought you *knew* all this, I guess you don't. See, that's sort of where we are right now. You and me. We're like those mobile homes I talked about. We're here, but we're just not all the *way* here. I mean we aren't all the way downtown."

"Sue Jean, I don't know what you got in mind, but I don't want to live in Fort Worth," Doug said. "Not downtown or anywhere else. I wouldn't like it there at all."

Sue Jean closed her eyes. "For God's sake, Doug, it's an *analogy,* okay? Sometimes I think I am speaking to a wall. I am not talking about downtown Fort Worth or downtown anywhere else. What I'm telling you is *this* is not all there is. There's something else. You can sit right here if you want but I *don't* think that's what you want to do. I think you want to get your shit together's what I think. Hon, that's what takin' classes and going back is all about. It isn't just to pass the time or heap trouble on your head. The sooner you go and get it all done, why the sooner you can move on up to somethin' better. That's what it's all for, don't you see?"

Doug felt a pause then a beat, one, *two,* as Sue Jean's words seemed to break through roadblocks in his head. He felt dazzled and marooned. Stupefied and oddly in the groove. Mystified and pleasantly at sea.

"I'm in a mobile home park," he said aloud and to himself. "I thought I had it all made. What I got is a trailer on the ass end of town like Otta Gee."

"Hon, you haven't got anything of the sort," Sue Jean said.

"Why didn't somebody tell me all this?"

"Isn't anyone supposed to *have* to tell you, Doug. You're supposed to kinda figure it yourself."

"Well thanks a whole lot," Doug said. "You could've given me a hint."

"Babe, giving you a hint's like shoutin' at a rock. It don't always get the thing to move."

"I'm real tired, Sue Jean. I think I'd like to go to bed."

"I think that's a fine idea." She came around and put her arms around his neck and kissed him lightly on the cheek. "I sure love you, hon, you know that."

"I guess I do."

"You come over standing up and then you sort of petered out. I think you might've thrown a rod. You're going to be just fine, you wait and see."

Doug lay in bed with Sue Jean in his arms and heard the first drop of rain upon the roof. He heard an ant do a jig, he heard a beetle brush his teeth. He heard the grass start to grow, he heard a spider have a Coke. He didn't dream about anything at all.

THE HEREAFTER GANG

There seems to be a lot to think about. Doug feels he might cure it with a walk. Walking has a way of kind of working things out, bringing issues to a head, making problems crystal clear, pushing answers to the fore. Either that or maybe blow it all off and look it up another day.

He leaves Sue Jean bare and tangled in the bed, sees the morning chart a cheery market swing across her back and down her thigh, leaves his cookie baking happy in the sun. On the way he makes a quick turn about and passes by the Kid's house. Everything looks just the same. He doesn't think that's the way it ought to be. It looks as if Billy might appear any minute on the porch and tell Doug to come and sit and have a beer. He waits to see if this will happen, then walks on down toward the square.

The rain has left the town washed bright, left the birds clean shirts, left the pleasant wet and dusty smell of brick. Doug waves at friends and takes a stroll around the square. At the ice cream store, he winks at the sweetie at the counter and orders up a peanut butter cone. The shops look nice and there are things he'd like to buy, but he's decided that today is just a walk. A walk around and think day without any stuff to carry home.

Coming out of the hardware, Doug spots a figure bearing quickly down the street, walking in a gait like a stork who wants to pee. He knows the man at once, knows the polyester suit, the bow tie, the bare feet without any socks to match. He tries to duck back in but too late. The man waves and shifts into second gear and catches up with Doug at once.

"Philo Akers," says the man, "I bet you don't remember me."

"I bet I do," Doug says.

"Well grand," Akers says, "this is working out fine. You decided on the tenor sax or not? I kinda think you'd be a piccolo whiz."

"I got a lot on my mind," Doug says. "I don't want to talk about the arts."

"How about the oboe or the flute? I'd say your woodwinds are coming back strong. Boy, I'd love to see you toot the old bassoon."

"I'll let you know," Doug says.

"I'll get you signed up quick," Akers says, and flips a clipboard from underneath his coat.

"I'm not about to sign a thing."

"How's Thursday sound to you?"

"I think I'll be out of town."

"I'll put you down for Monday noon. Say your cone looks swell. Is that chocolate fudge or what?"

"You have a nice day," says Doug.

Sue Jean's revelations over cheddar scrambled eggs flit about inside his head but can't find a place to light. It's like a creature in the zoo he's never seen. He knows what it is or what he thinks it ought to be, but where's the front and where's the back? He isn't sure he wants to know. He wants to think about it some but it won't settle down and sit still. He knows he'd feel a lot better if it wasn't there at all. He's still trying to figure out how to play the game and now they've gone and changed the rules. It's hard to think of all he's got to do, all he's got to be before he's done—before he gets someplace he already thought he was. Why can't they just leave things alone? Doug wants to know. Things seem to work fine the way they are. The town's just grand and the people really nice. And you can't beat the prices with a stick.

The people in the park have got the aimless saunter pat, they've got the random shuffle locked, they've got the haphazard zombie strut down without a flaw. Doug watches from the walk, astonished and amazed that the walkers don't collide. There's likely some equation for it all, but he wouldn't understand it if there was.

Doug looks again for the man who needs a train, but can't spot him anywhere. It's hard to pick faces from the crowd. He decides it's the walk that makes everyone the same. If they knew where they were and where to go and what to do they wouldn't all look alike, and they wouldn't be walking in the park.

And then all at once a familiar face seems to catch his eye. Doug looks again and isn't sure. Looks once more and then he is. He can't believe it, but he knows it has to be. The army overcoat dyed shoe polish black. The hair like a dog that's decided mange is fine. There can't be but one James McArthur Hill Dean.

He starts toward Dean in time to see him change his course, bearing south-southeast two degrees. Doug runs to cut him off. Stands in his path until Dean decides to halt.

"Get out of my way," says Dean, giving Doug a bleary eye, "I got a lot of stuff to do."

"The name's Hoover," Doug says. "We had coffee and pie a while back. Near Hempstead or Brenham I forget. They had a painting of some ducks on the wall. They didn't look right to me.

Dean studies Doug. Focal planes make corrections in his head. "I'm not your common vagrant or a tramp," he announces. "I'm an educated man fate has kicked in the ass. My name's James McArthur Hill Dean and I'm originally from El Paso, Texas. I ran a successful agency for the Prudential Life bunch for forty-one and a half years. I had a wife and a home and two kids. One boy and a girl. Their names were Axel and Mary Zane. My wife was the former Mavis Lee Loom of the Corpus Christi Looms, the daughter of Harold C. Loom of whom you've heard."

"You told me," Doug says.

"Say I remember you." Dean seems to brighten quite a bit. "We had coffee and pie together once. Is this Amarillo or what?"

"No it's not," Doug said.

"I was kinda 'fraid of that," Dean says. He stops and takes a look around the park. "I was walking on the Interstate Thursday afternoon. A white RV came along and knocked me flat. I don't recall what happened after that."

"I guess you don't."

"You got anything to eat?"

"I can fix you what you like, I got a fridge full of food."

"You got some Dutch apple pie?"

"I got a lot."

"You got some cheddar for the top?"

"I got all the cheese you want."

"Well let's hook it on out," Dean says, "I'd kind of like a place to sit."

Doug leads James McArthur Hill Dean out of the park and down the street. Dean seems to take in the sights or maybe not. He looks goofy in the eyes, he still tends to wander off.

"It might be Waco, I can't say for sure," Dean says. "They got a whole lot of parks and not anyplace to eat. I doubt if it's Wichita Falls. I'm eighty-three years old and I've led a life I doubt you'd believe. I took six thousand bucks and ran it up to a hefty illegal enterprise."

"That's what I hear," Doug says.

"You sure you got a lot of pie."

"I guess I do."

"We might be in San Antonio, I couldn't say."

"You feeling good?" Doug says.

"I'm feeling fine."

"You got a worry in your head?"

"I'm right as rain.

"Do you get along with dogs?"

"I think they're grand."

"Well there you are," Doug says. "You're going to make it just fine."

THE HEREAFTER GANG

Dean thought Sue Jean was a sweetie and a half. For the most part he wandered through the house and bumped into dogs and doors, muttered to himself about smuggling Cadillacs and the need for whole life, slick ways to quick shuffle Daffy Duck accounts. When he paused to catch a breath he'd sit down and eat a pie. Pie was his affliction and he didn't care for anything else. If he couldn't find apple he was satisfied with peach. Apricot and cherry and California plum would do fine. He didn't much go for lemon chess.

Dean still wasn't sure where he was. His first day at Doug's he ran out of larger towns and began to work his way through the Shell map in his head.

"I might be in Sulphur Springs," he'd tell Doug. "It kind of feels like Grand Saline. I wouldn't rule out Bleakwood or Hogg."

And so Doug got to hear about Votaw and Ace, Blackjack and Hilda and Wizard Springs and Vick. Lovelady and Gunsight, Veribest and Belk and Cut and Shoot. He thought he knew Texas towns but Dean clearly had him beat. The old man had wandered everywhere there was, and Doug hoped he'd never ventured out of state.

Everything changed when Sue Jean was on the scene. Dean's wits returned at once and his shuffle disappeared. He didn't bump into a thing. His vision was as clear as a bird dog on the point. He could tell where she was day or night. He knew when to catch her with her T-shirt off, where to be in that one bare instant when she wrapped up in a towel.

This irritated Doug no end. Sue Jean didn't seem to mind a bit. She thought Dean was cute and who cared what he saw?

Doug said *he* did was who, and suggested Sue Jean could be more careful where she dressed.

"Shoot, I could take off my skivies on the roof," Sue Jean said, "and that man would be hangin' from a tree. He's got a uncanny sense for T and A."

"He's got a real dirty mind is what he's got," Doug said.

"He reminds me of someone I know," Sue Jean said, "I can't recollect who."

The minute Sue Jean left the house, Dean slipped into a coma once again. Cataracts clicked into place. Dogs ran for cover and the cats hid in the yard. They knew Dean was lethal as a truck.

At first Dean kept to the house. He didn't like to get far from his pies, and Sue Jean might return at any time. Then, after two or three days, Doug began to find he'd wandered off. He'd catch Dean halfway down the street muttering his litany to himself: "Streeter Doss Pawnee, Petus Wink Geronimo..."

Doug wondered if he'd maybe taken Dean out of the park too soon. It might be a good idea to take him back, let him walk around some more. The idea appealed to him a lot. Sue Jean said absolutely not. Dean would do just fine. That living there with Doug would really help. Dean would get better quick, Doug would see.

Doug had his doubts about that, but Dean surprised him now and then. He'd find a station on his dial, and appear to know exactly where he was.

"You think that gal from Texas Tech might be around?" he asked Doug, suddenly alert and on the beam. "Boy, she flattened me good. Hit me with a tire iron and nearly broke my head. Knocked every one of them secret bank numbers all to shit, why I can't recall a one. I never seen honkers like that before or since. Had legs up to here and a baby duck crotch. The doctor took twenty-two stitches in my head. I'd sure like to try and get a date."

"I'll ask around," Doug said, and a minute after that Dean was semi-zonked again.

Doug began to appreciate Thack. Thack kept to himself and never said anything at all. If you had to go and take people in, there was much to be said about your introvert recluse. It sure beat horny old men who ate pies and had a head full of minor Texas towns.

In the late afternoon, Doc Holliday dropped by for a chat and he and Doug sat around out front and had a beer. Dean wandered out with a boysenberry pie. He told Doc about his mother-in-law the speedboat whiz. How he'd made nearly eight-hundred mil and wound up in a Pepsi plant in Wichita Falls.

"Is that a fact," Doc said, which didn't seem to please Dean at all.

Dean said, "Poncho Sandusky Doole," and stumbled out to the gate. He stood there looking down the street in case Sue Jean happened to appear.

"Real peculiar cuss," Doc said. "Reminds me some of old man Clanton. Does he fart a whole lot?"

"He better not," Doug said.

"You might get some citronella, that'll help."

"What he does is follow Sue Jean around. Stays right on her all the time."

"Imagine that," Doc said, who didn't find this strange at all.

Dean started off up the street. He didn't usually get far, and Doug decided to let him go. Maybe someone down the block would head him off.

"Max says he's going to get you in the air," Doc said. "Says he thinks you got the knack, says he feels you oughta fly."

"If I do, I'll sure get a leather suit," Doug said. "I'm not wearing any golf outfit."

"I guess you can wear what you want."

"Well I don't see knickers in a Fokker now, Doc. I just wouldn't feel right."

"You got a point."

"I think you got to draw the line."

"Boy, isn't that the truth. Hey, I might go up with you myself. I got my eye on a sweet Albatros."

"Well I'll be," Doug grinned. "We could buzz 'em off the field, we could show them how it's done."

"I bet we could," Doc said.

Doug went in for more beer. Dean had left three fruit pies on the table, which wasn't a real good idea. Dean didn't think about the dogs, but the dogs thought a lot about Dean. They knew Dean did things that other people didn't seem to do. Like stepping on their tails and forgetting to close the fridge, or what he'd done just now which was leave the pies in easy dog reach. So that's how it was when Doug walked in the room, three dogs at the table in three dining chairs, scarfing up three fruit pies. He viewed the scene with some alarm. He felt slightly off center, maybe two or three inches out of line. Neurons wouldn't seem to fire. He had to stop and think if dogs did this every day. It appeared altogether too normal to the eye and he didn't think it should. He shook off the thought and grabbed his beers and retreated to the porch.

Doc had his feet on the rail and a thin black cigar in his hand. He pointed the cigar down the street.

"Your friend come by going back the other way," he told Doug. "Didn't seem to be doin' any harm."

"I guess he won't," Doug said. "He's looking for a girl from Texas Tech."

"Well ain't we all," Doc said.

Doug watched Dean avoid a tree. He seemed to be doing real good. Maybe practice was the key. Doug tried to sip his beer and missed his mouth. Backed off and tried again. It seemed a simple task but the act required engineering skill. He thought about that. His thoughts raced ahead at glacial speed. He wasn't feeling right at all. The pie scene had knocked his wheels out of line and he couldn't get them straight.

"Doc," Doug said, "do your dogs ever eat in a chair?"

"Dogs'll eat anywhere they can," Doc said.

"I guess they will."

"I had a cat once liked to wear a tie. Wouldn't touch a paisley, had to be a stripe."

This isn't what Doug wanted to hear. He didn't need confirmation that his head was on the blink. He looked down the street and saw Dean had disappeared. Good. Maybe he'd found a coed queen. Maybe he'd wander back to the park.

"Hoss, you all right?" Doc said. "I think your color's kinda off."

"I don't know," Doug said, "I'm not sure. I think I might've hurt my mind."

"You don't want to do that."

"I'm getting used to it, Doc. I forget how it feels to think straight and down the line. Sideways is how I got my compass set."

"Are we still talkin' about dogs?"

"I don't guess," Doug said. He considered that a while. "I think dogs are a kind of side effect. My head isn't working like it should. I'm getting lots of spillover stuff and the dogs are part of that. It's Sue Jean, is what it is. I haven't settled down since she knocked me off the track."

Doc grinned and gave a wink. "That cookie got your wits on the run, she got you dazzled to a tee? I don't see the harm in that."

"It isn't that at all," Doug said. "Being dazzled suits me fine. What it is is something else; it isn't her fault I guess it's me. When I got here, Doc, why I figured I was through. And that's fine because I like the place a lot. Then I come to learn you got to go out again. You don't, but that's what everybody does. Well I'm getting *that* straight, and Sue Jean comes up with this brand new stuff. I find out when you go out enough you don't stay here at all, you move on to something else, which Sue Jean says is a whole lot better than we got. It might be, I don't know. If it's like downtown Fort Worth, I'm not sure I want to go."

Doc looked at the yard a long time. He puffed his cigar and watched the smoke find a breeze. "Hoss," he said at last, giving Doug a kindly look, "you didn't know 'bout any of this at all?"

"Well I can't figure everything at once," Doug said. "The Kid told me you didn't have to do it real fast."

"He's as right as he can be."

"At least I came over standing up. I'm not bumping into stuff in the park."

"You're doing fine, you're doing good. And like you say you got all the time there is."

Doug felt another tug on his line. He might've hooked a baby perch. His head seemed half a second fast. He pictured dogs in Arrow shirts, he saw a cat that smoked a pipe, he blinked and found a proper gear.

"Does all this stuff work for you?" he asked Doc. "I mean, going in and out so you got to leave town?"

Doc showed Doug a lazy smile. "One way or other, I been gettin' out of towns 'bout as long as I recall. And this is the best ol' deal I ever had. Shoot, Doug, why you think we keep bustin' ass to get it done if there isn't something to it? You think anybody likes doing poet and outlaw and advertisin' shit? And all the crap that come before that? It sure ain't just to pass the time."

"That's sort of what Sue Jean said."

"Well then she must've told it right. Listen, you talk to the Chief about this?"

"I don't guess I've had the time."

"Well he's sure the man to see," Doc said. "I don't have to tell you that." Doc stood and stretched, picked his hat off the rail. "You and him have a talk. I'd say that's the thing to do."

"I guess I will," Doug said.

Doug walked him to the gate. He looked down the street and tried to find James McArthur Hill Dean.

"You hang in there," Doc said. "I don't see any cause for alarm. Shoot, you got your PR stuff at your back. It kinda goes downhill after that."

"Maybe so," Doug said. "I'd just like to get it all straight."

Doc laughed at that. "I reckon you tied it up and said it all. That's the whole bit wrapped up and in a box."

Doug found Dean in Cole Younger's front yard. He was sitting on the porch watching Cole prune a Tammy Bakker pink.

"I was just about to give you a call," Cole said, giving Doug a puzzled look. "Near as I can make out this fella belongs to you."

"I hope he didn't get in the way," Doug said.

Cole stood up. "Wanted me to get him a date. Said I shouldn't tell Sue Jean. What the shit is he, a railroad engineer? I'm gettin' dizzy hearing towns."

"Come on now," Doug said to Dean, "we got to get on back."

"Newburg Gustine Clairette," Dean said. "Grayback Moravia Sublime."

Doug had forgotten about the dogs and what they'd done. Dean went right to the kitchen and spotted empty plates at once.

"Say, where the fuck are my pies?" he asked Doug. "You didn't have to eat 'em all."

"I didn't touch your pies," Doug said. "The dogs got to them, not me."

"You sure run a loose ship."

"You shouldn't have left them sitting out. A dog sees a pie, he's not going to let it go to waste."

"This place looks a lot like Myrtle Springs to me," Dean said. He sniffed out the pantry and found another pie. "Where's that girl, she ought to be back soon."

"You just keep your mind on that pie."

Dean walked into the den, turned on the TV and settled down on the couch, something Doug had never seen him do before. He set the pie in his lap and watched the screen. A right end went out for a pass, missed and got clobbered on the ten.

Dean's face brightened. "Well I'll be. It's Tampa Bay and the Giants. Shoot, New York'll chase 'em off the field."

"You like the Giants?"

"Can't stand 'em," Dean said. "I'm flat wild about the Bucs."

"They'll win," said Doug, who'd watched football here before. He stood behind Dean for a while and watched the game. Wondered why he hadn't thought of TV. Dean was transfixed. His pie hand was frozen at a point midway above his lap. All the dogs were outside, and Doug had never seen a cat eat a pie. There might be time for a nap. It couldn't hurt and might clear out his head. He felt he might be adrift, felt his moorings weren't secure. Thursday was vaguely out of synch, Friday coming up on the rail. Two days at once made the house steer slightly to the right. He tried to remember whether mice liked to eat tomato soup and knew he'd better hit the hay.

The back porch is cool and the bed sags just the way he likes. He picks up *Weird Tales* for August 1943 and reads a page. The game sounds like bees deep inside a hollow tree. He thinks about Cully Jean Moon. He thinks about his Fort Worth girl and Cindy Nance at fourteen. He thinks about an Alabama girl and he dreams about blood in Tennessee. He dreams about sweet creek water and he sees it turning red, sees a man with a bullet hole painted on his face, sees Missouri fade away. He walks with a girl through clover to his knees, a patch so wet and morning fresh his pants are cold against his skin. He holds the child up high and sucks its toes like early corn, feels it laugh against the sky. At night the girl lays very still while he slips her gown aside. He can't see her eyes but knows she watches every move, knows she watches with the same awe and wonder as their child; he's seen this very look when the first drop of rain begins to fall. On a farm outside Alpena, Arkansas, a dog goes mad with hunger and abuse and eats the man who gave it only rye to drink. Doug knows with some surprise the fear that comes and finds him out, simply walks right up and says hello, seeks him out in the full light of day on the hot and dusty street. He thinks he sees a friend die, and can't remember why they came. He hears the shouts like hounds far behind him in the trees. Branches cut him like a Kansas City barber and he sees a horse bleeding through the eye. He feels the shiver and the cold, and wonders if he'll ever see the night. A man in St. Joseph had a real fine wit; he could do sly tricks like find a silver dollar in your ear. He got shot because of this and nothing more. He's too tired and sore with the bullet in his leg, too tired to pee straight and he gets it on his shoe. He finds a squirrel but it's too dead to eat; he can't risk a shot and he eats it anyway. Spends the night trying to toss it back up. Even whiskey won't make it go away; the squirrel's too dead and doesn't really care to move. And now in his dream he's aware that there's someone in his head, that there's someone by his side. He can almost see a face, a dull reflection of himself but not the same. The mirror's pocked and seared, like he poked through the ash and picked it up with a piece of china cup, with a letter like a spider sucked dry. He's glad to know that he isn't all alone. He feels a warmth he can't define, the joy of a treasure put aside and found again, like a twenty dollar bill in a coat you never wear. Bread tastes good when you toast it in a pan. Never try to boil an owl. He remembers riding in on the white-legged sorrel, how the hoofs sounded hollow when they crossed the town bridge and they all remarked how fine a day it seemed. Well there you go, that's that. You can't be right all the time, some days don't work the way they should. An old man who'd spent his life trapping beaver with Shoshonis on his ass said he wouldn't eat chicken on a bet. Then someone told him that it tasted like snake and he was purely satisfied. He found them somewhat easier to catch and got a house in town and settled down. A girl Doug knew in Carolina had opals in her eyes.

Then Doug woke up and felt fine, felt like a banjo with brand new strings, felt contained and incomplete, felt detached and in accord, felt as if he might drink a case of 7-Up. Yet something held him back, pressed him flat and held him down, weighed heavy on his chest. He lifted up his head and saw goofy yellow eyes, saw the wisdom of the East, saw a bright confetti thought or maybe not.

"Mousebreath!" Doug cried out. "Say is this a big surprise, I'm sure glad to see you here." He scratched the cat roughly on the chin. Mousebreath shook him off at once and jumped down to the floor, sniffed the air and found the kitchen right away. Doug got up and followed her in. Opened up Tender Vittles and put them in a bowl and set the bowl on the floor. Other cats converged from every corner of the house. Mousebreath seemed appalled. She look accusingly at Doug.

"Do the best you can," Doug said. "You're going to have to learn to share."

Fuck you, said Mousebreath with her eyes.

The TV was still on and Dean had finished all his pie.

"What's the score?" Doug said.

"Sixty-three to six," Dean said, "second quarter, first down."

"Tampa Bay?"

"They got wings on their shoes, they got the Giants on the run. Say, I think this might be Marble Falls. It looks a lot like Kirbyville or Kountze. Everything came back to me a little while ago. I know where I got all my secret fund accounts, I got all the numbers too. Don't expect me to tell you what they are 'cause I won't. I got money in the Caymans, I got special Swiss accounts. I got millions in Bermuda, I got more in Martinique. I can walk in and get that money any time. I expect I'll be a rascal on a spree."

"Good," Doug said. He walked back to the kitchen to see if the other cats had left Mousebreath anything to eat.

THE HEREAFTER GANG

Leaving Dean with a clear Buc slaughter in the works, Doug grabs a 7-Up and beats a hasty retreat to the yard. The late afternoon is a wonder, a green and gold delight, and retreat doesn't seem the proper word. It might be withdrawal or attack. It has the feel of sly advance. Definition seems open to debate. There's nothing really new about that, but as he steps out back he feels the sweet inebriation of the day, feels he's found himself a fix, feels he's on a certain high, feels he's got the mental sniffles on the run. In a small back pocket of his heart next to Ellis County lint and a broken Ace comb, he understands his snooze has cracked a door he's never used, opened windows stuck with paint, left his senses magnified. He feels distinctly on the verge, feels perception on the wing, feels a breakthrough on the way or maybe not. The world before him now is edged in sharp illumination, sharp enough to hurt the eyes. Every leaf and blade of grass seems enhanced with polar light, every atom seems to dance, every ant exhalation seems a fog. He feels shattered and complete, he feels aware and out of synch, he feels symmetric and awry. And he knows somehow in a way he can't define that a cat in a mirror is a mouse, that a sharp and a flat are all the same, that discord gives harmony a hug. The dream has clearly jogged him loose, shaken mental nuts and bolts, added daffy resolution to the game. He's got a Kodak projector in his head, he's got a megaton bulb and Dolby sound, he's got a popcorn and a Coke. He sees a hundred sixty-two feature films with every blink. He sees his mother on a spree, sees a Navajo squaw behind a Ute behind a Creek behind a Celt behind a Greek behind a Sikh behind a Chink behind a nun behind a fairly distant aunt from Navarone. Previews of semi-past attractions hurry by. He watches Sunny D'Angelo chase a Spanish pig, sees him take a break at Ghent, sees him steal a Turkish goat at Erzurum. He watches Sarah Dee bite a Roman on the nose, sees her love a Saxon maid, sees her sink a Danish fleet. Mach 7 movies make him dizzy as a duck. He watches Stew and Erlene he watches Ham and

Aimilee. He watches Cully Jean Moon and Pastor Jack. He watches Parker Symmes the proctologist and Nazi car king, follows him from Belgorod to Bern, from Konigsberg to Kokonor, learns an asshole man is committed to his trade right from the start. And while the circus gallops by, while the spectacle unfolds, while every face he ever knew rushes by in heady flight, he very nearly finds himself. It's right there and then it's not, he only misses by a hair, it takes the bait and runs deep and snaps the line. He thinks his Fort Worth girl looks fine in Persian silk, he thinks Amos Fevre's silly in a kilt. In the streets of Eiriksjord, you could buy frozen mice on a stick. The Hittites and Medes invented Dr Pepper twice, and forgot how to do it both times.

Doug was relieved that Dean had found a new diversion in the tube. When the Bucs whipped the Giants he went on to let the Colts drop the Bears. After that in a college-pro match of Dean's design, Idaho U. brought the Redskins to their knees.

Doug didn't care if the Vatican played Arizona State. As long as Dean was off his back. There seemed to be enough pies for the dogs and Dean both, and peace and quiet descended on the day.

With Dean occupied, Doug thought he might safely wander off. Go downtown and see the sights or have a beer with Doc and Cole. The cinematic spree had left him dazed. Special effects were fine but they could wear a man down. He felt a need to see stuff outside his head. Anything that didn't move or wasn't bright—no color that didn't come in a dime Crayola box. Expanding your mind was real good, but it had a lot of drawbacks, too.

Doug had a beer and ate a piece of Dean's pie and decided not to go. He felt good, he felt fine, he felt enlightened and complete, he felt his compass was entirely on the blink. He could walk fairly well, but one direction or the other seemed the same. The back door and the front were both alike. Town was straight up or maybe not. Dyslexia was a new way of life. Insight was a pain in the ass. It irked him that he wasn't much better off than Dean. Some but not a lot.

He was really glad to see Sue Jean. Dean sensed her first, catching labial drift fully half a block away. Rising from his chair, he started for the door in a ten-degree list.

"Just hold it," Doug warned. "Don't you grab a thing."

The screen door slammed and Sue Jean stepped in over dogs. She looked slick and fine in her cutoffs and one of Doug's old shirts. Dean began major oscillation. Started humming like a top.

"Well hi there, hon," Sue Jean said, giving Doug a passing kiss. She dropped a package on the chair, opened up the fridge and got a cold 7-Up. "You have a good day, babe? Lord, I saw a fox on the way back from class. Looked just like one of them wraps. Ernst Udet's got a Rolls. He's sportin' that Arkansas girl, the one's got her hair in a twist. Dean, you got blueberry pie on your teeth. Go in and brush right now."

"You and me are going on a date," Dean grinned.

"We'll see," Sue Jean said.

"I'm thinking on dinner and a show. I expect you'll lose control."

"I am going to be checking those teeth," Sue Jean warned.

"I got more money than you think," Dean said, and wandered off.

"That man is driving me nuts," Doug said.

Sue Jean laughed. "Hon, he don't mean any harm. He's just kinda unsettled in the head. Damn, I flat forgot. I picked up a new outfit at the store. You are just goin' to *love* it. Now stay right there and don't move." She gave Doug a bawdy wink, grabbed her package and bounded up the stairs.

Doug felt slightly unhinged. The stairs seemed to go both ways. Dean strolled back in. "Where's that girl?" he asked Doug. "She's not here."

"Sit down and watch your game," Doug said.

"I don't care for football at all."

"Yes you do."

"I got gold in a Frankfurt account. I'm catching Lufthansa out at dawn. I'll warn you right now I can spot a tail quick. Don't try and follow, won't do you any good."

"Fine," Doug said. Dean hadn't brushed his teeth. He might've missed the john. Sometimes he wandered in a closet and just stood there till someone let him out.

Doug heard Sue Jean on the stairs. A moment later she appeared. His heart gave a quick little lurch. She was so sweet and pretty he wanted to cry.

"Well, what do you think?" Sue Jean asked. She whirled in a circle so Doug and Dean could see. Dean's eyes took on a hard ceramic glaze. "In case you don't know it's a black jersey Halston with an off the shoulder look. The hardware had 'em on sale. Well I say black, it's Raven Wing Blush is what it is. Your high fashion house don't do just a black, they got to think of something else."

"It's real nice, you look as fine as you can be," Doug said, though he wasn't really sure of this at all. For no reason he could see, his head did a number on the dress. A PBS on the properties of wool and a whiz bang light show on the side. When he blinked and came back, Sue Jean was looking right at him with concern.

"Hon, you okay?" She pulled up a strap on the dress.

"I'm just fine," Doug said.

"No you're not. You got your mouth out of whack. You got slant and misdirection in your eyes. Dean, go over there and *sit."* Dean sat. "Doug, you come out back with me right now."

She took Doug by the hand and led him out to the porch, walked around him once, studied him up and down.

"I'm okay," Doug said.

"Oh I can see that." Sue Jean put her hand on her hips. "All right. What'd you get into, babe?"

"I don't know," Doug said. "I think I kinda hurt my head again."

"Oh, shit."

"No, it's all right," Doug assured her. "It's just fine." He sat down on the bed. "It wasn't bad and I learned a whole lot. I got some side effects is all."

"You learned a lot about what?"

"Well, me. That kind of stuff."

"About you."

Doug wasn't sure he ought to even bring it up. Going sideways in his head wasn't all that new, it likely didn't mean a thing. "I thought I nearly had it, Sue Jean," he said at last. "I mean who I was before. I felt like a deb coming out."

"You think so?" Sue Jean brought her eyes close to Doug's until their noses nearly touched. "You might be, babe, I don't know. You sure got a lot of whirlies in your head. You want to lie down a while? You want a burger and some fries?"

"A burger'd be fine," Doug said. He looked outside, at the dark and the trees. "Lord, Sue Jean. Insight and wisdom's got me flat. I hope I don't learn a lot more. I got about all the bliss and funny colors I can take."

"You're going to be just fine," Sue Jean said.

"Mousebreath's back, you know that? Erlene took her to the pound is what I think."

"Now you don't know that at all. There's all kinds of stuff can happen to a cat."

"Well I'm betting on abuse. That woman had it in for me. I don't expect she'll stop because I'm gone."

"Hush," Sue Jean said, "that's over with and done." She looked around the porch, peeked beneath the bed. "MB, you little scamp, come on out here and say hello to me."

"Now you know she isn't going to do that."

"I guess not." Sue Jean sat and kissed him on the ear. "Anyway, I'm glad your ol' kitty's come home. Just lie still, hon. I'll get a burger on the fire."

"Sue Jean, wait." Doug reached out to hold her hand. "I don't want you going off right now, I want you here."

"Well okay, babe."

"I guess you think I'm acting like a fool."

"I don't think any such thing."

"That nap got me rattled real good. I got all this stuff coming in and I'm running out of room. I think I might explode."

"Now you aren't goin' to do that."

"I just might. I'm not myself. At least I'm not yet. I wish I was. I'm tired of showing movies in my head. I don't care if Ham Bayliss was a Pict. I don't want to know if the Greeks had 7-Up. I wish I'd left Dean in the park. I wish the Kid hadn't gone and run off I need him here. I wish I didn't have to think about mice."

Sue Jean backed off, gave him cool appraisal and a five-degree squint. Cupped his chin in her hands and checked him out.

"Doug, get up right now," she said.

"What for?"

"Don't start asking me a bunch of dumb questions, just do it."

Doug started to protest but she jerked him to his feet, marched him past the kitchen to the den. Dean was still sitting in his chair.

"Fine," Sue Jean said, "you just stay right there. Eat your pie and watch the tube. Don't rile up the dogs. Don't go anywhere at all. You got that?"

"You and me have got a date," Dean said.

"You and me are going at it, old man, you don't brush those teeth like I said."

Dean grinned, delighted at this attention.

"I thought I was going to get a burger and some fries," Doug said.

"Hon, you're going to get a change of scene, you're going to rest up your head," Sue Jean said. "We'll talk about supper after that. If you're nice I'll throw in a little top-notch frolic on the side." She rolled her eyes at Doug. "Lord A'Mighty, love—you might've come over standing up, but you've switched into eighteen-wheeler overdrive. I got to get you settled down before you go and throw a rod."

Springs were unwinding in his head. Sue Jean's house had a gentling effect, and he felt at ease at once. Colors seemed to fade and he could name them all but two. He sat and drank a Coke, watched Sue Jean slice potatoes at the stove, turned all his attention to the act, relieved to have this simple thing to do. He watched her drop them in the skillet, heard them sizzle with surprise. It was all he could handle at the time. Entertainment for the partially impaired. Fun for a twenty-watt mind.

Her house wasn't home but it was close enough to count. He liked the red tile floor, liked the old brick walls, liked the mortar squeezed out like the filling in a cake. He liked the dust in the halls, the faded paper on the walls, the natty Pawnee rug in the den. He liked the colors like coffee and burgundy and lime. He admired her choice of books, the stuffed ocelot lamp, the dried buffalo grass in a shapely Cretan urn. He liked the framed picture of a girl named Kelly Blue. He liked her dogs, he liked her cats, he liked her Herbert Hoover autographed tie. He liked the way the kitchen seemed to fit him like a shoe.

"Say, I think your place is neat," Doug said. "How come you never asked me here before?"

"Hon, you never asked to come," Sue Jean said, taking burgers off the stove. "Sit and eat. Besides, you were doing real fine where you were. It's kinda best to get your own surroundings straight right off. Get yourself settled in your head."

Doug put down his knife. "Sue Jean, I don't *feel* like I'm settled in my head. Or anything close to it. I feel like I fell down and broke and got glued together wrong. Now that's how I feel, you want to know."

"Shoot, you're doing fine," Sue Jean said. "That isn't so at all." She forked hot fries on his plate. "You just had a hard day is what you did.

My Lord, Doug—gettin' insight and all is going to wear you down some.

Isn't any two ways about that. It's something everybody's got to do. And you're getting close to it, why you said so yourself."

"I guess I am," Doug said, though he wasn't near as certain as he'd been that afternoon. The nap might not mean a thing at all. It didn't seem like a big deal now. Just a lot of bright lights and old movies in his head. Finding out your mother's been a Ute doesn't tell you much at all. It doesn't seem like the road to higher truth. Doug didn't care if a gangster caught a goat. What he wanted was the Doug Hoover story, no Movietone News or Daffy Duck. Who he was and who he'd been. Who he might want to be. It didn't have to be color or a big budget hit. Black and white with a real simple plot would do fine.

And later with the dogs put away and the dishes in the sink, with the lamp turned low so the cats can get some sleep, Sue Jean leads him up the stairs and down the hall and into bed. Doug feels a quick thrill as if he's seen the room before, as if he might get caught, as if he might have to run, because it's Waxahachie window-peeking, prowl-around time on a hot September night. She walks across the room and pulls the sweater off her head and he prays the bra away, wipes the sweat that stings his eyes. There's a dog out back, and the dog knows he's there, but there's nothing on earth could move him now. And through an inch between the window and the shade he sees a heart-stopping sight, sees a cheerleader tit that no mortal's seen before. It's there and then it's gone, and he knows he can't tell a soul at school because she goes with the captain of the team. The room is Cindy Nance and his Fort Worth girl and his mobile home sweetie all in one, every love he's ever known. It's permeated and distilled with every sweet and musty moment of his life, every hillbilly motel morning aftertaste, every pillow with the smell of yellow hair. The girl comes home and runs quickly up to bed, scatters late goodnights upon the stairs because the prom and after that was a lot more exciting than she planned. And if her dad walks in, he'll let the light in from the hall and see a look upon her face that he's never seen before. The look will tell him ice cream is not enough, that a teddy bear won't cut it anymore. He sees her tender and abused, he sees her tangled in the sheets, he sees a secret trail of down and looks away; he sees the boy next door has stolen all the fine sugar he was saving for himself, all the hugs and chocolate kisses gone away.

And Sue Jean locks Doug in the sweetest vise of all, takes him down for the count, sends him off on a spree in the magic of her room. The spell creeps out beneath the door into the hall and down the stairs. Cats perk their ears and a dog rolls over with a sigh. Three blocks down Dean wakes with a start, and can't believe he's done what he almost forgot he couldn't do.

"I got to get my head straight," Doug mutters half asleep, "I got to find my way to class."

"Just take it easy, hon," Sue Jean whispers in his ear. "You got a case of Grapette, you got a brand new car. You got your mean ol' cat back home, you got me."

Doug can't quite hear her but he can, and he knows this is true as it can be.

THE HEREAFTER GANG

The dream seems real, clear enough to cause alarm. No Milk Duds here, no safety in the dark, just Clay County dirt peeling up behind the plow. The mule shits while he walks and there's nothing you can do about that. Forget the smell and try to hop. There are other smells too, spring rain and buttermilk and pine. At night in a corner of the house, Doug's brother seems to stink worse than him. You can't wash off a week's work. A Chink in Kansas City eats gravel every day and never has any trouble with his bowels. Missouri locust summer turns to gold and then ice pushes water up funny from the pail. He lies awake and feels his brother close by, hears his mother down below, tries to draw a naked girl in his head. Tries, but he's missing all the parts. A man in Centralia said his calf had his dead wife's eyes. The calf watched him all day and he finally took to drink. There's trouble all around. Bluecoats ride to the farm. They're looking everywhere for Jayhawkers hiding out. He won't say a thing and they whip his ass good. His brother's been riding with the bunch for some time. Mr. Quantrill seems polite, a man with some reserve. He thinks maybe Doug's too young but Bloody Bill likes his spunk. A man in Independence gets drowned three times in one day, then sits down to salt ham and beans. Bloody Bill Anderson drags twenty-three bluecoats off a train, and slaughters twenty-two. Doug sees girls are even better than he dreamed. He kills Major Johnson on his horse. Shoots Captain Goss in the brain. He thinks about the farm, about the trees behind the house, about a sweet-eyed girl at the Liberty Baptist church. Wartime's bad, but peace in Missouri is despair, and the winners surely love to rub it in. Banks and trains seem a likely occupation for the poor; men who never knew his name know it now. A woman in Columbia, Missouri, grew carrots devoid of any color. They resembled the male organ, or so the woman said, though she'd clearly never married and had no great knowledge of the male. Doug and his brother and the others ride in across the bridge. The town seems quiet, but that's as wrong as it can be. Bill

Chadwell takes a bullet in the heart and Clell Miller falls and dies. Cole goes down with a bullet in his thigh and his luck starts to go the other way. In two weeks Charlie Pitts is dead, and Cole has eleven holes to count. His brother Bob falls, and Captain Vought shoots Jim's mouth and jaw away. All three are taken back alive, and that's a sorry end for sure. Nothing seems quite the same after that. A man in Little Rock finds blood in his well and charges half a dime to look. His chickens seem to thrive, but their eggs are an awful thing to see. Doug wakes every night with a mouthful of dirt. He doesn't let the woman know. Water doesn't help much at all. The woman holds him close and pretends she doesn't see. He walks through clover, throws the children up high. They laugh and flap their arms as if they might begin to fly. When his brother comes by, he brings onions and tomatoes from the yard. He thinks about hot Missouri days, about brown water creeks and the smell of summer night. Once he found an owl in a tree. It didn't seem to care, didn't try to fly away. When he touched it with a stick the end poked right out the back. Something had eaten it clear through and left a shell; it didn't weigh any more than a mouse. He gives the two men breakfast and some laughs. He fails to smell their fear, fails to see their sly deceit. The woman loved him good last night and he still tastes the moonlight on her skin, sees the wonder in her eyes. He turns and knows he's gone, doesn't hardly feel a thing, tries to call his brother's name. Dirt pours from his mouth and fills the room, leaves him hollow as a log. The woman never tells a soul, and no one ever writes about that. A lady in Kansas City found a piece of granite stone with the profile of Lincoln on the side. Her husband said he saw no resemblance at all, and ran off to St. Louis with a girl he used to know.

THE HEREAFTER GANG

Doug woke with a start. He felt dazzled and aware, he felt crafty as a fox, he felt scattered and complete. His head seemed clear, like he'd hatched and broken free.

"I did it, Sue Jean, I got it right!" he cried out, and woke her up and took her in his arms.

Sue Jean laughed aloud, held him off and looked him over good. "Well I see you did, babe, how you feel?"

"I feel great, I feel fine," Doug said. "I might get a white suit. I'd like to buy a pair of boots with some silver on the toes. Say, let's go and do it now."

"Hon, I'd wait till morning if I was you." She pushed him playfully back down. "They like to open up the stores before you shop."

"I guess you're right, that's what we'll do. Sue Jean, I never felt like this before. I'm seeing things I never did, I'm thinking stuff I never knew."

"I knew you'd get it, love. You just had to let 'er go."

"I guess I did."

"I could kinda see it comin' on, Doug. That's why I brought you over here, thought it might jog you through. Lord, I'm as proud as I can be, you did fine." She kissed him on the mouth, tossed a neat cookie leg across his chest, wriggled in till she found a spot she liked.

"Boy, that feels as good as it can be," Doug said.

"I guess it does."

"Are we having fun or what?"

Sue Jean looked hillbilly sly. "I was thinking on some celebration lust. You being a brand new deb and sort of comm' out and all."

"Sounds fine to me."

"I thought it might."

Sue Jean leaned up, did some quick fine tuning with her hand, sat back easy with a sigh. "Oh, babe," she said, grinning like a cat, "I think I'm ready for a spin."

"I kinda think we got it right, I think you're cute as you can be, I think you're honey on a stick."

"I think you ought to shut up and let me ride," Sue Jean said. "I didn't put my nickel in to hear you talk."

He held her hipbones tight, he let her ride, he let her rock, he let her slide to second base. He knew where he was and where he'd been and maybe who he'd like to be. He had his head on straight, he had his babe, he had his love, he had his apple tit girl, he had his carhop queen slick and hard and country wild, sweet and soft as baby ducks. He let her shine, he let her howl, he held her legs, he held her thighs, he held whatever he could find. He let her moan, he let her glide, he held her crazy yellow hair, he held her cheeks between his hands, he saw her lips, he saw her mouth, he saw the freckles on her nose, he saw his brother's blue eyes blue as winter river slate, saw his firm and steady jaw, felt his beard between his hands, bucked and tossed his little sweetie off the bed and on the floor.

He sat up straight and stared. "My Lord," he cried, "what's happening to me? Just what is going on in this bed!"

Sue Jean sat in a tumble on the floor. She blew her hair back and stood. Put her hands on her hips and gave Doug a flinty look.

"Shit, Doug. I thought you said you got it straight."

"I did," Doug said, "but I didn't get *that.*" She was Sue Jean again but he blinked to make sure. He didn't know what to do; he just looked at his cookie in dismay. "Good God, Sue Jean, what's everybody goin' to say? I been having sexual commerce with my brother!"

"Doug, you haven't done any such thing." She sighed and rolled her eyes. "I'm who I am now, not then. All right? Doug, you look at me right now."

Doug tried. The effort seemed to wear him down. Sue Jean sat on the bed and turned his face up to hers. "You got you, but you didn't get me."

"I guess not."

"You didn't even have a clue."

"I just figured you were you," Doug said. "Lord, Sue Jean, I wasn't looking for a girl named Frank."

Sue Jean read confusion in his eyes and held him tight. "Doug, just once I wish you'd get the whole picture in your head. You pick up scraps like a squirrel. You got nests all around the damn yard and that sure makes it hard on me."

"I don't mean to," he said.

"I know you don't, hon." She kissed him firmly on the mouth. "And you're as fine as you can be. You always have been, Doug. Sometimes you're kinda slow to get the beat, but I wouldn't have you any other way."

He looked in her eyes just then and saw something that he'd never seen before. Something happened in his head, or maybe something in hers or maybe both, which seems the way it ought to be. She drew him down deep, drew him further than he'd ever been before, and he saw in an instant who they were and who they'd been, like a mirror reaching back, a bright reflection that never seemed to end. His eyes blurred then and his feelings rose up with such intensity and strength, with such power that he feared they'd overwhelm him, burn him up and carry him away.

He held her close, put his hands behind her head and drew her tight against his chest. "Oh God, Sue Jean," he said, "I didn't know I'd loved you so long. I didn't know but now I do."

"We been through a whole lot," Sue Jean said. "Now you got a leg up and you know that, too. We're going to make it just fine you and me."

Doug had a sudden thought and his heart skipped a beat. "Sue Jean, I am not going to go back out without you. I just flat won't do it."

Sue Jean held him off and laughed. "Well you silly ol' goose." She pressed a finger to his nose. "What you think I been doin' here, hon, except waiting around for you? Babe, goin' back in twos is where it's at. We fucked our timin' up good last time, but it don't always work the way it should. When it doesn't, why you just got to try and get it right."

"Well that's the way it's going to be." Doug looked her straight in the eye. "I don't care if I got to take tap or the flute. I'm not going to do fourth grade without you. There wasn't anyone but fat girls in my class."

"Shoot," Sue Jean said, "you'll likely run through fifty-two honeys 'fore you get around to me. Wouldn't be the first time." She sat up. "You want something to eat or go to sleep?"

Doug looked crafty in the eye. "What I'd like is to finish up where I left off."

"I'm not real fond of getting tossed out of bed."

"Now you know I'm not going to do that."

"You better not."

"Sue Jean, going back's one thing. No one said a thing about changing your sexual persuasion."

"You don't *have* to do it 'less you want," Sue Jean said. "I tried it out that once and I don't guess I'll do it anymore. It didn't feel like me, and I kinda missed my tits. I guess I might be your basic girl."

"You think so?"

"I surely do."

"We'll see about that," Doug said.

In the kitchen Sue Jean made post-carnal omelettes while Doug fried sausage and fixed the toast. They hauled all this plus orange juice and jelly back to bed. The cats looked perplexed, like they do when people fail to follow normal eat and sleep habits cats know is the proper thing to do.

"What I think," Doug said, "is Bob Ford might've been Otta Gee. He had the same kind of eyes. You get eyes like that on a sow when it hasn't got to rut."

"Just because you don't like someone don't mean they done you wrong," Sue Jean said. "That's not the way it works."

"It might've been Erlene," Doug said, picking jelly off his eggs. "She'd go for a back shot every time."

"Doug, just stop."

"Well it doesn't hurt to think."

"It does sometime when it's you." Sue Jean started putting dirty plates on the floor and brushing crumbs off the sheet.

"I guess we're kinda famous," Doug said. "I guess we're just about as famous as the Kid."

"Don't let it go to your head."

"I was just saying it, is all."

"Well don't."

Doug looked surprised. "Now don't tell me you never thought how everybody knows who you are. That they've done us up in all kinds of books and movies and TV."

Sue Jean turned off the light. "What I'm telling you, Doug, is you want a smooth trip out and back, staying out of books is a start. Now go to sleep, hon. You've had a big night and I don't want you fucking up your head."

THE HEREAFTER GANG

The day was clear and bright, the summer sky scrubbed clean as old jeans. Sue Jean loaded up the picnic basket with ribs and fried chicken, deviled eggs and chips, pickles and mayonnaise and anything left in the fridge. Doug packed the drinks in ice, *Tres Equis* beer and Beck's, Grapette and 7-Up, Nehi Orange and some Delaware Punch, and five or six bottles of Moët. It wouldn't all fit in the trunk, and Doug piled what was left in the backseat with Dean. Dean complained there wasn't room to sit, that he didn't much care for crunching up. Doug said there'd be lots of room without his pies. Dean shut up at once, but as soon as they got underway he began to mutter minor Texas towns.

"You can just hush," Sue Jean warned, turning halfway around in her seat. "I won't put up with that."

Dean hushed, but glared at Doug in the mirror when he could.

The Cord rolled along with a satisfying sound, a sound that Doug could feel like a big St. Bernard beneath the hood. Sue Jean looked pretty as a peach. The wind caught her wispy summer dress and blew her hair. Doug liked a dress with straps, as they clearly had a tendency to fall.

"You ought to come up too," Doug said. "It's going to be a lot of fun."

"There isn't no way," Sue Jean said. "It's your cusp, babe, not mine.

"You don't have to be on any cusp. Anyone can do it if they want."

"Well you just wave. I'll be in a pink dress. I'll be sittin' in a lawn chair drinking 7-Up."

"Sue Jean, I can see what color of dress you've got. I don't have to look down, I can see it right now."

"I used to have my own plane," Dean said. "I had maybe two or three. I can buy as many as I want."

"That's fine," Doug said.

He saw the familiar sign that said *Jagdstaffel 11* and turned in. Cars were parked all about. Some by the hangars, others simply pulled off the road or right on the runway itself. Doug felt a quick chill at the planes lined up in neat angles in a row, fierce and boxy shapes that seemed eager to leave the ground. People were gathered in the shade. There were lawn chairs and rockers, and tables stacked with food.

Doug found a spot to park. Cole Younger saw him, waved and strided over double time. He swept Doug up in a hug, pulled him off his feet, and grinned from ear to ear.

"Jesse, you old son of a bitch," he said, "it's good to see you, friend. I hear you got it all straight, I hear you did it up proud. Hey, Jesse or Doug, what's it goin' to be?"

"I guess I'll stick with Doug," Doug said. "Jesse's kinda new." He showed Cole a silly smile. "I got the whole thing, Cole. You and me and Frank and all the guys. I got everything there was."

"I knew you would, hoss."

"That Northfield job was the pits. We shouldn't have ever rode in."

"You picked a fine time to tell me that." Cole laughed and looked at Doug's load. "Shoot, that's just what we need. More stuff to eat and drink. I'll give you a hand with this shit."

Doug hauled baskets and ice chests from the car. Cole gave Dean a wary look.

"Tell that dude I don't need my roses picked," he told Doug.

"Doug's going to class," Sue Jean said. "He's going to do just fine."

"I bet he is."

"Now I'm just thinking on that, Sue Jean."

"Well you just think real good," Sue Jean said sweetly, "'cause you're going to do it, hon."

"I sure like your leather suit," Cole said. "I like your boots and them goggles is a hit. You look like a Hun on a spree."

"You're going to burn up in that thing," Sue Jean said. "It's about a hundred and ten."

"This is what you're supposed to wear," Doug said. "It's a regular flying suit. You look at a picture you'll see that's what you do."

Sue Jean didn't comment on that. As they reached the big corrugated hanger, everyone stood to say hello. There were girls from Kentucky, and Alabama and Tennessee. Richthofen was there, and Werner Voss and Udet,

Boelcke and Immelmann, too. Doc Holliday and Bitter Creek Newcomb and Charlie Pierce. John Wesley Hardin and all the Dalton boys. Everyone was dressed in cutoffs and jeans, shower sandals and Nikes and Hush Puppies worn at the heels. Everybody was polite, and no one said a thing about his suit.

Doug got a Coke and was talking to Udet when a car horn made him look around. He turned in surprise and saw his mother in a '49 Ford. The car was packed with girls into state politics. Doug didn't feel they were contenders, but you never could tell.

He walked over to the car, and his mother turned her cheek up for a kiss. "Well hi there," Doug said. "What you doing out here?"

"This is my son Doug, who's only been to see me once," his mother said. The other women clearly understood.

"I been real tied up," Doug said.

"I'd give some thought to your appearance."

"This is what you're supposed to wear."

"The Hoover men don't run much to shoulders," Mother said. "I saw a suit coat slide right off your father's back."

"Mother, did you come out here to tell me that?"

"Don't be an old grouch." She formed a little kiss. "I heard you got your head straight. Is Sue Jean a nice girl? Try to eat something green. Doug I'd give some thought to the flute. Stay away from brass."

Mother ground gears and the Ford leaped off. Doug was still surprised by her arrival, trying to work on that. He walked back and Sue Jean met him with some ribs.

"What was that all about?"

"She said were you a nice girl."

"What'd you say?"

"I said you fucked like a fish."

"Now that's sweet. You want something else to eat?"

"I think I'll go and see the planes."

"Sure sounds like fun to me." She waved a rib and walked away, practiced hip exaggeration, knew he'd have to stop and watch.

Doug felt the same familiar thrill as he strolled among the planes, saw the clumsy old Rumpler, saw the chubby Albatros, saw a Halberstadt that seemed no more substantial than a kite. He found von Richthofen's apple-red prize and ran his hand down the Fokker's stubby wings, the canvas hot beneath the sun. He smelled the grease and castor oil, he heard a heated engine ping, he saw a Roland with a silver bottle nose. Albert Ball was waiting up there and maybe

Billy Bishop, too. Major Mannock would be high above Ypres, his SE-5 against the sun. Good Limey pilots but he'd have to bring them down. You got your duty and there's nothing else to do.

"Hi there, Jesse, you going to burn up the clouds, you going to win the Blue Max?"

The voice startled Doug out of his thoughts. He turned and saw the Chief, lazing up against the hangar wall, hands in the pockets of his white jump suit. He wore white Adidas shoes, he wore a white pilot's helmet and goggles on his head.

"Well I'll be," Doug said, taking in this nifty gear, "I guess you're going up, too. I didn't know you liked to fly."

"I sure do," the Chief said, and a big smile spread across his face. He came to Doug and spread his arms, embraced him with a hug that made Doug feel like a hundred dollar high. "I'm real proud of you," he said. "You went ahead and got it done, you came through like a pro."

"I wasn't real sure for a while," Doug said.

"Shoot. I wasn't worried for a minute. You run sideways now and then, you got some plays I've never seen, but you get there and that's the name of the game."

Doug felt his face get warm. "I been wanting to come and talk. I started out once, and forgot what it was I didn't know. I've been a little fuddled in my head."

The Chief smiled. His fine blue eyes caught the sun. "You're sure a caution, boy. I said so all along. You got it all clear now?"

"All except going out and coming back all the time because there's some place finer than the town—which is like a trailer court except it's not. I know you got to get a lot of stuff off your list so you can leave the place you like and go somewhere better than where you are. But no one'll tell me just what kind of better that is. I don't go along with this downtown Fort Worth stuff, I'll tell you that. If that's what it is, hardly anyone'd ever want to go. What I wish is you had some brochures, like the cruise ships and Pan Am do. Lots of color and a little slick copy on the side. Give folks an idea just what they're working for. What do you think?"

The Chief gave him a curious, sort of halfway penetrating look. "Jesse, where did you hear this stuff?"

"I kind of pick things up and try to piece them all together in my head."

"I see."

"We could talk about it some if you like."

"Well sure, that's fine." He showed Doug a nice smile. "We'll have lunch." He led Doug down the hangar in the shade, past the baron's red plane to a 7-Up machine. Found a pair of nickels, and handed Doug a drink.

"I got a favor I'd like to ask," the Chief said. "You haven't been here long so it's kinda up to you.

"I'll sure be glad to help," Doug said.

The Chief took a swallow of his drink and looked out across the field. "A.V. Annie's coming in," he told Doug. "She's out in Abilene now, going to get struck down by a Continental bus."

"Well I'll be."

"I'd be obliged if you'd go out and bring her in. You got her through her advertising stint and she's sort of drifting now. Bitter Creek Newcomb said he'd like to go along. Him and Annie go a long ways back, and he can show you how it's done."

"I'll be real glad to do it," Doug said. "I like Annie a whole lot. We had some good times; I kind of feel like we were close."

"Loving one another's where it's at," the Chief said. He showed Doug a warm smile. "That's the whole idea right there, if folks'd just come to see it. Say, I sure do appreciate what you did for Dean. It's mighty nice of you to take him in and help."

"The man's got a lot of funny stuff in his head," Doug sighed. "I sure hope he'll straighten out."

The Chief grinned. "Well *you* did, boy."

"Yeah, I guess you got a point."

"Come on down here with me," the Chief said, "there's something I want you to see." He tossed his empty can in a bin in a nifty long shot, took Doug by the arm and led him down the hangar wall. At a corrugated door, he stopped and stepped aside.

"There you go," he said. "Just step right in."

"In there?" Doug said.

"Hey. Trust me, okay?"

Doug walked in; for a second, everything seemed dim after the brightness outside. Then he saw them all there, everyone looking at him with a grin. Ernst Udet and Cole Younger, Doc Holliday and Boelcke and Immelmann and Voss, and the cookies from the Pronghorn Saloon. Charlie Pierce and Bitter Creek Newcomb, Sue Jean and James McArthur Hill Dean, Hardin and the Daltons, and Mannie Richthofen in his ratty bathrobe. And off to the side looking just as slick and shiny as could be was a biplane beauty with a shark-tail fin, a pug-nosed wonder painted bright willow-green with lemon trim.

"Oh my Lord," Doug cried, "it's a real Siemens-Schuckert D III, my favorite plane in all the world!"

The crowd laughed and gave a cheer. Champagne corks echoed off the walls. Doug was too stunned to talk, he couldn't move. Immelmann came up and led him over to the plane. Doug could smell the fresh paint, smell the varnish on the prop.

"Well what you think, Jesse," Max said, "does she look okay to you?"

"It's just like my picture," Doug said, still marveling at the sight, "the one I got from Uncle Billy Dale."

"Better'n that," Max said. "This one'll take you wherever you want to go."

"It's for your coming out, Jesse," Cole said. "She's all yours." He laid a hand on Doug's shoulder. "Says it is right there."

Cole pointed, and Doug saw the letters painted on the side. It read *High Lonesome* in a fine Kraut script. Above that was a cowboy hat over two crossed ribs dripping sauce.

"Kinda figured you'd like it," Boelcke grinned.

Doug looked past him to the crowd gathered in a half circle around the plane. "It's just great," he said. "It's the nicest thing anyone ever did."

"Hey," the Chief said, and tried to look hurt and surprised, "I thought *I* did the nicest thing anyone ever did!"

The crowd howled at that; the Chief looked shy but you could tell he was pleased. Sue Jean stepped up and broke a bottle of Moët on the bright green cowl and gave Doug a big kiss. Dean asked an Alabama girl if she'd like a piece of pie. "It's not a Fokker," Richthofen told Doug, "but next to that she's the sweetest little plane I ever saw."

Doug feels the wind, he feels the power in his bones, he hears the wires begin to whine, he hears the engine start to sing. The sky is sharp and clear with a blue that hurts his eyes; the sun's as bright as silver with a shine. He sees the wonders down below, he sees the hangar and the Cord, he sees the courthouse and the creek, he sees a pretty spot of pink. He sees Immelmann and Manny up above, sees Boelcke and Doc down below. To his right he sees Cole, sees him grin and wag his wings. Off to port he sees the Chief looking nifty in his whites, looking fine with his long hair whipping in the breeze. He gives Doug a thumbs up and neatly peels his craft away, a white bird against the blue. Doug rolls and feels giddy in the head, feels dizzy as a duck, sees Cole right on his tail.

And as he screams through the sky he wonders what he'd like to be, if the flute would treat him right, if the clarinet's the thing, if he could tap his way to fame. He's feeling good, he's feeling fine, he thinks he'd like to get a Jeep, he thinks he'd like to have a pizza with a little extra cheese. He thinks he'll really try to learn, discover what it's all about, why he really ought to go where it's nicer than the town.

He thinks he'll be nicer to Dean,

try to understand a cat,

Thinks he might try and settle down,

and really get it right this time...